The ENCYCLOPEDIA *of*
Two-Hour
Craft Projects

The ENCYCLOPEDIA of Two-Hour Craft Projects

Leslie Allen, Patrice Boerens, Linda Durbano,
Ann Benson, Susie Steadman, McKenzie Kate

Sterling Publishing Co., Inc.
New York

10 9 8 7 6 5 4

Published by Sterling Publishing Co., Inc.
387 Park Avenue South, New York, N.Y. 10016

Distributed in Canada by Sterling Publishing
c/o Canadian Manda Group, One Atlantic Avenue, Suite 105
Toronto, Ontario, Canada M6K 3E7
Distributed in Great Britain and Europe by Cassell PLC
Wellington House, 125 Strand, London WC2R 0BB, England
Distributed in Australia by Capricorn Link (Australia) Pty Ltd.
P.O. Box 6651, Baulkham Hills, Business Centre, NSW 2153, Australia

Printed and Bound in China
All rights reserved

Sterling ISBN 1-4027-1137-9

CONTENTS

Two-Hour Appliqué Projects

• *Welcome to* Two-Hour Appliqué •

This chapter is divided into three sections.

Section 1 contains the general instructions. The first section describes the appliqué process from beginning to end. The next section contains step-by-step instructions and photos illustrating several different appliqué techniques. Following is a section containing step-by-step instructions and illustrations for several embroidery stitches and dimensional ribbon work used with the appliqué.

Sections 2 and 3 are projects and patterns chapters. Each section contains a photograph of a finished project or projects followed by patterns for that project plus additional designs. The additional designs can be finished in the same way that the photographed pieces were finished. However, the finished pieces are meant only as ideas—every design can be finished in many ways.

• History •

Appliqué is both a simple way to embellish fabric and an easy and efficient means of repairing clothing. It is a nearly international art and craft. It has long been a part of both classic and folk art traditions. In fact, the history of appliqué is almost as old as the history of textile making itself.

Appliqué is a central part of textile traditions all over the world. The most ancient example of appliquéd cloth is a ceremonial canopy dating from approximately 980 B.C. Appliqué was used to decorate wall hangings in ancient Gobi desert cultures and in ancient Egypt. In medieval Europe, appliqué was used mainly to decorate banners, horse trappings and ecclesiastical vestments. Appliqué has long been a part of the quilting traditions in the United States and Europe. There are, of course, many other examples of the use of appliqué in history—too many to list here, in fact. There are many books available about the history of appliqué specifically and textile arts in general should you wish to learn more.

• Definitions •

Appliqué: The art of applying fabric cutouts or other materials to a background in order to create a decorative pattern.

Background: Material to which motifs are appliquéd.

Basting: Stitches used to hold motifs in place on the background until secured by some means.

Decorative Stitch: A stitch used to decorate an appliqué piece as opposed to a stitch used to secure the motif in place.

Dimensional Ribbon Appliqué: Tacking pre-made ribbon-work flowers and other pre-made ribbon designs to a background.

Double-Sided Fusible Web: Often used to secure a motif to a background before stitching. A web with weak adhesive can easily be removed if desired. Different webs are made for different types of fabric.

Free-Standing Motifs: A three-dimensional design attached to a background at only one or two points.

Fused Appliqué (Bonded Appliqué): Use of fusible fabric adhesive or iron-on interfacing to bond the design to the background.

Hand-Stitched Appliqué: Hand-stitching fabric cutouts to a background.

Inlay (Mosaic): Setting a pattern into a perfectly cut background.

Iron-on Interfacing: Used to stiffen loosely woven fabrics and knits, to prevent a dark background from showing through a light foreground, or to make frayable fabrics more manageable. Creates a crisp look. Different weights are made for different types of fabric.

Machine-Stitched Appliqué: Machine-stitching fabric cutouts to a background. Good for heavy fabrics that are difficult to hand-stitch or for items that will be used heavily or laundered frequently. Has a sharper appearance than hand-stitched appliqué.

Mixed-Media Appliqué: Use of other materials in combination with fabric to create a design. Can also refer to the use of dying and hand-painting techniques in combination with appliqué.

Motif: A piece of the appliqué design.

Padded Appliqué (3/D Appliqué): Use of some type of padding to make the appliqué more dimensional.

Reverse Appliqué (Multilayered Appliqué): Layering two or more fabrics and cutting the design out of the top layer or layers of fabric to reveal the colors beneath. It is a process of removing fabric, rather than adding fabric.

Shadow Appliqué: Placing solid-colored fabrics on a background, then covering those fabrics with sheer fabric to create a shadow effect.

Template: A reference drawing of the desired finished appliqué. It is also used to make patterns.

Turned-Edge Appliqué (Blind Appliqué): The edges of the cutout fabric turned under or hemmed before or during appliquéing them to the background. There is no stitching around the design in this method.

Step-by-step instructions for each appliqué method start on page 16. Step-by-step instructions and definitions for embroidery stitches and ribbon work start on page 21.

• Tools •

Note: The tools used are dependent upon on the means of transferring the design and the method of appliqué used for the project.

Basting thread
Cotton thread or similar synthetic thread in standard and quilting length
Craft knife
Double-sided fusible web
Dressmaker's carbon or chalk
Dressmaker's ruler
Fabric glue
Fabric marker
Florist's wire
Frame or embroidery hoop for accuracy
Iron, ironing board, pressing cloth
Iron-on interfacing
Needles: beading, embroidery, small quilting, and hand sewing; size should be appropriate for fabric
Paints and colored pencils
Pencils: hard and soft, depending on use
Photocopy machine
Pins
Ruler
Scissors: embroidery, fabric, fine-point, paper, pinking sheers, etc.
Sewing machine with embroidery function
Tape measure
Thimble
Tracing paper

• Fabrics and Threads •

All kinds of **fabrics** can be used for appliqué–plain, patterned, smooth, textured, thick and thin. The type and style of fabric used depend on the desired look of the finished product and the skill of the crafter. Cotton fabrics are the most commonly used in appliqué, and are among the easiest to use. Unwoven fabrics, like felt and leathers, are particularly easy to cut and handle and can be used by both beginner and expert alike. Other fabrics, like silks and satins, require skill and care to use but add sophistication to a piece.

The type of fabric used should be appropriate for the use of the finished piece. For instance, a piece that needs to be washed frequently should not be made from nonwashable fabrics! Furthermore, it is best to use like background fabric with like motif fabric, because they will react and behave the same way.

The type of fabric should also match the style of the piece. For example, a bright-colored felt would be just right for use in a child's wall hanging but inappropriate for a Victorian piece.

It is also important to take into account the scale of any patterns printed on fabric. Small motifs can be very versatile and will "read" even in a small piece. Larger motifs have a limited number of uses and cannot be seen if the cutout is small.

Also keep in mind how easily a fabric frays. A fabric that frays very easily may be hard to work with, and the edges will have to be secured in some way.

The above considerations for fabric choice also apply to **thread** choice. The type of thread used should be appropriate for the use and style of the finished piece.

All kinds of embroidery threads can be used for appliqué. The color and character of the thread are usually subservient to the fabric used, but not always. Sometimes contrasting stitching adds as much to the design as the material itself.

Another consideration in choosing threads is the type of fabric used. Like threads should go with like fabrics. Natural threads should be used with natural fabrics, and synthetic threads with synthetic fabrics.

• Preparing Fabrics •

All fabrics should be clean and pressed (if possible) before using. Make certain the fabric used is preshrunk and colorfast if the finished piece will be washed. Also, check to make certain the grain line is straight by pulling out a weft thread near the edge of the fabric and cutting along the gap.

• Backing Fabrics •

A backing fabric is used as a support for fabrics that need extra firmness and strength. Most wall hangings and panels need a backing fabric, as do lightweight and stretch fabrics. The backing fabric should be pre-washed and correspond in weight to the fabric it is applied to. Cut the backing fabric larger than the finished design of the appliqué to allow for seams, finishing and/or mounting. Iron-on interfacing can also be used to give body and strength to a thin fabric.

• Positioning the Design •

Most designs may be positioned simply by eye, but some need more precision. To find the center of the design, fold the paper pattern into quarters and mark two pencil lines along the folds. To check if the exact center has been located, draw a diagonal from corner to corner. If it intersects the middle of the crossed horizontal and vertical lines, you have found the exact center of the design.

The center of the fabric can be found in a similar manner. Fold the fabric in quarters and mark the lines with basting stitches. When transferring the design to the fabric, use the pencil and basting lines to check the alignment.

• Transferring the Design •

Note: It is easier to transfer the design to the back of a fabric with a pile. Make certain that you transfer a mirror image of the design.

Template: The first step in transferring the design is to make a full-scale outlined drawing of the design on tracing paper (template). Enlarge the design as needed, using a photocopier, or by hand, using dressmaker's grid paper. Number each separate part of the design in a logical order of assembly, usually starting with the background and moving to the foreground. Use this full-scale template to mark the background, to make patterns for the motifs and as a reference during the construction of the piece.

Window or Light Table: The simplest means of marking the design on the background is tracing, using a light table or a bright window. Of course, this method only works if the background is lightweight and/or light colored.

Dressmaker's Carbon: Another means of marking the design on the background is to use dressmaker's carbon paper. Do not use office carbon paper as it will leave indelible marks. Since dressmaker's carbon comes in many colors, choose a carbon paper that is closest in color and tone to the background fabric. Be certain to follow the manufacturer's directions.

Patterns and Chalk: Another way to transfer the design is to make cardboard or paper patterns and use dressmaker's chalk, fabric markers or a soft pencil to mark the design. This method is not quite as accurate as the first two, and it is harder to mark the placement of motifs if they are not a part of the outer edge of the design.

Tracing Paper: Tracing paper can also be used to mark the outline. Pin the tracing paper to the background fabric, then pin or baste along the lines. Tear the paper away. This method is also not as accurate as tracing the design directly onto the fabric or using dressmaker's carbon.

• Making Patterns •

Note: Plan the construction of the piece carefully. Sometimes it is easier to overlap pieces than to fit them together exactly.

The tracing or the dressmaker's carbon methods can be used to transfer the design on the motif fabrics as well as the background. If neither method is feasible, patterns must be made for the motifs to ensure they are cut precisely. The pattern can be made from a variety of materials. X-ray film, stencil plastic or thick tracing paper are all good choices because they are semitransparent.

First, trace each piece of the design from the full-scale template onto tracing paper. Copy the design numbers and mark the grain lines on each piece of the design. Cut out each pattern piece. The pattern can then be transferred to a thicker material if desired.

• Cutting Out Motifs •

Cut on a flat surface so that the fabric does not pucker or draw. Be certain to add seam allowances if necessary. If using a paper pattern, pin the pattern to the fabric and cut out as with any other pattern. If using a thicker pattern, place the pattern on the fabric, pin in place, and mark the design with dressmaker's chalk, fabric markers, or a soft pencil.

• Assembling Appliqué •

When the design has been transferred to the background by tracing or with dressmaker's carbon, simply place the motifs over the marked outlines. If another means has been used, the motifs can be positioned by eye, using the full-scale template for positioning. Another way of placing the motifs is making a tracing of the design and placing it on top of the background. Then, slide the motifs between the two and pin or baste in place.

• Keeping Fabric Flat •

When doing machine appliqué, appliqué tissue is often used to hold fabric in place and prevent tiny puckers in the fabric. It is placed on the bottom layer of the fabrics to be stitched. When the stitching is complete, the paper is torn off. If no appliqué tissue is available, thick tissue paper or typing paper can be used. Even newspaper can do in a pinch.

When doing hand appliqué, good basting is essential. A motif should be basted in place with stitches running both directions to prevent the fabric from puckering. First, find the center of the fabric, then baste from the center in each direction toward the outside. Additional basting may be needed, but be certain to always start from the center to prevent any puckering of the fabric.

An embroidery hoop can be used to further hold fabric taut. If the area to be appliquéd is too large for an embroidery hoop, a frame can be used to pull fabric flat.

• Changing a Design •

The colors in the diagrams in this book are only suggestions. Remember that a design can look completely different simply by changing the colors. Also remember that the pattern and texture of the fabric used in a design will make it look different as well. Feel free to change colors, patterns and textures as desired. Many wonderful new looks can be made with the same pattern by using your imagination.

The designs in this book can also be easily mixed and matched to create new designs. Motifs from one design will often work well with motifs from another. For example, in the next column we have taken two designs and combined them to create a new design.

(1)

+

(2)

=

(3)

• Appliqué Methods •

The following pages contain step-by-step instructions for several different methods of appliqué. Keep in mind that appliqué techniques are often used together and one project can incorporate several methods of appliqué. The quickest method of appliqué is to combine the fused method with the machine-stitched—fusing the motifs to a background and then machine-stitching over the edges.

The more work done by hand and the more complicated the method used, the more time-consuming a project will be. A two-hour machine-stitched project would be a day's work done with hand-stitching.

Some methods of appliqué are more appropriate for certain designs than others. Choose an appliqué method that fits both the chosen design and desired finished product.

15

• Hand-Stitched Appliqué •

1. Place pattern right side down on wrong side of fabric. Trace and cut out shape. Label.

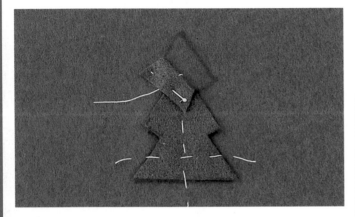

2. Mark design on background. Pin motif in place. Baste. If fabric frays easily, secure edges with overcast stitch, backstitch, or running stitch using matching thread. Remove basting stitch.

3. Stitch over edges with desired decorative stitch to conceal securing stitches. If edges do not fray, motif can be secured with stab stitching.

• Turned-Edge Appliqué • (Blind Appliqué)

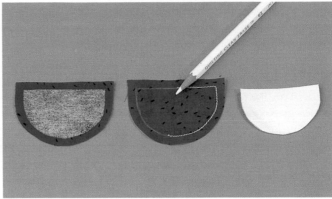

1. Trace design to fabric. Cut out motif, leaving a ⅛" to ½" seam allowance, depending on the weight of the fabric being used. (Lighter-weight fabrics need a larger seam allowance.) Machine-straight-stitch along actual motif line, or cut out iron-on interfacing to actual motif size and iron onto fabric.

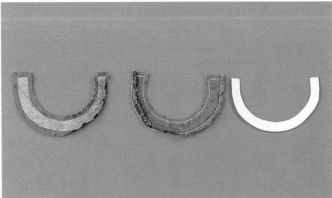

2. Fold seam allowance to wrong side, using stitching or interfacing as a guide. Snip, notch, or trim allowance as needed. Baste edges in place. Iron for a crisp, flat edge, or leave unpressed for a slight relief.

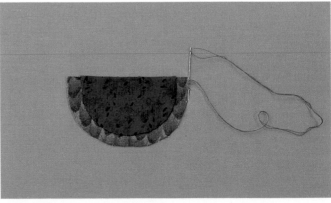

3. Mark design on fabric. Pin and baste prepared motif in place. Secure with chosen stitch. Remove basting stitches.

• Machine-Stitched Appliqué •

• Fused Appliqué •

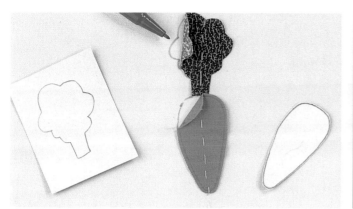

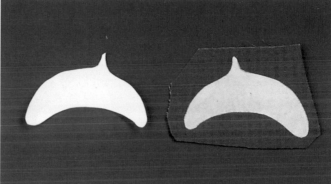

1. Trace motif pattern onto fabric. Cut fabric a little larger than actual design. Mark placement of motif on background. Baste onto background fabric to minimize puckering.

1. *Note: This method is most often used as a preparation for sewing rather than an independent method. Use this method without securing stitches only for infrequently used items.* Trace reverse design on nonadhesive (paper) side of double-sided fusible web (outline will be a mirror image of motif). Cut out web motif, allowing a small margin.

2. Sew over exact line with straight stitches. Trim away extra fabric. Go over stitching with a short, close zigzag or satin stitch.

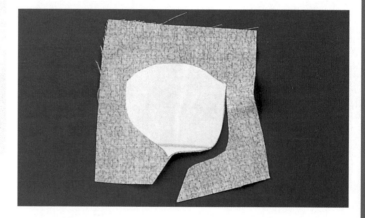

2. Iron unbacked (adhesive) side to appliqué fabric, matching grain lines and following manufacturer's instructions. Cut out motif with sharp embroidery scissors.

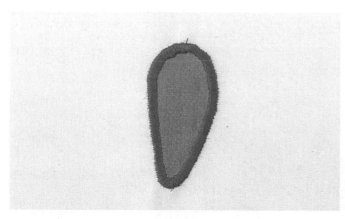

3. Trim away all visible basting threads. Press to ease out any small wrinkles. Snip off raw edges and bits of thread with embroidery scissors.

3. Mark placement of motif on background. Peel away backing paper, and iron motif to background, following manufacturer's instructions. Go over edges with machine- or hand-stitching or paint, depending on the desired finished effect and amount of use.

• Reverse Appliqué •

1. Make a template that clearly indicates colors. Cut desired pieces of fabric into identically sized pieces. Tack fabrics together. Transfer template to top layer of fabric with dressmaker's chalk. Baste around outline. Using sharp embroidery scissors, cut out layers of cloth to reveal desired color.

2. For a blind edge, leave a ¼" margin to turn under. Slip-stitch edges in place through all layers of fabric. Continue until desired effect is achieved.

3. For stitched edges, cut fabric to design outline. Machine- or hand-stitch over edges to secure. Continue until desired effect is achieved.

• Inlay •

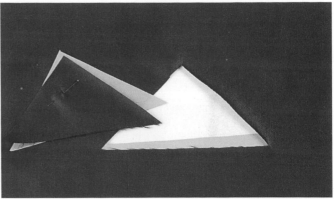

1. Mark design on right side of background fabric. Lay background fabric on top of motif fabric. Place both on a cutting board and pin in place to hold steady. Cut through both layers of fabric.

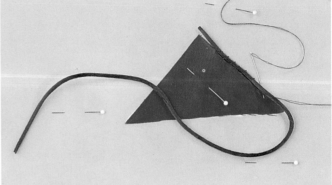

2. The traditional method of inlay is reversible. Pin and baste the fabric to a temporary backing of brown paper. Join raw edges with couched cording or button-hole stitch, interlocking the second row with the first. The stitching should not pierce the paper. Remove paper.

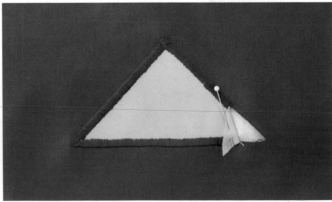

3. The modern method of inlay has a backing and is not reversible. Stitch both fabrics onto backing material. Feather-stitch along joint, catching both edges and backing (a machine zigzag stitch can also be used if it is wide enough to catch both edges).

• Shadow Appliqué •

Method One: Baste a sheer fabric on top of desired shadow motif, matching grains. Draw design on sheer fabric and stitch over lines (in hand-stitching, use a pin stitch). Cut away excess sheer fabric close to stitching line. Apply to background as desired.

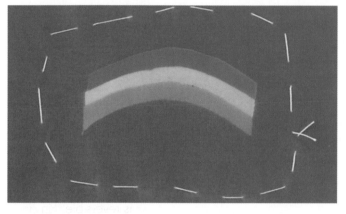

Method Two: 1. Cut motifs and secure to background as desired. Pin sheer fabric over entire design and baste around edges.

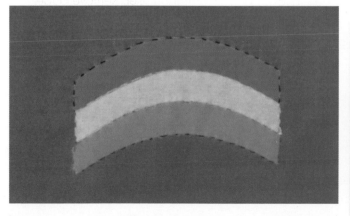

2. Work small running stitches around the edge of motifs. Either cut away fabric at lines of stitching or stitch around edges of finished piece to achieve a quilted effect.

• Padded Appliqué •

Felt: Cut out several pieces of felt the same shape as motif, each slightly smaller than the other. Starting with the smallest piece, pin and stab-stitch to center of area to be padded. Repeat with other pieces. Sew the motif* on top with turned-edge method.

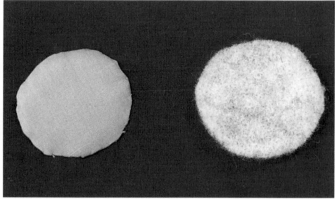

Batting: Cut required batting the same size as motif and the required thickness. Stitch batting to background with loosely tensioned straight stitches. Stitch motif* on top of batting, using turned-edge method.

Cardboard: Cut fabric between ¼" to ½" larger than motif*. Center cardboard on wrong side of fabric. Wrap edges to back and secure with fabric glue. Slip-stitch to background around edges.

*Motif must be cut slightly larger than pattern to accommodate padding.

• Mixed-Media Appliqué •

1. Buttons, beads and sequins should be sewn on in the traditional manner.

2. Other objects (like tiny mirrors or stones) can be secured with buttonhole stitching.

3. Most objects can be secured with fabric glue, tacky glue, or industrial-strength adhesive. Check to make certain the glue used will not stain fabric and will hold for desired use.

• Free-Standing Motifs •

Fusible Web: Adhere two fabrics to each other, wrong sides together. Mark design on top side and cut out shape. Stitch any details. Stiffen with fabric stiffener if desired. Motif can be shaped by inserting florist's wire between layers of fabric before bonding. Tack to background with small, invisible stitches.

Raw Edges: 1. Mark design on top fabric. Place over bottom fabric with wrong sides together. Insert layer of batting or felt between layers if desired. Baste together. Machine-stitch along outline.

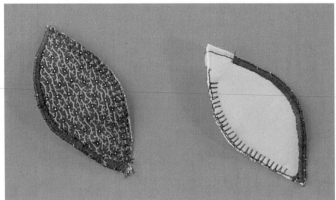

2. Cut out motif close to stitching. Work machine satin stitch or close zigzag stitch along edge, or cover with hand-stitched buttonhole stitch.

• Dimensional Ribbon Appliqué •

1. *Note: Ribbon work instructions are on page 23.* Make all desired ribbon pieces, such as flower, leaf or bow. Mark placement on background, taking care to note which layer should be attached first if necessary.

2. Tack ribbon piece on background, using small invisible stitches, like a slip stitch or hem stitch.

If you do not wish to make your own dimensional ribbon items, several companies offer pre-made ribbon flowers and bows for purchase. These can be found at most sewing, needlework, and crafts stores.

Silk, velvet, and lace flowers can also be appliquéd, using the dimensional ribbon technique. You can also mix and match ribbon, silk, velvet, and lace flowers for an interesting design.

The ribbon flowers and motifs used in this book are described beginning on page 23. If you cannot find the kind of ribbon flowers you want to make in our instructions, there are several good ribbon craft books that illustrate how to make many kinds of dimensional ribbon crafts. Feel free to explore and experiment!

• Embroidery Stitches •

The following are instructions for many common embroidery stitches, but there are many, many more. Several excellent stitch dictionaries are available that catalog hundreds of different stitches if a different stitch is desired.

• Backstitch
Come up at A; go down at B, to the right of A. Come up at C, to the left of A. Repeat B-C, inserting the needle in the same hole.

• Blanket Stitch
A blanket stitch is worked like a buttonhole stitch, except a space is left between each upright.

• Buttonhole Stitch
(1) Bring needle up at A, down at B. Bring needle up again at C, keeping thread under needle. (2) For second stitch, go down at D and back up at E. (3) Completed Buttonhole Stitch.

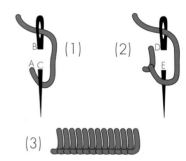

• Crossed Buttonhole Stitch
(1) Come up at A, go down at B and up at A. Go down at C and up at D, with tip of needle over thread, and pull to complete stitch. (2) Go down at E and up at D. Go down at F and up at G, with tip of needle over thread, and pull to complete stitch. Continue to end of row. (3) Completed Crossed Buttonhole Stitch.

• Chain Stitch
(1) Bring needle up at A. Put needle down through fabric at B and back up at C, keeping thread under needle to form a loop. Pull thread

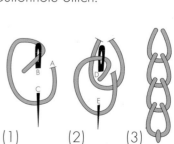

through, making a loop.
(2) To form the next chain loop which holds the previous one in place, go down at D and back up at E. Continue to form each loop in the same manner.
(3) Completed Chain Stitch. Finish with a short straight stitch over the bottom of the last loop to secure.

• Couching Stitch

(1) Complete a straight-stitch base by coming up at A and going down at B (the desired length of the straight stitch).
(2) Make a short, tight straight stitch across the base to "couch" the straight stitch. Come up at C on one side of the thread. Go down at D on the opposite side of the thread. The straight-stitch base is tacked at varying intervals.
(3) Completed Couching Stitch.

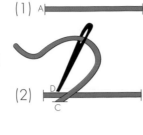

• Feather Stitch

(1) Come up at A. Go down at B and back up at C, keeping the thread under the needle to hold it in a "V" shape. Pull flat.
(2) For second stitch, go down at D and back up at E.
(3) Completed Feather Stitch.

(1)   (2)   (3)

• Running Stitch

A line of straight stitches with an unstitched area between each stitch. Come up at A and go down at B.

A B A BA BA B

• Satin Stitch

(1) Come up at A and go down at B, forming a straight stitch. Then come up at C and go down again at B, forming another smooth straight stitch that is slightly overlapping the first.
(2) Repeat to fill design area.

(1)   (2)

• Slip Stitch

A small straight stitch worked from the background fabric into the edge of the motif, at tight angles to the motif's edge.

• Stab Stitch

A Stab Stitch forms a dotted line, with tiny stitches evenly spaced in a line. It differs from running stitch in that the needle pierces the fabric vertically instead of diagonally.

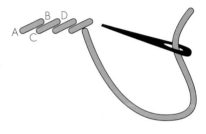

• Stem Stitch

Working from left to right, make slightly slanting stitches along the line of the stem. Come up at A and insert needle through fabric at B. Bring needle up at C (halfway between A and B). Make all stitches the same length. Insert needle through fabric at D (half the length of the stitch beyond B). Bring needle up at the middle of previous stitch and continue in the same manner.

• Whipped Running Stitch

(1) Complete the Running Stitches first.
(2) To whip the running stitch, go under the first running stitch from A to B. (Be careful not to pierce the fabric or catch the running stitch.) Come up on the other side of the stitch. Wrap the thread over the stitch and go under the next running stitch at C. Continue in the same manner. The effect can be varied by how loosely or tightly the thread is pulled when whipping.

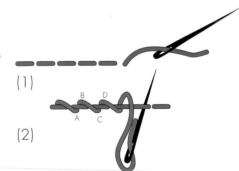

Note: When working whipping, it is good to use a blunt-end needle or put needle through running stitches eye first to avoid catching the thread.

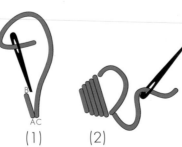

• Ribbon Work •

Individual instructions will include ribbon required for the project and other information as needed.

• Cascading Stitch

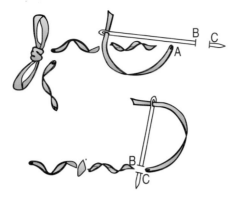

The Cascading Stitch can be done starting with a bow or just using ribbon to "cascade" streamers through design. If starting with a bow, tie bow, leaving streamers long enough to work "cascade" through design. Thread streamer on needle, stitch down through fabric where bow placement is desired and come back up at start of "cascade" effect. This will hold the bow in place.

(1) Come up at A and go down at B. Come back up at C, allowing ribbon to twist and lay loosely on the fabric.

(2) Go down again at B and come up at C, making a small backstitch. This keeps the cascading in place.

• Daffodil

(1) Petals: Cut six 2¾" lengths from 1½"-wide sheer yellow to orange ombré wired ribbon. To make one petal, cut the short sides at an angle so that top edge is 2¾" and bottom edge is 1" (bottom edge is bright orange). Gather-stitch side and bottom. Pull gathers and secure. Make five more petals. Chain petals together, pull gathering thread lightly and secure. Join last petal to first petal.

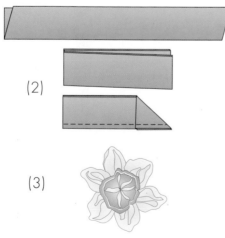

(2) Center: Cut a 5" length from the same ribbon. Fold in half, then fold in half again. Fold raw edge at a 45° angle and gather-stitch folded edge. Pull gathering thread tightly and secure. Sew the gathered edge to the center of the petals.

(3) Completed Daffodil.

• Folded Leaf

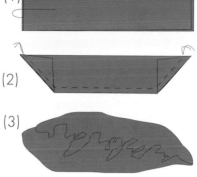

(1) Fold a 7" length of 1"-wide ombré ribbon in half.

(2) Fold corner to form 45° angles. Gather along darker edge of ombré.

(3) Pull slightly and tie off. Trim bulk from corners and open leaf.

• Free-Form Flower Stitch

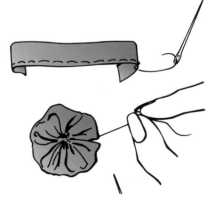

(1) Use a 2" piece of ribbon. Fold each end under about ⅛". Baste along one long edge of the ribbon with one strand of sewing thread or floss.

(2) Gather ribbon tightly to create a flower. Knot to secure ruffled effect. Stitch ribbon in place along the gathered edge.

• French Knot

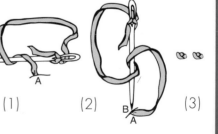

(1) Bring needle up through fabric at A; smoothly wrap ribbon once around needle.

(2) Hold ribbon securely off to one side, and push needle down through fabric at B.

(3) Completed French Knots.

• Fuchsia

(1) Cut a 6½" length of 1½"-wide wired ribbon. Fold ribbon in half with short ends together. Crease ribbon on fold to mark center. Fold one end of ribbon to center, overlapping ¼". Fold remaining end down ¼". Fold to meet center and pin.

(2) Draw a diamond with disappearing pen. Points are $\frac{1}{16}$" from edge. Knot end of 2mm ribbon. Stitch through center of ribbon for stem. Fold stamen in half and hot-glue to inside of fuchsia. Gather-stitch diamond. Pull tight and tie off.
(3) Completed Fuchsia.

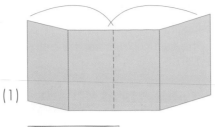

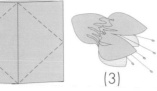

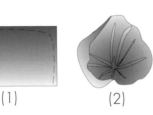

• Ivy Leaf

(1) Cut 1"-wide ribbon into a 7" or a 5" length. Gather-stitch each as shown.
(2) Pull thread tightly. Appliqué in place, shaping petal like an ivy leaf.

• Layered Pointed-Petal Flower

(1) Cut $1\frac{1}{2}$"-wide wired ribbon into fifteen 6" lengths.
(2) Make pointed petals by folding one edge at a 45° angle and the other edge over first angel at a 45° angle. Gather-stitch below the salvage.
(3) Chain together, pull gathers as tightly as possible and secure. Join to first petal. Secure thread and tie off.
(4) To make second layer, cut $1\frac{1}{2}$" striped wired ribbon into twelve 6" pieces. Make 12 petals. Gather-stitch, catching salvage. Chain together, pull gathers as tightly as possible and secure. Join to first petal, secure thread and tie off.

Sew second petal layer to first. Using industrial-strength adhesive, glue a charm in the flower center.

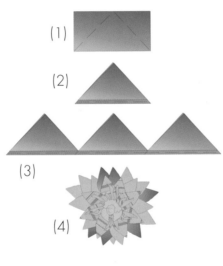

• Lazy Daisy

(1) Bring the needle up at A. Keep the ribbon flat, un-

twisted and full. Put the needle down through fabric at B and up through at C, keeping the ribbon under the needle to form a loop. Pull the ribbon through, leaving the loop loose and full. To hold the loop in place, go down on other side of ribbon near C, forming a straight stitch over loop.
(2) Completed Lazy Daisy.

• Japanese Ribbon Stitch

(1) Come up through fabric at the starting point of stitch. Lay the ribbon flat on the fabric. At the end of the stitch, pierce the ribbon with the needle. Slowly pull the length of the ribbon through to the back, allowing the ends of the ribbon to curl. If the ribbon is pulled too tight, the effect of the stitch can be lost. Vary the petals and leaves by adjusting the length, the tension of the ribbon before piercing, the position of piercing, and how loosely or tightly the ribbon is pulled down through itself.
(2) Completed Japanese Ribbon Stitch.

• Mum

(1) Cut a $22\frac{1}{2}$" and a $17\frac{1}{2}$" length of ribbon. Measure and mark $22\frac{1}{2}$" length of ribbon following diagram.
(2) Fold downward at each mark. Gather-stitch as shown. Pull thread tightly and secure. Repeat with $17\frac{1}{2}$" length of ribbon with only five $2\frac{1}{2}$"-long intervals. Stitch larger petals in place with embroidery floss, then stitch smaller petals on top. Make small stitches throughout flower for texture.
(3) Completed Mum.

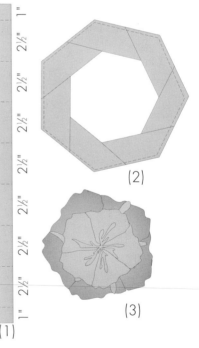

• Rosette

(1) Cut a 12" piece of 9mm ribbon. Fold ribbon at a 45° angle with $\frac{1}{2}$" tail. Fold again.

(2) Fold edge of ribbon diagonally back and wrap around center. Secure each wrap with thread. Continue to wrap and roll for half of the ribbon.

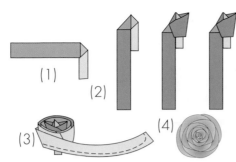

(1)
(2)
(3)
(4)

(3) Gather bottom edge of remaining ribbon tapering thread at end. Pull up gathers and wrap around rose. Secure.

(4) Completed Rosette.

• Straight Stitch

This stitch may be taut or loose, depending on desired effect.

(1) Come up at A. Go down at B, keeping the ribbon flat.

(2) Completed Straight Stitch.

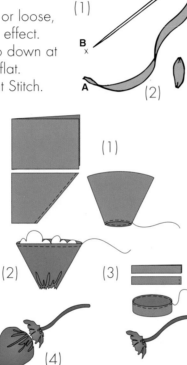

(1)

B
x

A
(2)

• Strawberry

(1) Cut a 4" length of 1½"-wide red ribbon and a 3" length of ¼"-wide single-faced light olive satin. Fold red ribbon in half. Make a diagonal cut in the ribbon so that the bottom measures ¾" and the top 2". Stitch the diagonal together and turn to right side. Make a running stitch along the bottom. Pull tight and secure gathers.

(1)

(2)

(3)

(4)

(2) Lightly stuff strawberry with a small amount of batting. Gather-stitch top edge of strawberry and secure gathers.

(3) Fold ¼"-wide olive satin in half. Stitch seam and turn. Gather-stitch top edge. Tie a knot in one end of 2mm rattail, and place throughout center of olive gathered edge so that the knot is on the inside for stem. Stitch gathers and rattail securely in place.

(4) Tack olive satin to strawberry. Pin completed strawberry to background, being careful to make tacks as invisible as possible. Lightly shape and mold strawberry with french knots, using three strands of olive brown embroidery floss.

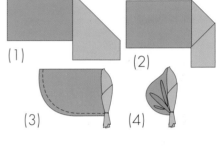

(1)

(2)

• Violet

(1) Cut a 7½" length of 1"-wide shaded violet silk ribbon. Fold in half lengthwise and press. Trace a half circle five times on ribbon, leaving ¼" at beginning and end. Gather-stitch along each half circle. Pull as tight as possible and secure thread. Join to first petal and secure thread. Adjust petals as needed.

(2) Completed Violet.

• Wisteria

Make twelve 3" petals like a rosette.

(1) Fold 1½"-wide fabric at a 45° angle.

(2) Fold again. Roll fabric three times. Stitch to secure.

(1)

(2)

(3)

(4)

(3) Gather remaining ribbon, tapering thread at end and leaving a ¼" seam allowance.

(4) Pull tight and tie off. Stitch to rosebud. Arrange petals, following diagram on page 122.

• Painting Techniques and Tips •

Painting on fabric requires a textile medium. A textile medium is mixed with acrylic paint to make it glide better over fabric and make it permeate the fibers. It prevents paint from bleeding and makes the painting, when dry, permanent.

Fabric should be washed before painting and then ironed smooth. The fabric should then be stretched taut to prevent any bubbling or puckering. See page 11 for ideas on keeping fabric flat.

To use a textile medium, first pour a small amount of desired paint onto palette. Place a few drops of medium onto paint. Mix well. The paint will become more transparent as more textile medium is added. Paint can also be diluted with water. Paint. After the paint is dry, most fabrics painted with textile medium can be heat-set in a dryer or with a warm iron on the reverse side of fabric. *Make certain to read and follow manufacturer's instructions when using a textile medium.*

Model Information

Method: Machine-Stitched
Enlargement: 125%
Fabrics: Cottons and Muslin
Note: Star charms were used on bottom right house.

FOR SALE
APARTMENT FOR WRENT
VISITORS WELCOME
HOUSE HUNTING

Framed Birdhouses Patterns

Additional Designs

Every seed after its own kind

Be one of a kind

Model Information

Method: Machine-Stitched
Enlargement: Actual Size
Fabrics: Cotton Calicos
Note: Charms were added to ap-pliqué to go along with heart sayings.

Framed Heart and Broken Heart Patterns

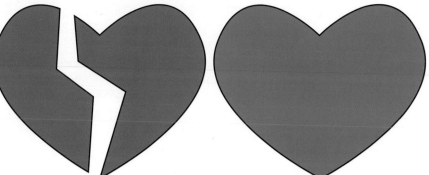

Additional Designs

Framed
Picket
Fence and
Birdhouses
Pattern

Model Information

Method: Machine-Stitched
Enlargement: 190%
Fabrics: Printed Cottons
*Notes: Picket fence was stenciled
on fabric with diluted white
acrylic paint. Buttons were used
for flower centers.*

Additional Design

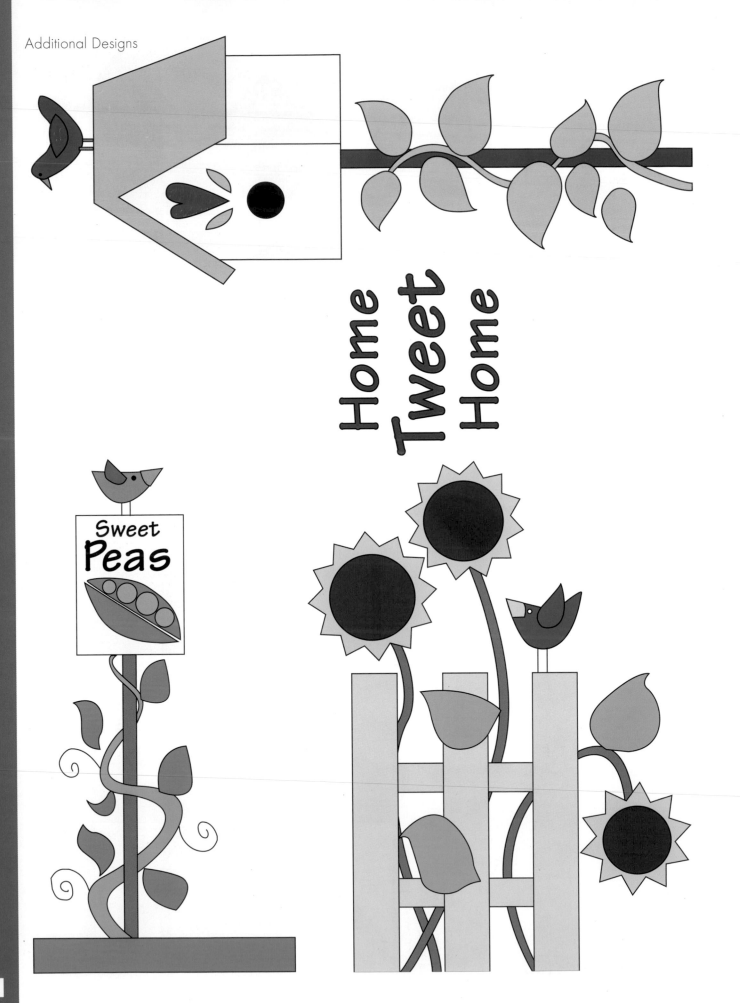

Additional Designs

COME IN

OUT OF THE RAIN

HOME SWEET HOME

FACE

HANDS

Model Information

Blueberry and Strawberry
Method: Fused and Machine-Stitched
Enlargement: 180%
Fabrics: Cotton and Poly-Cotton Blends

Hands and Face
Method: Fused and Machine-Stitched
Enlargement: 210%
Fabrics: Cotton

Sunflowers
Method: Fused and Machine-Stitched
Enlargement: 190%
Fabrics: Cotton Calicos

Additional Design

It all starts
with a
little miracle!

Blueberry and Strawberry Pattern

Hands and Face Pattern

A B C D E F G H I J K
L M N O P Q R S T U
V W X Y Z

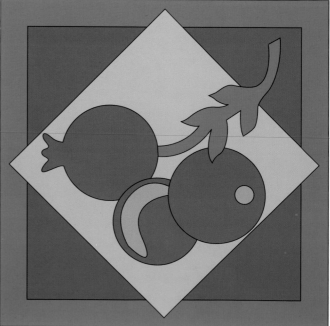

Sunflowers Pattern

Additional Designs

Model Information

Rex Rabbit Sweatshirt
Method: Fused
Enlargement: 215%
Fabrics: Cotton Blends

Rex Rabbit Tote Bag
Method: Fused and
   Machine-Stitched
Enlargement: 230%
Fabrics: Cotton Blends

Rex Rabbit Sweatshirt Pattern

Rex Rabbit Tote Bag Pattern

Share my garden

Share my heart.

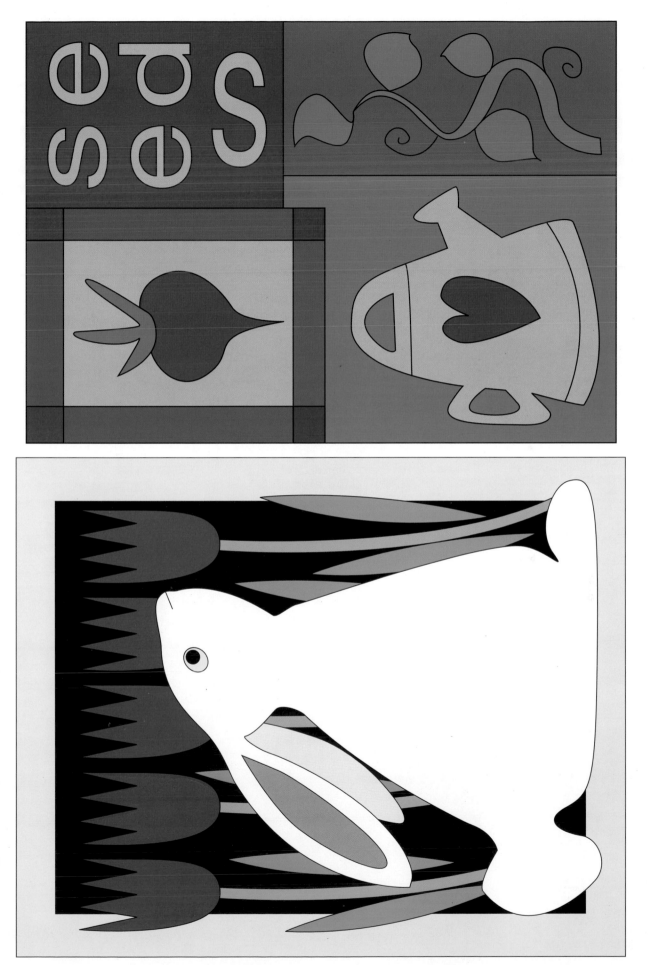

Additional Designs

Model Information

Forever Friends
Method: Padded, Fused, and Machine-Stitched
Enlargement: 510%
Fabrics: Screen-printed Cottons and Cotton Calicos

Joy to the World
Method: Fused and Machine-Stitched
Enlargement: 230%
Fabrics: Cotton Calicos

Apple of My Pie
Method: Fused and Machine-Stitched
Enlargement: 190%
Fabrics: Printed Cottons
Note: Lazy Daisy stitches and a button were stitched on pie crust.

Happy Halloween
Method: Fused and Hand-Stitched
Enlargement: 225%
Fabrics: Poly-Cotton Blends and Screen-Printed Background

Forever Friends Pattern

Unlikely Friends

Joy to the World Pattern

Apple of My
Pie Pattern

Happy
Halloween
Pattern

You're the apple of my pie

TO MY LITTLE PUMPKIN

HAPPY HALLOWEEN

Model Information

Juggling Cat
Method: Fused
Enlargement: 200%
Fabrics: Poly-Cotton Blends.
Note: Ceramic buttons were used as juggling balls

Jester
Method: Fused with Painted Stitch Lines
Enlargement: 170%
Fabrics: Screen-Printed Cottons
Note: Jester's face was made with acrylic paints.

Birdhouse
Method: Fused and Machine-Stitched
Enlargement: 250%
Fabrics: Cotton Calicos and Lace

Patriot Bears
Method: Fused with Fabric Pen Stitch Lines
Enlargement: 175%
Fabrics: Cottons (Screen-Print, Polished, Broadcloth, etc.)

Jester Pattern

Juggling Cat Pattern

Birdhouse Pattern

Patriot Bears Pattern

Model Information

Method: Fused and Machine-Stitched
Enlargement: 220%
Fabrics: Cotton Calicos
Note: Ceramic animal buttons were stitched to pockets.

Noah's Ark Pajamas Pattern

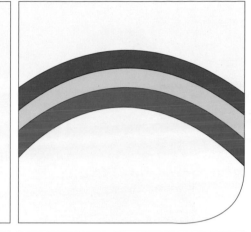

Additional Designs

• Traditional Appliqué

Model Information

Method: Hand- and Machine-Stitched
Enlargement: 200%
Fabrics: Cotton Calicos

all hearts go home
for **Christmas**

All Hearts Go Home Pattern

Model Information

Merry Christmas Wreath Banner
Method: Fused and Machine-Stitched
Enlargement: 240%
Fabrics: Printed Cottons
Notes: Washable taffeta ribbons were used on the banner. Metallic red machine embroidery thread was used on berries.

Snow Angels Banner
Method: Fused and Machine-Stitched
Enlargement: 340%
Fabrics: Felts and Screen-Printed Cottons.
Notes: Sequins were used for snowflake centers and seed beads for snow angels' eyes and mouths.

Merry Christmas Wreath Banner Pattern

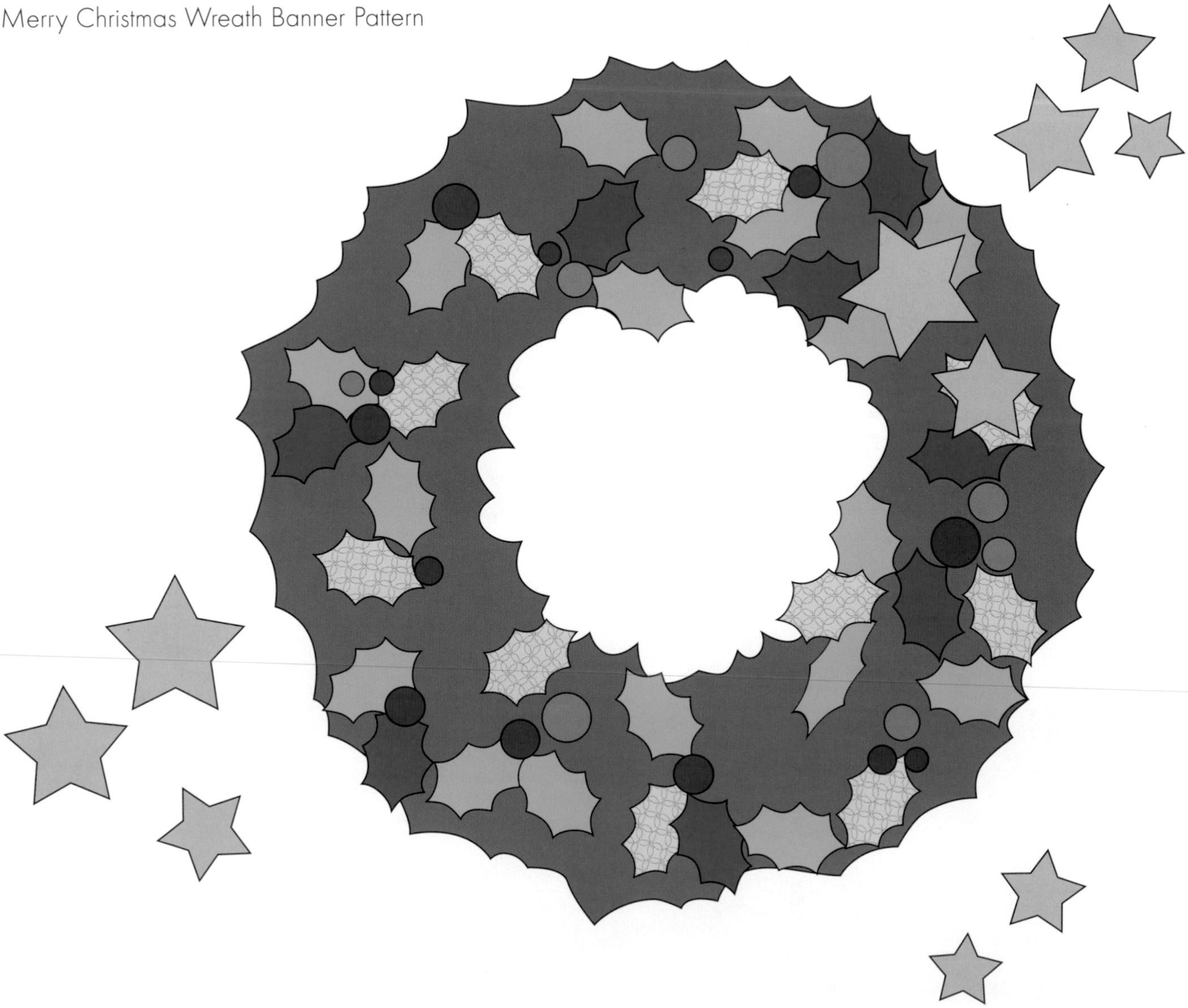

Additional Design

Snow Angels Banner Pattern

Additional Designs

LIGHTS FADE
STARS APPEAR
EVENING ANGELS
GATHER HERE.

Alleluia

Model Information

Method: Fused, and Hand- and Machine-Stitched
Enlargement: 200%
Fabrics: Cotton Calicos on a Cotton Rug

Additional
Designs

Yuletide Table Runner
Pattern

HO
HO
HO

Model Information

Cowboy Bags

Method: Fused Appliqué
Enlargement: 145%
Fabrics: Denim, Bandanna,
and Gold Metallic

Holiday Ornaments Bag

Method: Fused Appliqué
Enlargement: 190%
Fabrics: Vinyl Coated Metallic
or Wrapping Paper, and
Gold Metallic Lace
*Note: Cording was used for
ornament "hangers."*

Cowboy Bags Patterns

KICK UP YOUR HEELS

These boots are made for walking-

Holiday Ornaments Bag Pattern

Additional Designs

Share my garden

Share my heart...

Here
Kitty
Kitty

HEARTS
over easy

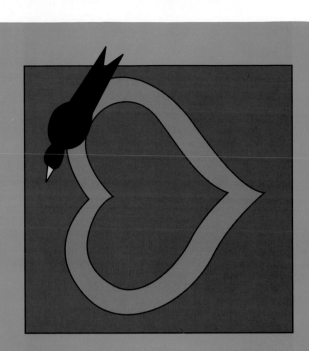

Hearts & Sunflowers Panel Pattern

Model Information

Hearts & Sunflowers Panel
Method: Fused Appliqué
Enlargement: 290%
Fabrics: Cotton Calicos

Sunflower Clock
Method: Fused Appliqué
Enlargement: 150%
Fabrics: Cotton Calicos

• Clocks •

Materials

¾"-thick wooden circle (model was 9" in diameter)
Clock movement and hands
Acrylic paints
Paintbrushes and sponges
Drill

Instructions

1. Paint clock face as desired with acrylic paints (model was sponge-painted). Let dry. Apply double-sided fusible web to appliqué motifs, following general instructions and manufacturer's instructions. Iron motifs onto clock face, being careful not to touch painted surface with hot iron.

2. Drill a hole for clock movement in center of clock face, according to size of clock movement and manufacturer's instructions. Assemble clock movement and attach clock hands, according to manufacturer's instructions.

Additional Design

Sunflower Clock Pattern

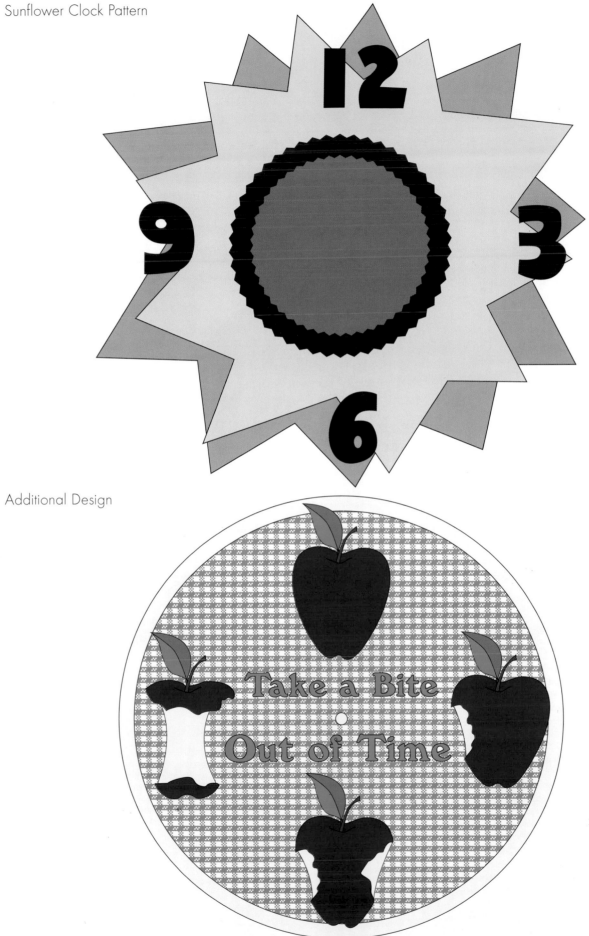

Additional Design

Model Information

Row of Hears Pocket
Method: Mixed Media and
  Machine-Stitched
Enlargement: Actual Size
Fabrics: Cotton with Acrylic Paints
  mixed with Textile Medium
  and Ink

Wacky House Shirt
Method: Mixed Media and Hand-
  Stitched
Enlargement: 125%
Fabrics: Cotton with Acrylic Paints
  mixed with Textile Medium

Hidden Hearts Shirt
Method: Mixed Media and Hand-
  Stitched
Enlargement: 160%
Fabrics: Cotton with Acrylic Paints
  mixed with Textile Medium

Elegant Lace Shirt
Method: Mixed Media and
  Dimensional Ribbon Embroidery
Fabrics: Lace Motif; Burgundy, Blue,
  Green, Orange, and Terra-Cotta,
  4mm silk ribbons

Row of Hearts Pocket Pattern

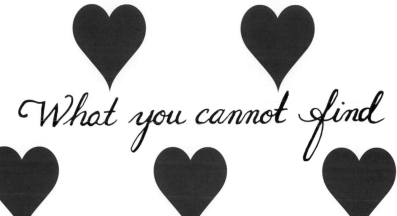

What you cannot find

on earth

is not worth seeking

Wacky House Shirt Pattern

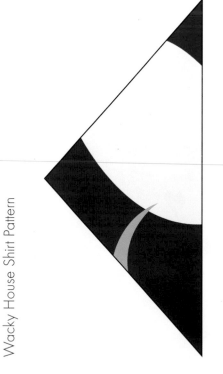

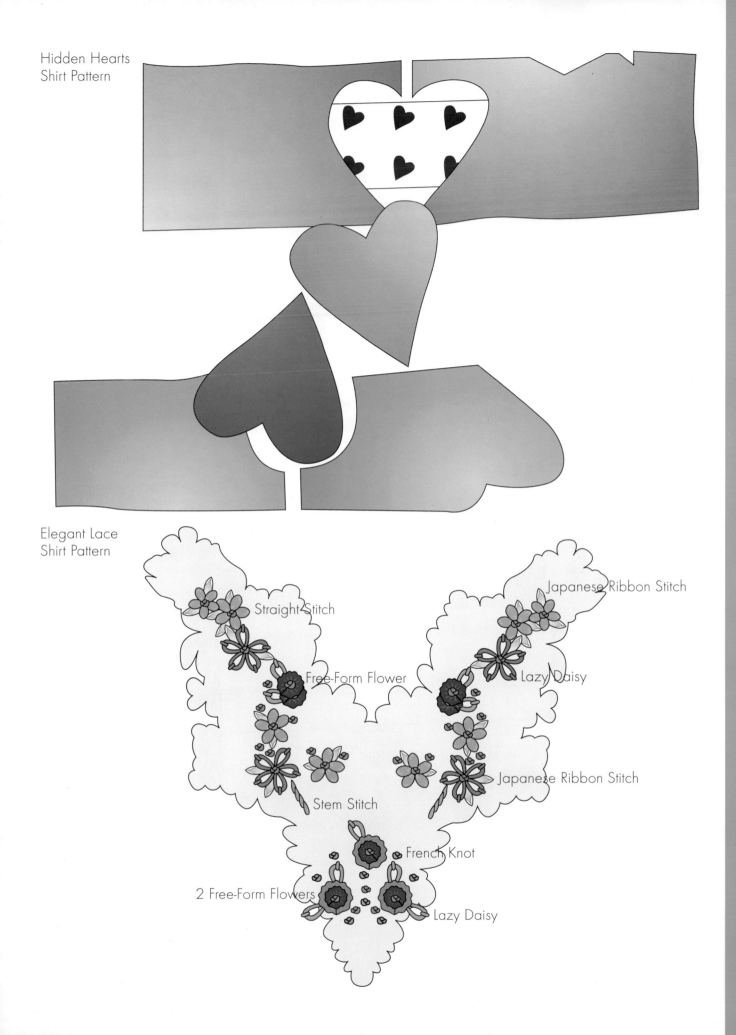

Hidden Hearts
Shirt Pattern

Elegant Lace
Shirt Pattern

Straight Stitch

Japanese Ribbon Stitch

Free-Form Flower

Lazy Daisy

Japanese Ribbon Stitch

Stem Stitch

French Knot

2 Free-Form Flowers

Lazy Daisy

Model Information

Gold Ribbon Towel
Method: Dimensional Ribbon Appliqué
Ribbons: 1"-wide Gold Sheer, ⅝"-wide Gold Sheer, 1"-wide Brown Ombré Wired, and Blue/Grey and Gold 4mm Silk

Spiral Flowers Towel
Method: Machine-Stitched (straight stitch along center of ribbon)
Ribbons: 7mm Rayon

Additional Design,

Gold Ribbon Towel Diagram

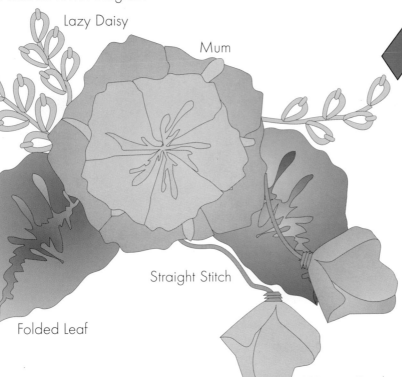

Lazy Daisy

Mum

Straight Stitch

Folded Leaf

Wisteria Petal

Spiral Flowers Towel Diagram

Model Information

Floppy Daisy Jumper
Method: Free-Standing Motifs, Machine-Stitched
Enlargement: 250%
Fabrics: Muslin and Cotton, and Denim Jumper

Floppy Daisy Jumper Pattern

Notes: Long strips of muslin were cut for daisy leaves and left to flop. Buttons were sewn to center of flower for texture.

Additional Designs

Flowerpot Apron
Method: Machine-Stitched
Enlargement: 245%
Fabrics: Polished Cottons

Flowerpot Apron Pattern

Additional Designs

• Daisy Jumper •

Materials

1 yard 60"-wide denim; matching thread
¼ yard muslin
2" x 45" torn strip of green cotton fabric; matching thread
2½"-diameter circle of tan fabric; matching thread
1 package of ½"-wide elastic
¾"-wide flat bias tape
15–20 old buttons

Instructions

1. From denim, cut two jumper straps 30" x 3½". Cut two jumper ties 60" x 2". Cut one jumper piece 28" x 45".

2. Hem long edges of straps with a ¼" rolled hem, top-stitching in place. Place a length of bias tape down center on wrong side of each strap. Stitch down both sides of bias tape to form casing. Thread elastic through casing and stitch ends down.

3. Fold tie strips in half lengthwise and press. Fold each edge in to center and press again. Topstitch down both sides through all layers.

4. Lay jumper piece flat and mark center with a pin at the top and bottom. Zigzag all edges of jumper. Fold top edge down 2" and press. Repeat for bottom edge.

5. Tear muslin into 1" strips and cut into 5" to 7" lengths. Start flower in center of jumper about 6" down from top. Layer muslin strips in a spoke fashion, mixing lengths together. Pin tan fabric circle in center and satin-stitch around edge. Sew buttons in center, allowing buttons to overlap. Tear green cotton fabric in half lengthwise. Cut pieces desired length for stem and leaves. Arrange on jumper, letting them twist and curl. Sew a straight stitch down center of stem and leaves.

6. Mark and sew a buttonhole 3" up from bottom edge of jumper in the center of front. Mark and sew two buttonholes 3" down from top edge and 1¼" in from side edges.

7. With right sides together, bring sides together and sew up back seam. Sew the 2" hem in the top and bottom. Stitch a casing in each hem at the 1" mark. Thread ties through casings and out through buttonholes. Sew straps in place, adjusting for size desired.

• Flowerpot Apron Pocket •

Materials

½ yd. terra-cotton polished cotton; matching thread
Ruler or yardstick
Fabric-marking pencil

Instructions

1. Cut a 16½" x 15" piece of polished cotton. Fold top edge down 3¾", wrong sides together. Press. Sew ¼" from raw edge through both layers to secure. Fold top edge over 3" to right side to form top of flowerpot.

2. Fold bottom edge up ½". Press.

3. Using ruler and marking pencil, mark a center line on the wrong side of fabric. At top edge, mark two ¼" intervals out from center. At bottom edge, mark ½" and ¾" out from center. Draw a line connecting top and bottom marks. Fold at lines to make box pleat. Bar-tack at top of pocket.

4. Mark ½" from bottom left and right edges. Mark a line from top edges to bottom marks.

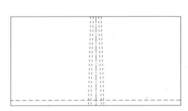

5. Cut along line. Fold edges in ¾". Press. Pin pocket in place on apron. Sew along sides and bottom. Tack at center top. Fold in pleat again and press.

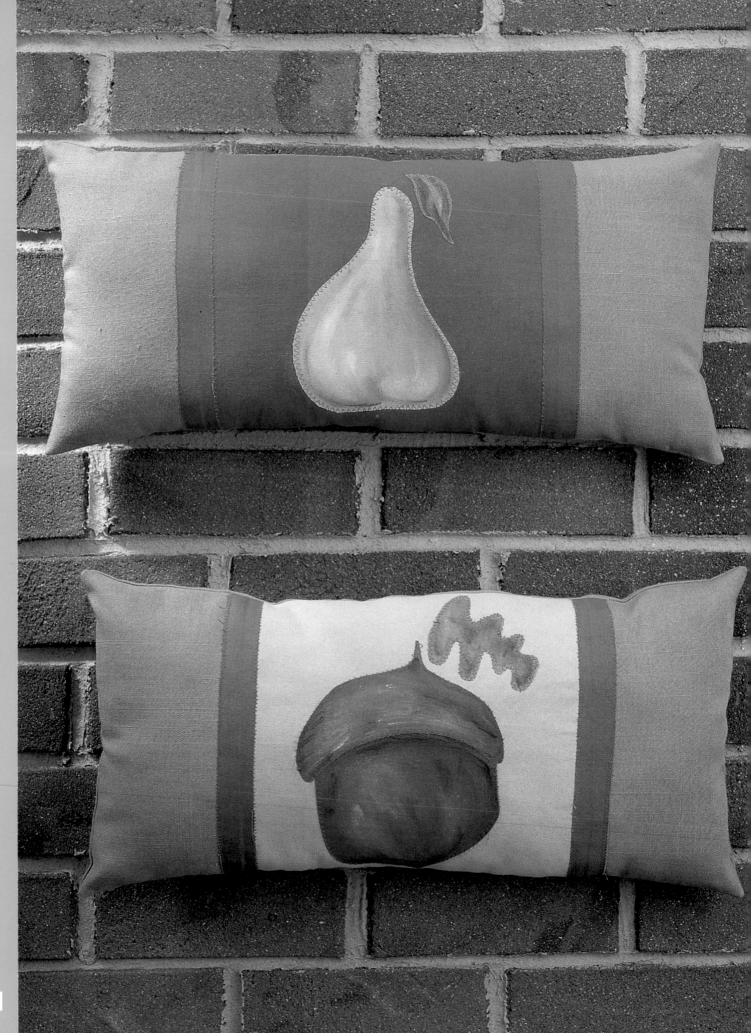

Model Information

Pear Pillow
Method: Machine-Stitched, Mixed Media
Enlargement: 155%
Fabrics: Cotton Twill

Pear Pillow Pattern

Acorn Pillow
Method: Machine-Stitched, Mixed Media
Enlargement: 220%
Fabrics: Cotton Twill

Acorn Pillow Pattern

Additional Designs

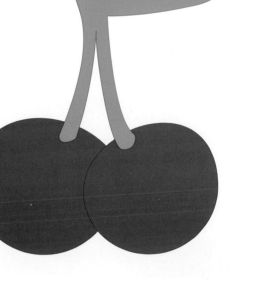

Model Information

Flowerpots
Method: Fused Appliqué
Enlargement: 135%
Fabrics: Cotton Calicos

Gardening Gloves
Method: Fused Appliqué
Enlargement: 180%
Fabrics: Printed Cottons

Flowerpots Patterns

Additional Designs

Sew the seeds of love!

Appliqué designs onto fabric or paper seed packets. Fill packets with seeds. Give the seed-filled packets to someone who needs extra love, joy, time, or hope.

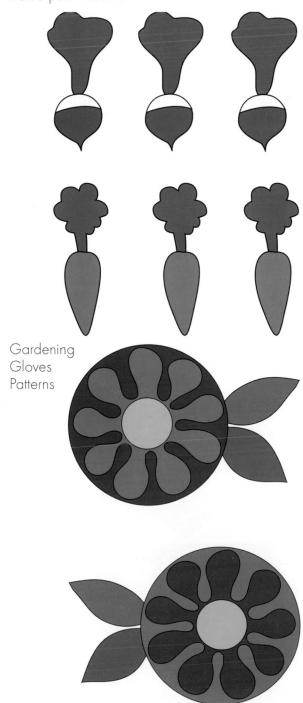

Gardening
Gloves
Patterns

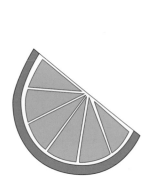

Two-Hour Beaded Projects

introduction ...

The history of traditional jewelry and its decoration began with the pieces worn by hunters and gatherers in their caves. It spans thousands of years and not only connects every continent, but every civilization of the world.

The story begins with necklaces that were made from the bone and teeth of animals and from the flowers and fruits that were gathered. It progresses through the ages to the gold, silver, and precious stones that were used to make the collars, crowns, and goblets for kings and noblemen.

There is a tale, told during these same years, that is of decorative objects and jewelry made and worn for folk and ethnic costumes and for decorating the homes of the more common people and tribesmen.

These pieces were ornaments whose makers had no rules or customs, whose style was dictated by the time, the event, the place, and the artist.

The making and wearing of jewelry and special objects that are adorned by jewels has always been prompted by vanity, status, religion, and superstition. They have been used throughout time for trading, for the expression of love, and for the giving of gifts. These pieces that are so admired and so sought after have sometimes been extravagantly ornate and sometimes priceless, yet have sometimes been made of the simplest of materials and in the shortest amount of time. Descendants of the latter are the pieces that are presented here. Those pieces that are much admired and constantly worn or displayed by the receiver yet inexpensive and quickly made by the giver.

Here in TWO-HOUR BEADED PROJECTS, not only can traditional pieces of jewelry such as necklaces, bracelets, and earrings be found, but unique styles have been created to suit many personalities. Hair accessories have been included as have many ideas for embellishing wearables. There are also ideas for creating home decorative accessories, such as adorning candle holders, glass vases, stationery boxes, suncatchers, decorative bottles, and much more.

Here are pieces that can be made for a daughter, a mother, or a friend. Here are pieces that are perfect for gift giving or for keeping for oneself. Here are pieces that are beautiful in their simplicity and practical in their monetary value.

It is hoped that what is within these pages will give hours of enjoyment not only in the making, but in the giving and receiving.

bead shapes ...

bugle beads

Bugle beads are essentially very long seed beads. They are long thin tubes which come in a variety of lengths. Bugle beads are available in many finishes, but the color selection is limited. Some bugle beads are twisted in the manufacturing process.

faceted beads

Faceted beads are often referred to as "crystals." They are made in many different shapes and colors.

Faceted beads are classified as molded crystal and cut crystal. Cut crystal is more expensive and comes in a wider range of shapes than molded crystal.

Finishes can be applied to any faceted bead. Molded crystal beads are available with metallic finishes — usually in silver or bronze.

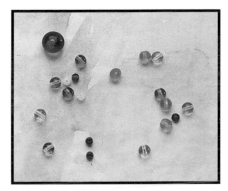

round beads

Round beads, of course, are spherical. They come in many sizes and are measured in millimeters. They can be found in numerous colors and finishes and can be made from polymer clay.

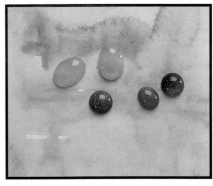

cabochons

Cabochons are flattened beads without holes and are usually mounted in a bezel cup (refer to page 95). They are available in a wide range of sizes and can be made from almost any material, including polymer clay. There is a good selection of cabochons available in semiprecious stones.

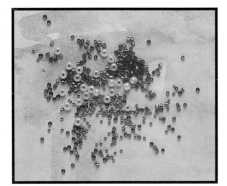

seed beads

Seed beads are small glass beads and are the most common type of bead used. They are available with many finishes and are made in many, many colors. They come in a variety of sizes — the larger the number, the smaller the bead.

fancy shaped beads

Fancy shaped beads can vary from cylindrical, cube, and oval to twisted disks and tubes, triangles and tear drops, lozenges, and donuts. Many of these beads make great centerpieces on all varieties of jewelry.

a little about beads ...

glass beads

Glass beads are available in an unbelievable range of size, shape, and color. It is no wonder glass beads are used more often than any other type of decorative bead.

Glass beads can be molded or hand-blown. Molded glass beads can be made in almost any color of glass and are readily available in any bead store. Hand-blown glass beads can be exquisitely beautiful.

plastic beads

Some of the most exciting beads available are plastic beads. Plastic beads can be pale and translucent or wildly colorful, and their variation is nearly endless. Because they are almost always molded, the holes in the beads are uniform in size.

Besides affordability, plastic beads offer many advantages to the serious beadworker. Plastic beads are lightweight and consistently strong. This makes plastic beads an ideal candidate for use on heavier-weight cords and multiple strand cords.

metal beads

The price of metal beads is largely determined by their precious metal content. Sterling silver, gold-filled, and gold-plated beads can be costly.

There are, however, several styles and sizes of metal beads that are available in surface-washed base metal beads. These beads are readily available, lightweight, and inexpensive.

natural beads

Natural beads include wood, stone, and bone beads. These beads have a special beauty.

Wood beads are lightweight, relatively inexpensive, and widely available. Many varieties of wood are used to make wood beads, and each is unique because of its grain and finish. Unlacquered wood beads can be soaked in vanilla or fragrant oils and worn as perfume.

Stone beads are very popular and include turquoise, pearls, and semiprecious stones. Because the are derived from nature, they are available in a myriad of sizes, shapes, and colors.

Bone beads are made from bone or tusk. These beads are often made into disks, which are usually side-drilled for use in making jewelry pieces.

ceramic beads

Ceramic beads can be either rough or decorated. Both beads are made from the same materials; however, the differences lie in the way the surfaces are treated.

Rough ceramic beads can be glazed, but because of the rough, grainy surface after firing the beads, they appear to be unglazed.

Decorated ceramic beads are often glazed before firing, but some decorated ceramic beads are painted with permanent colors after firing. Decals are often added to the surface of the fired ceramic bead.

Most ceramic beads tend to have a soft, natural color, but some varieties have dye added to the clay before the beads are formed. Therefore, colors are literally unrestricted.

Ceramic beads come in an unlimited variety of shapes and sizes but can be quite heavy.

clay beads

Polymer clays are used to make clay beads. Truly a modern wonder, polymer clay allows any bead to be made at any time in any shape, any size, and any color!

There are many fine instructional manuals on the subject of making clay beads.

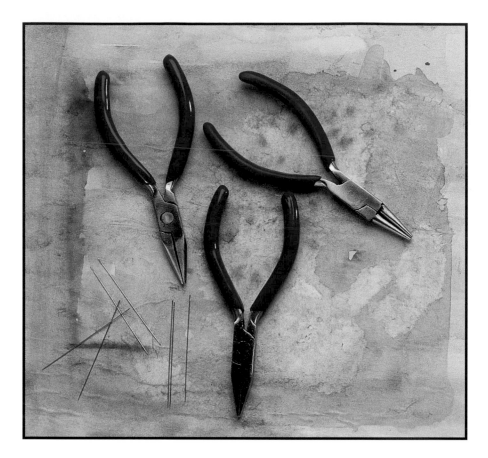

tools ...

Very few tools are required for successful beadwork. A good assortment of needles and sharp scissors are essential.

Wirecutters, round-nose pliers, and needle-nose pliers are necessary for making jewelry with headpins and eyepins.

bead sizes ...

Round beads: 4mm, 6mm, 8mm, 10mm, 12mm

Oval cabochons: 4x6mm, 5x7mm, 6x8mm, 8x10mm, 10x12mm, 10x14mm, 13x18mm, 18x25mm

Round cabochons: 25mm, 20mm, 16mm, 12mm, 10mm, 8mm, 6mm, 5mm, 4mm, 3mm

Seed Beads:	**Bugle Beads:**
6/0 seed beads	20mm bugle beads
8/0 seed beads	15mm bugle beads
11/0 seed beads	#5 bugle beads
14/0 seed beads	#3 bugle beads
12/0 three cuts	#2 bugle beads
hex beads	

Photos are actual size.

beading components ...

pre-strung beads

Pre-strung beads are available in a number of different varieties, sizes, and colors.

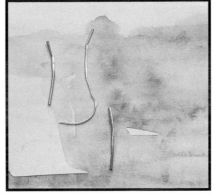

french wire

French wire is a tightly wound coil of very fine metal wire. It is available in a variety of diameters and finishes, and is extremely flexible. It can be cut with ordinary scissors without marring the cutting surface.

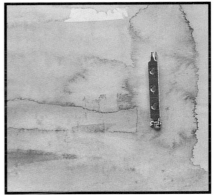

pin backs

Pin backs are available in a wide range of styles and sizes. They can be made from gold- and silver-plated metal.

Pin backs are generally glued to the back of the pin.

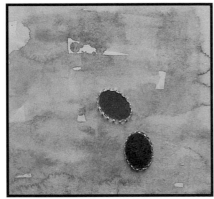

bezel cups

Bezel cups hold flat-backed cabochons and can easily be incorporated into simple jewelry designs. They are available in a variety of sizes.

The outer wall of the cup is a series of loops, which give it a lacy appearance. These loops can be bent and used as joining loops quite easily. The remainder of the loops can be bent inward in close contact with the cabochon to hold it in the cup, or a tiny dot of glue can be placed in the center of the cup to hold the stone in place.

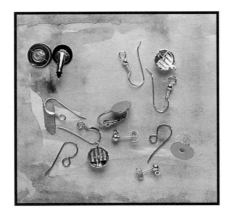

ear findings

Ear findings are available in a wide range of styles and sizes. They can be made from plated base metal or genuine gold and silver.

Ear findings include French ear wires, ear clips, and ear posts. Ear clips or posts can be glued to the back of the earring or to a bead. Ear wires usually come with a loop in order to hang an intended finding.

Niobium is a finish that is often used to enhance the look of a pair of earrings and can be found in a variety of bright colors.

button cover blanks

Button cover blanks are made from base metal and can be found in a brass- or silver-colored finish. The size is usually about 3/4" in diameter, and will accommodate buttons up to a slightly larger size.

findings & components ...

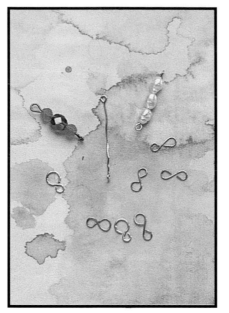

headpins & eyepins

Headpins and eyepins come in a variety of gauges, finishes, and lengths.

Headpins look much like nails with one flat end. This flat end keeps beads from falling off the pin.

Eyepins are used in the same manner as headpins, but they have a loop instead of a flat end. Eyepins are often used to make figure-eight connectors.

figure-eight & beaded connectors

Figure-eight connectors are small links in the shape of the number "8" which can be made from an eyepin or from metal wire.

Beaded connectors are extended figure-eight connectors that have beads in between the loops on the ends. Beaded connectors can also be made from headpins.

clasps

Clasps can be very ornate or very simple and they can act as part of the design. They come in a variety of finishes and shapes, but they must be coordinated with the beadwork.

It is recommended that barrel clasps not be used when assembling bracelets — they must be closed using both hands!

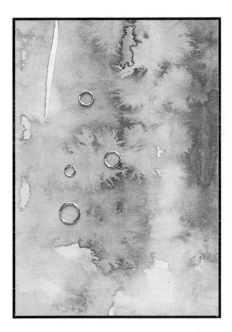

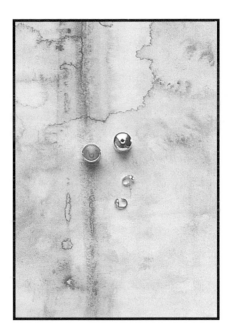

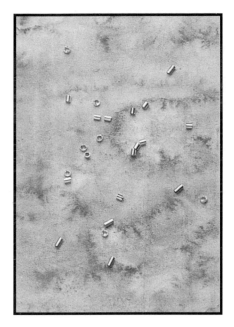

rings

Rings are used to join components, such as clasps or strung beads. They are available in a wide range of sizes and finishes.

Jump rings have a gap in the circle and separate easily with pliers.

Split rings are tiny key holders — the ring is doubled onto itself for better surety.

Unless crimps are used, rings are generally used when attaching clasps.

end caps & end cups

End caps can be found in cylindrical and conical shapes and in a variety of metal finishes. They are used to create a finished look on the ends of multi-strand necklaces, bracelets, and earrings.

End cups hold the knot of beading thread and are then attached to the clasp and jump ring on necklaces and bracelets. They come in silver-tone and gold-tone finishes.

crimps

Crimps are flattened over wire or leather with the use of pliers to secure a strand of beads to a clasp or other finding. It is important that the crimp being used is the proper size for the material being secured.

When possible, coordinate the finish of the crimp with the finish of the clasp.

general instructions ...

adding a new length of thread

When about three inches of thread remains unbeaded on the needle, it is time to add a new thread.

Remove the needle from the old thread and cut a new 30" length. Thread the needle so that a 5" tail remains. A longer thread tends to tangle, and a shorter thread necessitates frequent rethreadings.

Tie a square knot so that the knot lands about 1" from where the old thread emerges from the beadwork. Refer to the diagrams below.

Place a tiny dot of glue on the knot. Wipe off any excess glue, but the glue need not be dry before proceeding.

Continue beading as if one continuous thread were being used. Let the thread ends protrude from the work until the new thread is well established within the weave. Refer to the diagrams below. Pull gently on the ends and clip them close so that they disappear into the weave. It might be necessary to use a smaller needle until the area of the knot has been passed.

assembling beaded connectors

A beaded connector is an extended figure-eight connector with a bead(s) added in the middle. It can also be referred to when threading a bead(s) onto a headpin.

When starting with an eyepin, trim it to 3/8" beyond the last bead. Using round-nose pliers, form a second loop in the opposite direction as shown in the diagram below. Many eyepins can be beaded and joined together to form a necklace or bracelet. When working with metal wire, form the first loop, trim to 3/8", and form the second loop. Any wire used to make a connector should be substantial enough to retain the shape of the loops. If the wire can easily be shaped, it is probably not strong enough for use as a jewelry connector.

When starting with a headpin, simply thread on the beads and cut the headpin with wirecutters so there is 1/4" to 3/8" excess. Using round-nose pliers, form a loop in the top of the headpin as shown in the diagram below, then close it around the intended finding. Headpins are the most commonly used finding when assembling earrings. A headpin with beads can be attached to an eyepin and will dangle with a nice movement.

attaching clasps

Clasps have loops by which they may be attached. Depending on the type of material used for stringing, they may be attached to end caps or joined to the strand by crimping.

End caps are sometimes used to join multiple strands to a clasp. Some clasps have multiple loops and are designed for a specific number of strands, in which case you should attach the strand directly to the clasp loops using end caps or crimps to secure the fiber.

attaching end caps

Cover a final knot, holding several strands together, with cylindrical or conical end caps.

Open the loop on an eyepin, and insert it through the hole in the end cap. Close the loop around the knot. Pull the knot into the cap, then trim the excess eyepin to 3/8" and form another loop, which should be attached to your clasp.

Refer to the diagrams below.

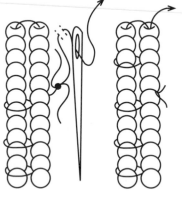

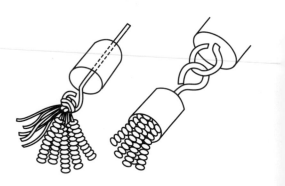

brick-stitching

Brick-stitch is a diagonal weaving technique in which the beads lay against one another like alternating bricks. All work progresses outward from a central foundation row. Each new row is looped into the previous row one bead at a time. The resulting weave is strong and flexible, and can be used for many different purposes.

The foundation row is worked with two needles. Cut a length of thread about 24" long, and thread each end onto a needle. Center the first bead of the foundation row between the two needles, then form the foundation row. Refer to the first diagram below.

Thereafter, you will work with one needle at a time. It is convenient to remove the needle from the thread end not currently in use, as it minimizes the tangling of the two threads. Refer to the diagrams below.

For rethreadings, refer to "adding a new length of thread" on page 16.

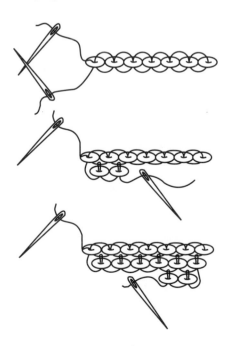

crimping

Secure tigertail or nylon to a jump ring or clasp, using a crimp which is squeezed tightly with pliers over the trimmed end to form a strong loop.

Refer to the diagrams below.

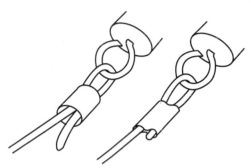

embellishing simple objects

Many simple pieces of jewelry can be dramatized with the simple addition of drops or hangers.

When planning to embellish jewelry, choose jewelry pieces that have openings suitable for inserting loops.

To make sure the drops or hangers move freely, make the loops a bit larger. When trimming the headpins, leave an excess of 1/2" instead of the usual 3/8".

finishing strands

The diagrams below show two methods used for finishing strands of beads that have been strung on sewing thread or beading cord.

Finish the knotted strands with one large knot — knotted over itself until it is of substantial size. With matching sewing thread, sew the knot to an attractive clasp (ring shown) or knot nylon thread into an end cup, then attach it with a jump ring to a clasp.

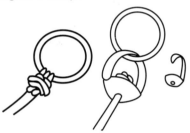

fusing fabric

To fuse fabric to beadwork, a thick white towel, completed beadwork, fusible webbing, fabric, a sheet of white paper, and an iron are needed.

Layer and center the components in the following manner, starting at the bottom: the towel, the beadwork face down, the fusible webbing with paper removed, the fabric right side up, and the sheet of white paper.

Press the iron down flat for five seconds. Shift the iron and press for two more seconds to eliminate any steam holes. Allow the piece to cool completely. With nail scissors, trim the excess from around the beadwork. Run a thin line of diluted white glue around the entire trimmed edge to secure.

needle-weaving

The work in needle-weaving always proceeds in the direction of the beadworker's dominant hand.

To begin, make a "stopper bead," which keeps the design pattern beads from slipping off the needle. Refer to the diagrams below. Cut a length of thread about 30 inches long and thread a needle so that a 5" tail remains.

Slip one bead over the needle and position it about 3 inches from the long end of the thread. Loop the thread back through the bead and pull it tightly. Secure the stopper bead to a flat or slightly curved surface to stabilize the thread. Remove the stopper bead after the first few rows.

Thread the beads of row 1 from top to bottom. Refer to the diagrams below. Skip the last bead threaded, inserting the needle back through all the beads on the thread. The needle should emerge from the top bead of row 1.

Thread the beads of row 2, again reading from top to bottom. Refer to the diagrams below.

Insert the needle into the loop exposed at the bottom of row 1. Pull the thread gently until the whole second row is taut, but not tight. It should rest against the first row without much puckering.

Insert the needle into the last bead of row 2, and bring the thread out until it is taut, but not tight. Loop the thread around row 1 so that it nestles in the space between beads 12 and 11 of row 2, bringing the needle out in the space between beads 10 and 9 on row 2. Again, the thread should be taut, but not tight.

Loop the thread around row 1 so that it nestles in the space between beads 10 and 9 of row 1. Insert the needle into the next three beads on row 2 — beads 9, 8, and 7 — and bring the needle out in the space between beads 7 and 6 on row 2.

Tighten the thread again, then loop it around the first row so that it nestles in the space between beads 7 and 6 on row 1. Insert the needle into the next three beads on row 2 — beads 6, 5, and 4 — and repeat the looping and inserting process until the thread emerges from bead 1 of row 2. After row 2, the work may no longer need to be stabilized. It gets easier and easier to handle as the weaving grows.

For rethreadings, refer to "adding a new length of thread" on page 16.

surface beading

Surface beading requires beads to be sewn on individually and may be done on any material through which a beading needle can pass (fabric, soft leather, paper, or card stock). The method used to make the stitch is largely determined by the type of bead being sewn.

Seed Beads:

Seed beads can be sewn on singly or in multiples. For tight curves and small areas, single beading is best. For larger areas or lines, two or more beads can be sewn on at one time.

The diagram below shows two excellent methods for sewing on a single seed bead.

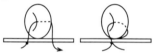

The diagram below shows how to sew on two seed beads at one time.

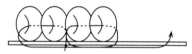

The diagram below shows how to backtrack a line of seed beads to stabilize them.

The diagram below shows a long row of seed beads being held in place by couching stitches.

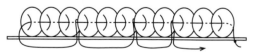

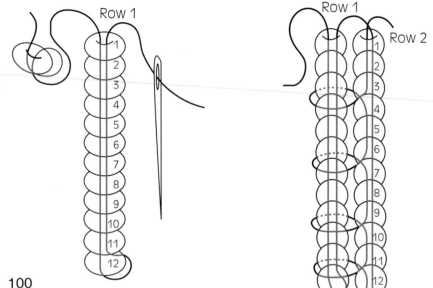

Row 1

Row 1 Row 2

Odd-Shaped Beads:

The method used to sew on these beads is largely determined by the shape of the bead.

Bugle beads, pearls, round beads, flat beads, and other odd-shaped beads can be sewn on using some of the techniques diagrammed below.

Note that in some cases the larger bead is anchored to the surface using a seed bead.

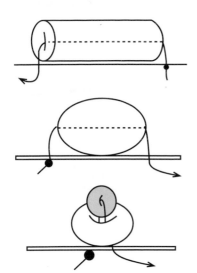

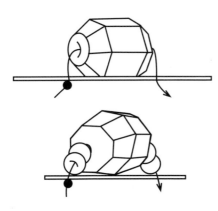

working with leather cord

Using leather cord as a foundation for the piece of jewelry makes the project extremely simple. The most important thing to keep in mind is that the beads chosen must have a large enough hole to accommodate the bulkiness of the leather cord.

Wood, bone, and metal beads tend to have larger holes than glass beads, and beads can always be made from polymer clay with custom-sized holes.

Cut the leather cord in the length needed. Then, simply thread the desired beads onto the cord and crimp on both trimmed ends.

Open the loops on the clasp, and close them around the crimp loops.

If necessary, refer to the diagrams below.

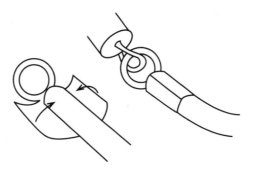

working with polymer clay

Working with clay:

Work the clay in your hands until it is soft and pliable. Form the softened clay into desired shapes. A rolling pin can be used to flatten the clay, or it can be run through the flattening wheels of a pasta machine. If the pasta machine does not create the correct thickness, combine two or more layers together. The thickness of the clay should be at least 1/8" for strength and stability. Do not use a pasta machine which may later be used to make edible pasta!

Form a U-shaped piece with the headpin scrap, and insert it into the top of the shape — be sure to leave enough space to slip the hanging cord or ribbon through.

Bake on a clean cookie sheet covered with aluminum foil at 200° F for 20 minutes. Allow to cool before handling.

If desired, coat the shape with varnish or clear nail polish.

Pressing beads into clay:

Lay the seed beads out on a flat surface in a tight layer with the bead holes up or down. Make the desired shape from the polymer clay. Roll the clay shape in the beads, and press the beads tightly into the surface of the clay. Repeat until the entire surface is covered with beads, filling in with individual beads as needed to cover the entire surface. Do not press the beads too deep into the clay or they will disappear.

Pictured from left to right: Turquoise Tube Necklace, Turquoise Drum Necklace, Lucky Elephant Necklace.

turquoise tube necklace

Materials:

Fifteen 6x14mm
turquoise tube beads
Thirty 6mm frosted
amethyst beads
Thirty metallic blue
11/0 seed beads
Thirty inches of
blue niobium wire
One silver-tone barrel clasp

Beading:

Cut the niobium wire into fifteen 2-inch lengths. Following the directions for assembling beaded connectors found in the General Instructions on page 98, assemble 15 links. Form a loop on one end of each niobium wire, and thread on the beads in the following order: one 11/0 seed bead, one 6mm bead, one turquoise tube, one 6mm bead, one 11/0 seed bead. Trim to 3/8" excess, then form a new loop from the trimmed ends.

Join the loops together to form the necklace. Following the directions for attaching clasps found in the General Instructions on page 98, attach one side of the barrel clasp to each end.

If necessary, refer to the photograph.

102

lucky elephant necklace

Materials:

One 2" cloisonne elephant
One 3x10mm
    turquoise tube
One 12x18mm
    turquoise barrel bead
One 8x10mm
    cloisonne bead
One 4mm blue
    round glass bead
Two gold-tone end caps
One gold-tone spring clasp
One gold-tone split ring
One gold-tone headpin
Three gold-tone eyepins
Twenty-four inches of
    5mm thick woven cord
Jewelry glue

Beading:

Sew the eyepins to the ends of the woven cord, and form the loops with the trimmed eyepins. Following the directions for attaching clasps found in the General Instructions on page 98, attach the eyepins to the spring clasp. Fill the end caps with glue, and glue them to the woven cord. Thread the elephant onto the remaining eyepin, and form a loop of adequate size to reach around the woven cord, trimming the eyepin first if needed.

Following the directions for assembling beaded connectors found in the General Instructions on page 98, assemble the beaded connector in the following order from bottom to top: 4mm round glass bead, cloisonne bead, turquoise barrel bead, turquoise tube. Add the drop below the elephant.

If necessary, refer to the photograph.

turquoise drum necklace

Materials:

One 13x25mm carved
    turquoise barrel bead
Two 6mm copol rondelles
Two 14x20mm amber beads
Four 8mm
    turquoise rondelles
Six 15mm square
    frosted plastic beads
Six metallic gold
    6/0 seed beads
Three gold-tone headpins
Two gold-tone leather crimps
One gold-tone spring clasp
One gold-tone split ring
Thirty inches of metallic
    green narrow leather cord

Beading:

Follow the diagram to assemble the necklace. First, thread on the square plastic beads and tie the knots, tightening them so that they will not loosen. Leave adequate space between the knots to allow the headpins to hang freely.

Following the directions for assembling beaded connectors found in the General Instructions on page 98, assemble the three headpins and trim to 1/2" beyond the last bead.

Following the directions for working with leather cord found in the General Instructions on page 101, attach the crimps to the leather, then attach the clasp and loop to the crimps. Form a loop in the excess using round-nose pliers and close the loop around the leather.

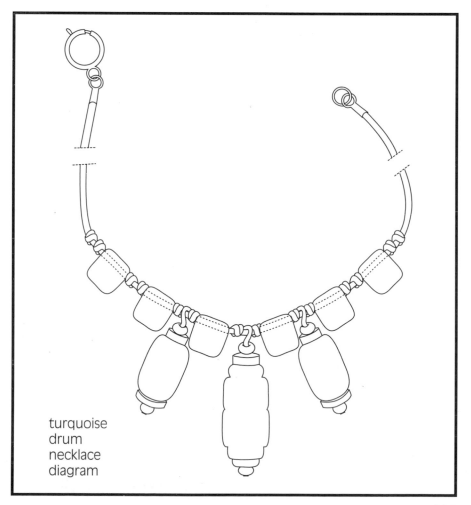

turquoise
drum
necklace
diagram

Pictured from left to right: Pastel Crystal Necklace, Bronze & Iris Crystal Necklace, Crystal Swirl Necklace.

pastel crystal necklace

Materials:

Nineteen 10mm aqua crystals
Thirty-eight 4mm green crystals
Seventy-six lavender color-lined
   11/0 seed beads
Thirty-four inches of
   green niobium wire
One silver-tone clasp

Beading:

Cut the niobium wire into nineteen equal lengths. Following the directions for assembling beaded connectors found in the General Instructions on page 98, assemble 19 links. Form a loop on one end of each wire, and thread on the beads in the following order: one 11/0 seed bead, one 4mm crystal, one 11/0 seed bead, one 10mm crystal, one 11/0 seed bead, one 4mm crystal, one 11/0 seed bead. Trim to 3/8" excess, then form a new loop from the trimmed ends.

Join the loops together to form the necklace. Following the directions for attaching clasps found in the General Instructions on page 98, attach one side of the clasp to each end.

If necessary, refer to the photograph.

bronze & iris crystal necklace

Materials:

Fourteen 8mm bronze crystals
Twenty-eight gold
   6/0 seed beads
Twenty-eight 5x7mm
   purple iris teardrops
Twenty-eight gold
   11/0 seed beads
Twenty-eight inches of
   purple niobium wire
One gold-tone barrel clasp

Beading:

Cut the niobium wire into 14 equal lengths. Following the directions for assembling beaded connectors found in the General Instructions on page 16, assemble 14 links. Form a loop on one end of each wire, and thread on the beads in the following order: one 11/0 seed bead, one teardrop, one 6/0 seed bead, one 8mm crystal, one 6/0 seed bead, one teardrop, one 11/0 seed bead. Trim to 3/8" excess, then form a new loop from the trimmed ends.

Join the loops together to form the necklace. Following the directions for attaching clasps found in the General Instructions on page 16, attach one side of the barrel clasp to each end.

If necessary, refer to the photograph.

crystal swirl necklace

Materials:

Nine 10mm
   color-swirled crystals
Sixteen 6mm
   color-swirled crystals
Six 8mm color-swirled balls
Sixty-two crystal AB
   6/0 seed beads
Thirty-two crystal AB
   11/0 seed beads
One gold-tone spring clasp
One gold-tone
Two gold-tone
   bead end cups
Nylon beading thread

Beading:

Beads of similar size can be used to create this necklace. Instead of swirled crystals, try iris crystals or aurora borealis finish crystals.

Once beads have been selected, assemble the necklace by stringing the beads following the diagram below. The diagram represents half of the necklace, starting at the center bead. Repeat the pattern on the other side.

Following the directions for attaching clasps found in the General Instructions on page 98, attach the clasp.

If necessary, refer to the photograph.

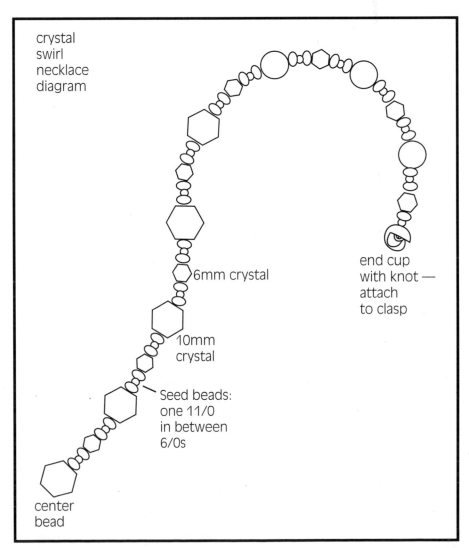

crystal
swirl
necklace
diagram

6mm crystal

10mm crystal

end cup with knot — attach to clasp

Seed beads: one 11/0 in between 6/0s

center bead

chevron necklace

Materials:

370 green iris 6/0 seed beads
Forty metallic silver
    6/0 seed beads
125 matte turquoise
    rainbow 6/0 seed beads
550 metallic silver
    11/0 seed beads
Thirty small turquoise chips
One gold-tone hook finding
Forty-eight inches of
    nylon beading thread,
    size 0
Fine beading needle or
    #10 quilting needle
Jewelry glue

Beading:

Assemble the foundation row. Thread the needle with the nylon beading thread. Slide one metallic silver 11/0 seed bead onto the thread; leave about 4 inches of excess, then loop back into the bead. Tighten this thread; it will be buried in the necklace later. Alternate green iris 6/0s and metallic silver 11/0s until there are 17 green iris 6/0s, then add one more metallic silver 11/0s and the hook finding. Run the needle back through all the beads on the thread, taking up the slack as you progress. Begin adding green iris and metallic silver beads, alternating the pattern as previously done, until there are a total of 104 green iris beads on the thread. Insert the needle back into the last metallic silver 11/0, then run it through the beads until the needle emerges from the 37th green iris 6/0. See diagram on page 107 for details of the foundation row.

Add the drops as shown in the diagram on page 107, and make 30 drops. Start each drop with one metallic silver 11/0, then add the 6/0 beads in the order given, alternating with metallic silver 11/0. Refer to the diagram. End with one turquoise chip and one metallic silver 11/0. Run the thread back through all the beads on the drop, and skip to the next 11/0 on the foundation row. Run the thread through the next 6/0 on the foundation row in preparation for beginning the next drop.

Finish the thread by running it through the foundation row until it meets the original 4" tail. Tie a square knot, and dab a small amount of glue on the knot. Run the thread ends through the foundation until they are secure, then clip close.

If necessary, refer to the photograph.

1 & 2: 7I
3 & 4: 1I, 5T, 2I
5 & 6: 1I, 2T, 2I, 2T, 2I
7 & 8: 1I, 2T, 3I, 2T, 2I
9 & 10: 1I, 2T, 4I, 2T, 2I
11 & 12: 1I, 2T, 2I, 1S, 2I, 2T, 2I
13 & 14: 1I, 2T, 2I, 2S, 2I, 2T, 2I
15 & 16: 1I, 2T, 2I, 3S, 2I, 2T, 2I
17 & 18: Repeat 13 & 14
19 & 20: Repeat 11 & 12
21 & 22: Repeat 9 & 10
23 & 24: Repeat 7 & 8
25 & 26: Repeat 5 & 6
27 & 28: Repeat 3 & 4
29 & 30: Repeat 1 & 2

foundation row

S = Metallic silver 6/0
T = Turquoise rainbow 6/0
I = Green iris 6/0

drops

square knot

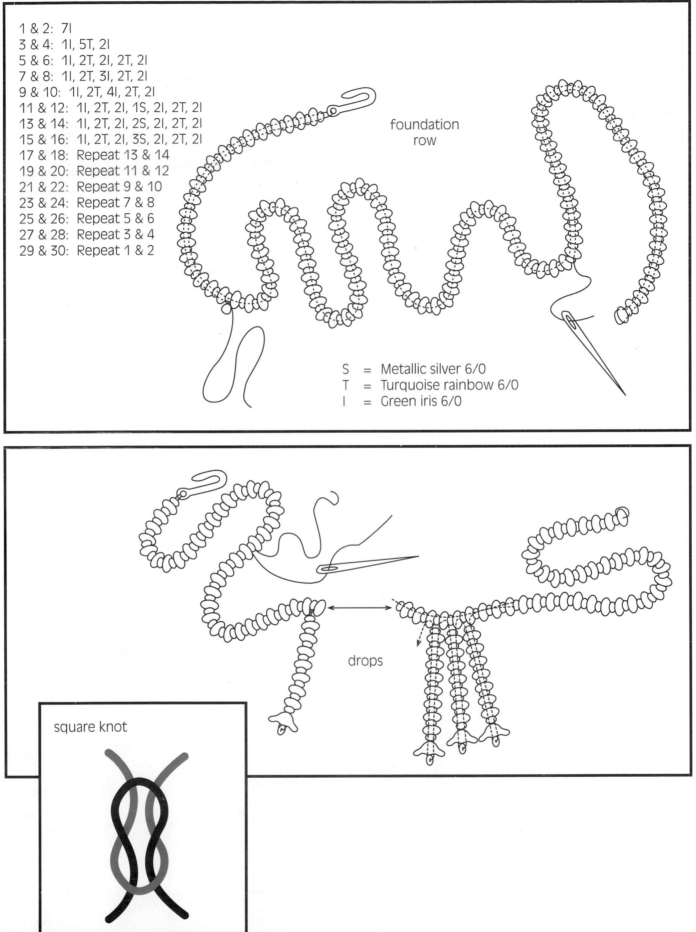

lilac tassel necklace & earrings

Materials:

Three 15mm sub-opaque white
  side-drilled plastic disks
582 lilac 11/0 seed beads
456 white 11/0 seed beads
Twenty-four bronze
  11/0 seed beads
Three gold-tone end caps
Two gold-tone headpins
Four gold-tone eyepins
Two gold-tone crimps
One gold-tone spring clasp
One gold-tone split ring
One pair of ear clips or posts
Sewing thread
25 lb. test nylon fishing line
Jewelry glue

Beading:

Make the three tassels. Each
tassel has eight rows of beads
strung onto thread. Use one
bronze seed bead to anchor the
bottom of each row of beads.
Following the bronze seed bead,
add three lilac seed beads, one
white seed bead, two lilac seed
beads, one white seed bead, one
lilac seed bead, two white seed
beads, one lilac seed bead, 12
white seed beads.

Following the directions for
attaching end caps found in the
General Instructions on page 98,
attach the tassels to the end caps.
Attach the end caps to the
side-drilled plastic disks.

String the lilac seed beads onto
the fishing line, making a 19"
strand. Following the directions for
crimping found in the General
Instructions on page 99, attach
the clasp using the crimps.

Attach one disk and tassel onto
the center of the strand. Glue the
ear clips or posts onto the back of
the side-drilled plastic disks.

If necessary, refer to the
photograph.

indian agate necklace & earrings

Materials:

Three 9x15mm matte gold beads
Two 7x13mm matte gold beads
Twelve 6mm matte gold beads
Fourteen 5x8mm
   matte gold beads
Ten 6x15mm matte gold beads
Ten 10mm indian agate beads
Twelve 6mm indian agate beads
Eighteen 4mm
   indian agate cubes
One gold-tone hook clasp
One gold-tone split ring
Two gold-tone headpins
One pair of matte gold-tone
   5/8" hoop earring posts

Beading:

The design shown uses round and twisted corrugated beads — lined surface similar to corduroy or box cardboard.

This necklace is made of graduated alternating matte gold and indian agate beads. Any pattern of stringing can be used, but start at the center of the necklace with the larger beads and gradually decrease the size as stringing out toward the clasp in an identical pattern on both sides. This will create a pleasing look which hangs nicely.

String the beads to a length of 22".

Following the directions for crimping found in the General Instructions on page 99, attach the clasp using the crimps.

Following the directions for assembling beaded connectors found in the General Instructions on page 98, assemble the earrings.

If necessary, refer to the photograph.

109

yin-yang necklace, bracelet & earrings

Materials:

Nine 3/4" metal yin-yang beads
Eleven 8mm black onyx beads
Two 1" silver tube beads
244 black 11/0 seed beads
Four 4mm silver-tone beads
Four blue 11/0 seed beads
Two silver-tone beehive clasps
Four silver-tone crimps
Two silver-tone headpins
One pair of silver-tone ear wires
25 lb. test nylon fishing line

Beading:

Cut a length of fishing line about 20" long. Place the center beads on the necklace. On each side of the center beads, add 7 inches of black seed beads.

Cut a length of fishing line about 10" long to make the bracelet. Start with one 8mm onyx bead, then add one yin-yang bead. Repeat the onyx/yin-yang pattern until there are six yin-yang beads. End with an onyx bead.

Following the directions for crimping found in the General Instructions on page 99, attach both ends of the clasp to the necklace and the bracelet using the crimps.

Following the directions for assembling beaded connectors found in the General Instructions on page 98, thread the beads onto the headpins in the following order: one blue 11/0 seed bead, one 4mm bead, one yin-yang bead, one 4mm bead, one blue 11/0 seed bead. Trim the excess to 3/8" and form a loop on each headpin. Close the loops around the loops on the wires.

jingle bells necklace & earrings

Materials:

Twenty to thirty small metal
open-end bells in
assorted colors and sizes
Thirty to forty metal
jingle bells in
assorted colors and sizes
Approximately twenty 6mm
cobalt blue faceted crystals
Two gold 6/0 seed beads
One 18" gold-tone chain
with large links
(4 to 5 links per inch)
Twenty-four inches of
green niobium wire
One gold-tone clasp
One pair gold-tone ear wires

Beading:

Lay out the design before
beginning to attach the bells to
the chain. Cut the niobium wire
in 3/4" lengths to make the
figure-eight connectors and
in 1 1/8" lengths for the
beaded connectors.

Arrange the bells so that the
pattern is roughly graduated.
Following the directions for
assembling beaded connectors
found in the General Instructions
on page 98, attach each large bell
with a cobalt blue crystal
beaded connector.

Between the larger bells,
attach smaller bells with simple
figure-eight connectors.

When attaching the bells, be
sure the chain links are flat and
untwisted so that they will
hang nicely.

Assemble two beaded
connectors that have one gold
seed bead each. Attach each one
to a jingle bell, and hang from
the inside of an open-end bell.
Attach to the ear wires.

pearl spray earrings

Materials:

One pair of silver-tone
   French ear wires
Two long silver-tone cone ends
Twelve silver-tone 2" headpins,
   .021 gauge
Two silver-tone 4" headpins
Fourteen 5mm fine-quality
   freshwater pearls

Beading:

Thread the pearls onto the headpins. Make two bunches — each will have six 2" headpins and one 4" headpin. Vary the ends randomly, and twist all seven headpins together. When the bunch is stable, trim all but the longest headpin so they will fit inside the cone end. Insert the longest end through the hole in the cone end, and trim so there is an excess of 3/8". Form a loop in the end of the headpin using round-nose pliers, and close the loop around the French ear wire.

If necessary, refer to the diagram below and the photograph.

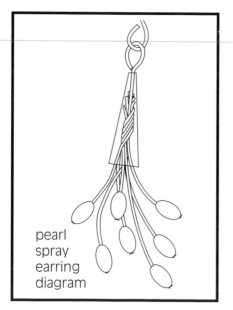

pearl
spray
earring
diagram

turquoise drop earrings

Materials:

One pair of silver-tone
   French ear wires
Two silver-tone 2" headpins
Two 7x15mm turquoise tubes
Four flat turquoise disks,
   10mm diameter x 3mm deep
Four dusty green ceramic beads,
   5mm diameter x 3mm deep
Four dusty blue ceramic beads,
   3mm cylinders
Four 2mm dark blue
   ceramic disks

Beading:

Following the directions for assembling beaded connectors found in the General Instructions on page 98, thread the beads onto the headpins in the following order: one 2mm ceramic disk, one 3mm ceramic bead, one 5mm ceramic bead, one 10mm turquoise disk, one turquoise tube, one 10mm turquoise disk, one 5mm ceramic bead, one 3mm ceramic bead, one 2mm ceramic disk. Trim the excess to 3/8". Form a loop in the end of each headpin using round-nose pliers, and close the loops around the French ear wires.

If necessary, refer to the photograph.

amethyst cabochon earrings

Materials:

One pair of ear clips or posts
Two 18x13mm
    amethyst cabochons
Two 18x13mm gold-tone
    lace-edged bezel cups
Two freshwater pearls
Two 10mm square
    turquoise matte glass beads
Two 12mm amethyst
    matte glass beads
Four 8mm amethyst
    matte glass beads
Six amethyst matte rainbow
    6/0 seed beads
Eighteen metallic gold
    11/0 seed beads
Twenty-eight matte turquoise
    rainbow 11/0 seed beads
Six gold-tone headpins
Jewelry glue

Beading:

Bend out three loops at the bottom of both bezel cups. Glue the amethyst cabochons in the bezel cups.

Following the directions for assembling beaded connectors found in the General Instructions on page 98, assemble the beaded connectors. Thread the beads onto the headpins. Refer to the photograph. Trim the excess to 3/8". Form a loop in the end of each headpin using round-nose pliers, and close the loop around the loops in the bottom of the bezel cups.

zuni bear earrings

Materials:

One pair of gold-tone
    French ear wires
Two 3/4" three-hole
    disk components
Six gold-tone 1" headpins
Two side-drilled turquoise chips
Ten turquoise chips
Two 8mm frosted
    amethyst rondelles
Four blue 6/0 seed beads
Two matte pink ceramic donuts
Four 12mm rose ceramic tubes

Beading:

Following the directions for assembling beaded connectors found in the General Instructions on page 98, assemble the beaded connectors. Refer to the photograph. Trim the excess to 3/8". Form a loop in the end of each headpin using round-nose pliers, and close the loops around the disk components.

Attach the ear wires to the disk components.

silver
heart
earrings

Materials:

One pair of five-hole
 silver-tone heart
 post earrings
Ten silver-tone 2 1/2" headpins
Twenty-two small dome-shaped,
 side-drilled freshwater pearls
Ten 4x10mm amethyst
 AB glass tubes
Two purple or amethyst
 fancy glass beads,
 about 12mm
Approximately 112 purple iris
 hex beads

Beading:

Following directions for
assembling beaded connectors
found in the General Instructions
on page 98, thread the beads
onto the headpins in the following order from the bottom: one
pearl, one tube, one pearl, hex
beads to fill the headpin. The
center beaded connector should
be beaded in the following order
from the bottom: one pearl, one
fancy glass bead, one pearl, one
tube, one pearl, hex beads to fill
the headpin. Trim the excess to
3/8". Form a loop in the end of
each headpin using round-nose
pliers, and connect the loops to
the ear posts.
 If necessary, refer to the
photograph.

turquoise
cabochon
earrings

Materials:

One pair of matte silver-tone
 3/4" ear hoop earring posts
Two silver-tone
 figure-eight connectors
Two 18x13mm
 turquoise cabochons
Two 18x13mm silver-tone
 lace-edged bezel cups
Jewelry glue

Beading:

Bend out one loop at either
end of both bezel cups. Glue
the turquoise cabochons in
the bezel cups, and secure the
loops around the bezel cups. Use
the figure-eights, and attach one
end of each connector to the
loops on the bezel cups. Attach
the other end of each connector
to the ear posts. Twist one loop
on each figure-eight connector
so the cabochons hangs facing
front, perpendicular to the
ear posts.
 If necessary, refer to the
photograph.

sun-star earrings

Materials:

One pair of gold-tone star
   ear posts with loops
Two gold-tone sun face
   drops with loops
Two gold-tone 1" eyepins
Two freshwater pearls

Beading:

If star ear posts cannot be found, make them from polymer clay.

Following the directions for assembling beaded connectors found in the General Instructions on page 98, assemble the beaded connectors using the freshwater pearls and the eyepins. Use the beaded connectors to attach the sun face drops to the star ear posts. Carefully close the loops.

sand dollar earrings

Materials:

One pair of silver-tone
   sand dollar ear posts
Two large floral lamp beads
Two white 6/0 seed beads
Two silver-tone 1" headpins

Beading:

Following the directions for assembling beaded connectors and for embellishing simple objects found in the General Instructions on pages 98 and 99, assemble the beaded connectors using the lamps beads, seed beads, and the eyepins.

Attach the beaded connectors to the sand dollar ear posts. Carefully close the loops.

If necessary, refer to the photograph.

115

french wire earrings

Beading:

These earrings are made using finely coiled wire, known as French wire. It is extremely flexible and can be slipped over a shaped headpin quite easily. All three designs are created by following these simple steps:

1. Slip on the bottom bead(s).
2. Shape the headpin into the desired shape.
3. Slip on the French wire, and cut it using wirecutters. Be careful not to cut through the headpin. Only the slightest pressure is needed to make enough of a nick to separate the wire.
4. Trim the headpin to 3/8" beyond the end of the French wire.
5. Form a loop in the end of the headpin using round-nose pliers, and close the loop around the ear finding.
6. Shape the wires as desired.

If necessary, refer to the photograph.

... with freshwater pearls

Materials:

One pair of 4mm
   gold-tone ball and
   loop ear posts
Gold-tone French wire
Two large freshwater pearls
Two 4mm gold-tone beads
Two gold-tone 2 1/2" headpins

... with purple crystals

Materials:

One pair of purple niobium
   French ear wires
Gold-tone French wire
Two 5x7mm purple iris
   teardrop crystals
Two gold-tone 2" headpins

... with goldstone beads

Materials:

One pair of 4mm
   silver-tone ball and
   loop ear posts
Silver-tone French wire
Two 4mm goldstone beads
Two metallic silver
   11/0 seed beads
Two silver-tone 2 1/2" headpins

polymer clay earrings

Beading:

Follow the directions for working with polymer clay found in the General Instructions on page 100.

Using a pasta machine or rolling pin, roll the clay flat to a depth of 1/16". Using the cabochon as a guide, cut a circle out of the rolled clay. Place this cut layer over another layer of clay, and trim the edges into the appropriate shapes. Gently shape the petals with your fingers to round them.

Insert the cabochon into the cut hole again. Form additional petals or tiny balls of clay, and place them around the edge of the cabochon hole.

Insert the eyepin into the clay between two petals prior to baking. Form additional beads if necessary. Insert the headpins through the clay beads.

Following the directions for assembling beaded connectors found in the General Instructions on page 98, thread the beads onto the headpins. Trim the excess to 3/8". Form a loop in the end of each headpin using round-nose pliers, and connect the loops to the eyepins.

Bake according to the General Instructions, and varnish before assembling.

If necessary, refer to the photograph.

... sunflowers

Materials:

One pair of ear clips or posts
Yellow polymer clay
Two 12mm black onyx
   round cabochons
Four black 6/0 seed beads
Two gold-tone 1/2" eyepins
Two gold-tone 1 1/2" headpins
Jewelry glue
Gloss varnish

... marigold

Materials:

One pair of ear clips or posts
Rose polymer clay
Two 18x13mm amethyst cabochons
Two 12mm amethyst glass crystals
Four small dome-shaped
   freshwater pearls
Two gold-tone 1/2" eyepins
Two gold-tone 1" headpins
Jewelry glue
Gloss varnish

... anemones

Materials:

One pair of ear clips or posts
Dark blue polymer clay
Two 12mm rose quartz
   round cabochons
Two 4x15mm rose quartz tubes
Two gold-tone 1/2" eyepins
Two gold-tone 1 1/4" headpins
Jewelry glue
Gloss varnish

... blue/white

Materials:

One pair of ear clips or posts
White polymer clay
Two 18x13mm blue-lace
   agate cabochons
Two 10 to 12mm blue-lace
   agate beads
Two gold-tone 1/2" eyepins
Two gold-tone 1" headpins
Jewelry glue
Gloss varnish

... english cut hex

Materials:

One pair of ear clips or posts
Seventy medium blue luster
    11/0 seed beads
Forty-six aqua luster
    11/0 seed beads
Sixty light green luster
    11/0 seed beads
Forty-two metallic gold
    11/0 seed beads
Ten 4mm aqua English cuts
Double-faced adhesive dots
    or jewelry glue

... black & turquoise hex

Materials:

One pair of ear clips or posts
Eighty-two matte black
    11/0 seed beads
150 matte turquoise iris
    11/0 seed beads
Ten matte turquoise iris
    6/0 seed beads
Double-faced adhesive dots
    or jewelry glue

... blue & silver hex

Materials:

One pair of ear clips or posts
154 crystal silver-lined
    11/0 seed beads
Forty-four light blue color-lined
    11/0 seed beads
Thirty-four gold silver-lined
    11/0 seed beads
Ten light blue English cuts
Double-faced adhesive dots
    or jewelry glue

hex earrings

Beading:

Following the directions for brick-stitching found in the General Instructions on page 99, weave the main body of the earrings.

Add the hangers when the body is complete. Attach the completed earring to the ear post using double-sided adhesive dots or glue.

If necessary, refer to the photograph.

... pastel crystal hex

Materials:

One pair of ear clips or posts
Eighty medium pink luster
    11/0 seed beads
Eighty lavender luster
    11/0 seed beads
Fifty-six light lavender luster
    11/0 seed beads
Twenty-six metallic gold
    11/0 seed beads
Eight 4mm clear lavender
    English cuts
Two 8mm clear lavender
    English cuts
Double-faced adhesive dots
    or jewelry glue

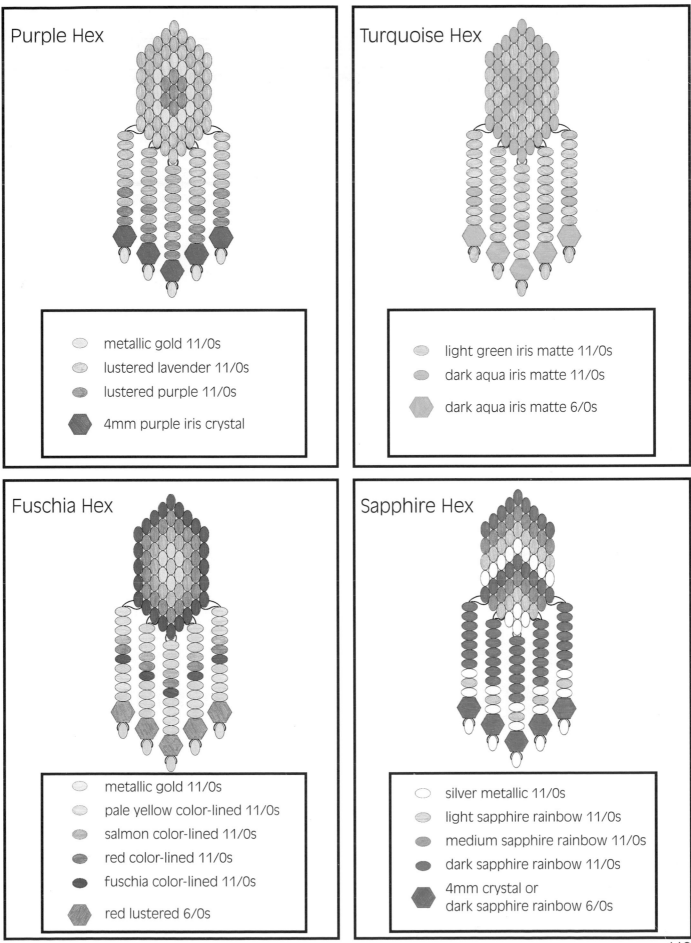

Purple Hex

- metallic gold 11/0s
- lustered lavender 11/0s
- lustered purple 11/0s
- 4mm purple iris crystal

Turquoise Hex

- light green iris matte 11/0s
- dark aqua iris matte 11/0s
- dark aqua iris matte 6/0s

Fuschia Hex

- metallic gold 11/0s
- pale yellow color-lined 11/0s
- salmon color-lined 11/0s
- red color-lined 11/0s
- fuschia color-lined 11/0s
- red lustered 6/0s

Sapphire Hex

- silver metallic 11/0s
- light sapphire rainbow 11/0s
- medium sapphire rainbow 11/0s
- dark sapphire rainbow 11/0s
- 4mm crystal or
  dark sapphire rainbow 6/0s

component earrings

Beading:

Simple components can be used to make elegant earrings. There is a nearly endless variety of types and styles of components. Each bead store and mail-order bead source will have a different variety, depending on the styles component manufacturers are making at the time. The techniques used in the styles shown will work with styles of the future.

Following the directions for assembling beaded connectors found in the General Instructions on page 98, assemble beaded connectors when necessary.

When using ear clips or posts, attach the completed earring to the ear post using double-sided adhesive dots or glue.

If necessary, refer to the photograph.

... decorative finding

Materials:

One pair of gold-tone
    stamped ear posts
    with three loops
Six gold-tone headpins
Twelve gold 11/0 seed beads
Six side-drilled amber chunks

... hollow cone

Materials:

One pair of silver-tone
    French ear wires
One pair of silver-tone cones
Two silver-tone headpins
Two spiral lamp beads

... hoop with interior drop

Materials:

One pair of silver-tone
    French ear wires
One pair of silver-tone hoops
Two silver-tone headpins
Two cinnabar beads

... cabochon mount

Materials:

One pair of silver
    stamped ear posts
    with bottom loops
    and 4mm cabochon opening
Two silver-tone headpins
Two 4mm amber
    round cabochons
Two freshwater pearls

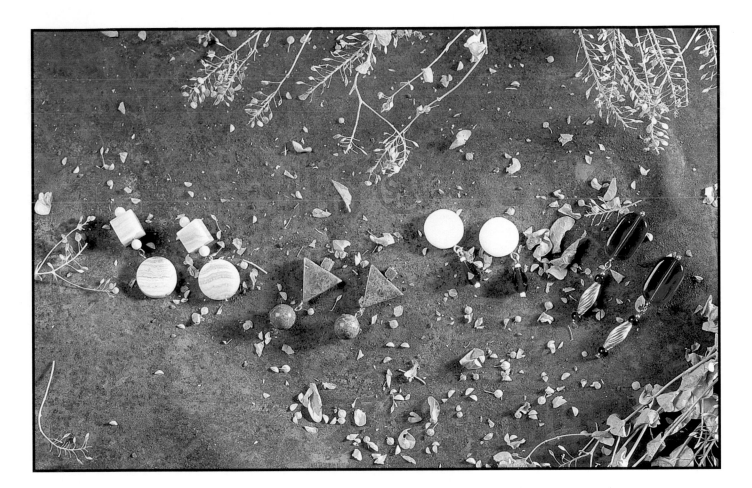

... blue lace agate

Materials:

One pair of ear clips or posts
Two 15mm side-drilled
   blue lace agate disks
Two 10mm blue lace
   agate cubes
Four 4mm blue lace
   agate round beads
Four silver-tone headpins
Double-sided adhesive dots
   or jewelry glue

... indian agate

Materials:

One pair of ear clips or posts
Two 18mm side-drilled indian
   agate triangular flat beads
Two 4mm indian agate cubes
Two 10mm indian agate
   round beads
Four gold-tone headpins
Double-sided adhesive dots
   or jewelry glue

... cobalt drop

Materials:

One pair of ear clips or posts
Two 15mm sub-opaque white
   side-drilled plastic disks
Two 7x10mm cobalt
   drop crystals
Four white 11/0 seed beads
Four gold-tone headpins
Double-sided adhesive dots
   or jewelry glue

... blue lozenge

Materials:

One pair of ear clips or posts
Two 12x20mm blue lozenge-
   shaped plastic beads
Two 5x15mm twisted gold-tone
   finished bicones

Four cobalt 6/0 seed beads
Eight gold 11/0 seed beads
Four gold-tone headpins
Double-sided adhesive dots
   or jewelry glue

artistic dangle earrings

Beading:

Following the directions for assembling beaded connectors found in the General Instructions on page 98, and following the diagrams on page 123, assemble the components on headpins. Trim all headpins to 3/8" before forming loops and assembling.

If necessary, refer to the photograph

... stars & stripes

Materials:

One pair of silver-tone
   French ear wires
216 red 14/0 seed beads
408 white 14/0 seed beads
Ninety-eight navy blue
   14/0 seed beads
Two 3/8" white glass star beads
Thirty-four silver-tone
   3" headpins

... yin-yang

Materials:

One pair of gold-tone
   French ear wires
304 metallic gold
   14/0 seed beads
178 black 14/0 seed beads
Ninety white 14/0 seed beads
Two 12 to 16mm yin-yang beads
Thirty-four gold-tone
   3" headpins

... treble clef

Materials:

One pair of silver-tone
   French ear wires
476 white 14/0 seed beads
128 metallic silver
   14/0 seed beads
136 metallic bronze
   14/0 seed beads
Two music note or clef charms
Thirty-four silver-tone
   3" headpins

... heart

Materials:

One pair of gold-tone
   French ear wires
134 salmon 14/0 seed beads
220 green 14/0 seed beads
120 blue 14/0 seed beads
240 white 14/0 seed beads
Two heart charms
Thirty-four gold-tone
   3" headpins

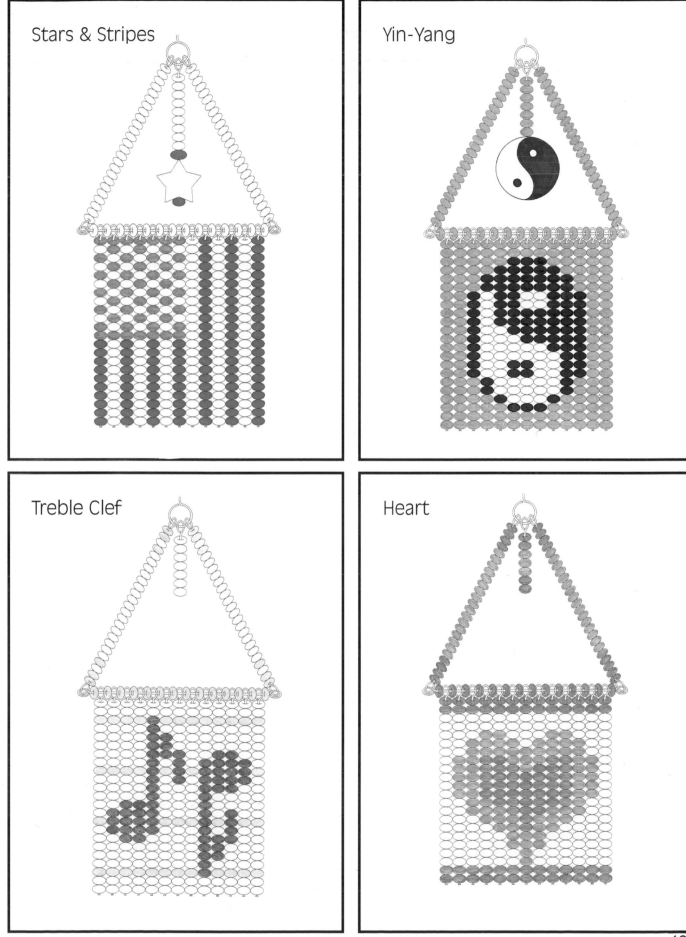

Stars & Stripes

Yin-Yang

Treble Clef

Heart

white disk bracelet

Materials:

Nine 15mm sub-opaque white
    side-drilled plastic disks
Assortment of colored
    6/0 seed beads
One gold-tone clasp
    with eyelets
Two gold-tone crimps
25 lb. test nylon fishing line

Beading:

Starting with a 6/0 seed bead, alternate disks and 6/0s on the fishing line, using the 6/0s in a random color pattern.

Following the directions for crimping found in the General Instructions on page 99, attach the clasp using the crimps.

If necessary, refer to the photograph.

button bracelet

Materials:

Eleven 1/2" antique buttons
One flat-link bracelet
Industrial strength glue

Beading:

Lay the bracelet out flat. If necessary, remove the shanks from the back of the buttons. Glue the buttons onto the bracelet. Be careful to evenly space the buttons.

If necessary, refer to the photograph.

peruvian bracelet

Materials:

Seven 15mm round
    peruvian style beads
Fourteen 6mm
    persimmon rondelles
Fourteen turquoise
    6/0 seed beads
Eight black 11/0 seed beads
One silver-tone beehive clasp
Two silver-tone crimps
25 lb. test nylon fishing line

Beading:

Thread seven repeats of beads onto the fishing line.

Following the directions for crimping found in the General Instructions on page 99, attach the clasp onto the ends using the crimps.

If necessary, refer to the photograph.

expansion bracelet

Materials:

One expansion bracelet blank
   with 40 links,
   each with three loops
About 120 headpins in a finish
   matching the bracelet blank
120 assorted beads, pearls,
   and crystals

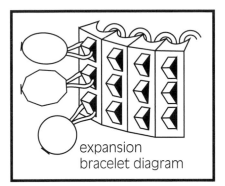

expansion
bracelet diagram

multi-bracelet bracelet

Materials:

One 2"-long bead in cup
   with loops
One 1" bracelet clasp
One 3/4" bracelet clasp
Eighteen to 20 bracelets
   and chains
Thirty-six 1/4" jump rings
Needle-nose pliers

Beading:

Using the needle-nose pliers,
shorten or lengthen the
bracelets and chains to the
same length.

Attach the bracelets to the
loops in the long bead using
the jump rings. Attach the
bracelet clasps.

If necessary, refer to the
photograph.

Beading:

The upper and lower rows are beaded with alternating pearls and
matte glass beads. The center row is beaded with a random assortment
of 6mm crystals.

Either complete each link of three beads, or work each row. It might
be easier to progress row by row or link by link. Trim each headpin so
there is slightly less than 1/2" of excess — more than the standard 3/8"
of excess will be needed. Form the excess into a loop, and close it
around the openings on each link.

If necessary, refer to the photograph.

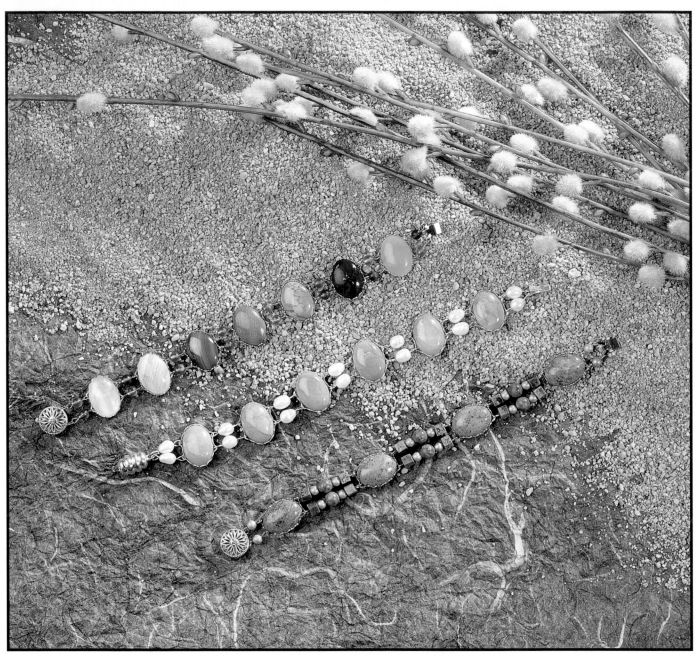

Pictured from top to bottom: Seven Cabochon Bracelet, Cabochon & Pearls Bracelet, Indian Agate Bracelet.

cabochon bracelets

Beading:

Bend four loops on each bezel cup, and mount and glue the stones as shown in the diagram.

Following the directions for assembling beaded connectors found in the General Instructions on page 98, assemble any beaded connectors that are needed and assemble the bracelet.

Following the directions for attaching clasps found in the General Instructions on page 98, attach the clasp to the bracelet.

If necessary, refer to the photograph.

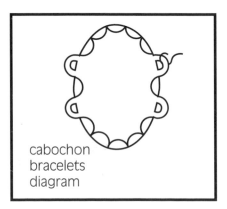

cabochon
bracelets
diagram

... seven cabochon

Materials:

Seven 18x13mm
  stone cabochons
  (model has rose quartz,
  blue lace agate, malachite,
  tigereye, turquoise, lapis lazuli,
  and serpentine)
Seven gold-tone
  lace-edged bezel cups
Sixteen 4mm fluorite
  round beads
Sixteen gold-tone 1" eyepins
One gold-tone clasp
  with double eyelets
Four gold-tone jump rings
Jewelry glue

... cabochon & pearls

Materials:

Six 18x13mm howlite
  dyed to look like
  turquoise cabochons
Six silver-tone
  lace-edged bezel cups
Fourteen freshwater pearls
Fourteen silver-tone 1" eyepins
One silver-tone beehive clasp
Jewelry glue

... indian agate

Materials:

Four 18x13mm
  indian agate cabochons
Four gold-tone
  lace-edged bezel cups
Twelve 4mm square
  indian agate beads
Six 6mm round
  indian agate beads
Sixteen 3mm gold-tone beads
Six gold-tone 1 1/2" eyepins
Four gold-tone 3/4" eyepins
One gold-tone clasp
  with double eyelets
Jewelry glue

silver & amethyst cabochon watch

Materials:

One silver watch face with
  five-loop side mountings
One silver bracelet clasp
Twelve 1" silver eyepins
Four 13x18mm silver
  lace-edged bezel cups
Four 13x18mm
  amethyst cabochons
Eight lavender
  6mm faceted crystals
Jewelry glue

Beading:

Make four figure-eight connectors, and attach one loop of each one to the second and fourth holes on the five-loop side-mounting.

On each bezel cup, bend out the loops as shown on page 126. Mount and glue the cabochons in the bezel cups.

On each of the remaining eight eyepins, slip on one lavender crystal. Trim the excess eyepin to 3/8", and form a loop to create a connector.

Assemble the watch band. Refer to the photograph.

liquid silver bracelet

Materials:

One 12mm ceramic tube bead
Two frosted amethyst
    6/0 seed beads
Two light green hex beads
Two aqua hex beads
Two lavender hex beads
Two pink hex beads
Two purple 11/0 seed beads
Sixty-four liquid silver beads
    (or more depending
    on desired length)
One silver-tone spring clasp
One silver-tone split ring
Two silver-tone crimps
Lightweight nylon fishing line

Beading:

Thread beads onto the fishing line in the following order: one purple 11/0 seed bead, one pink hex, one lavender hex, one aqua hex, one light green hex, one 6/0 seed bead, one ceramic tube, one 6/0 seed bead, one light green hex, one aqua hex, one lavender hex, one pink hex, one purple 11/0 seed bead. Add liquid silver beads to each side of the center motif to desired length.

Following the directions for crimping found in the General Instructions on page 99, attach the clasp at the ends using the crimps.

If necessary, refer to the photograph.

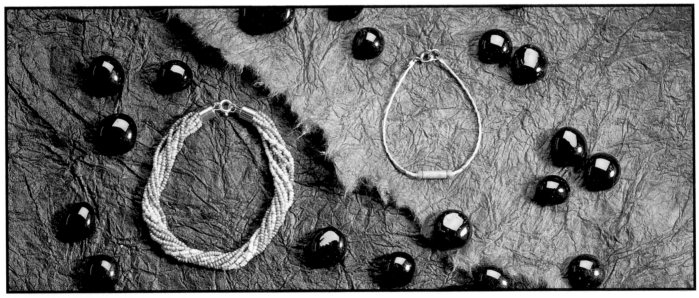

twisted bracelet

Materials:

392 gold 11/0 seed beads
Approximately 100
    11/0 seed beads in each
    of the following colors:
    turquoise, light aqua,
    champagne, teal iris,
    light green, dark purple,
    light gray iris, dark gray iris
Two gold-tone end caps
Two gold-tone
    figure-eight connectors
One gold-tone spring clasp
One gold-tone jump ring
Nylon beading thread

Beading:

String the beads on the nylon beading thread using the following pattern: one gold bead, two colored beads. Make eight 7 1/2"-long strands — one from each color.

Following the directions for attaching end caps and attaching clasps found in the General Instructions on page 98, attach the end caps and the clasp.

If necessary, refer to the photograph.

pearl anklet

Materials:

Thirty to thirty-five
   freshwater pearls
Forty silver-lined
   amber 14/0 seed beads
One gold-tone clasp
   with double eyelets
Two gold-tone crimps
Lightweight nylon fishing line

Beading:

Cut a 10" length of fishing line.
Start with a silver-lined amber
14/0 seed bead, then alternate
pearls and 14/0 seed beads until
the desired length has been
reached.

Following the directions for
crimping found in the General
Instructions on page 99, attach
the clasp using the crimps.

If necessary, refer to the
photograph.

coral anklet

Materials:

Forty to fifty-five coral chips
100 to 120 gold 11/0 seed beads
One gold-tone barrel clasp
Two gold-tone crimps
Lightweight nylon fishing line

Beading:

String the coral chips onto the
fishing line alternately with two
gold seed beads until the desired
length has been reached.

Following the directions for
crimping found in the General
Instructions on page 99, attach
the clasp using the crimps.

If necessary, refer to the
photograph.

liquid silver anklet

Materials:

Enough liquid silver beads
   to make a 10" strand
One 8mm floral lamp bead
One silver-tone barrel clasp
Two silver-tone crimps
Lightweight nylon fishing line

Beading:

String 4 1/4" of liquid silver
onto the fishing line. Add the
glass bead, and continue with
4 1/4" more of liquid silver.

Following the directions for
crimping found in the General
Instructions on page 99, attach
the clasp using the crimps.

If necessary, refer to the
photograph.

floral
oval
pin

Materials:

Card stock paper
One freshwater pearl
Three light pink 6/0 seed beads
Four lavender 6/0 seed beads
Sixty-six gold #2 silver-lined
    bugle beads
11/0 seed beads:
    220 metallic gold
    150 black
    55 purple
    45 pink
    55 light blue
    35 aqua
    15 medium blue purple
    20 dark green
    20 medium green
One gold-tone pin back
Fusing web and backing fabric
Jewelry glue

Beading:

Transfer the design to the card. Following the directions for surface beading found in the General Instructions on page 101, stitch the metallic gold border outlines and the bugle beads first. Backtrack the outer gold row. Stitch the pearls and 6/0 seed beads in the center motif, then add the additional seed beads. Fill in the background with black seed beads.

Following the directions for fusing fabric found in the General Instructions on page 99, fuse the fabric backing to the back of the pin. Carefully trim away the excess card.

Glue the pin back to the center back of the pin.

If necessary, refer to the photograph.

Pictured from top to bottom: Floral Oval Pin, Oval Flower Pin, Petite Paisley Pin.

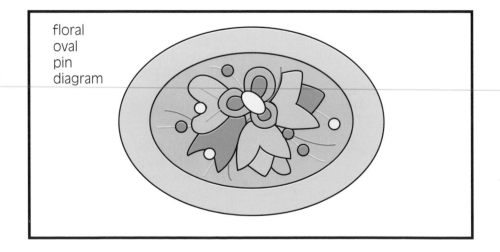

floral
oval
pin
diagram

petite paisley pin

Materials:

Card stock paper
Four freshwater pearls
Eight matte topaz rainbow
   iris #2 bugle beads
11/0 seed beads:
   Fifty-four matte purple iris
   Forty-four cream
   Fifty-five matte amber
   152 metallic gold
Sewing thread
One gold-tone pin back
2 1/2" square fusing web
2 1/2" square backing fabric
Jewelry glue

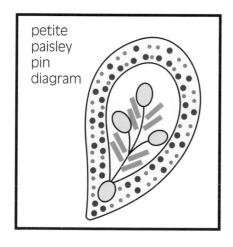

petite
paisley
pin
diagram

Beading:

Transfer the design to the card. Following the directions for surface beading found in the General Instructions on page 101, stitch the metallic gold outlines first, then add the pearls and bugle beads. Fill in the center background with the cream 11/0 seed beads, then stitch the three-bead clusters in the border.

Following the directions for fusing fabric found in the General Instructions on page 99, fuse the fabric backing to the back of the pin. Carefully trim away the excess card.

Glue the pin back to the center back of the pin.

If necessary, refer to the photograph.

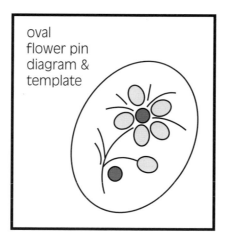

oval
flower pin
diagram &
template

oval flower pin

Materials:

Card stock paper
Six freshwater pearls
Two gold 6/0 seed beads
Fifty-four metallic gold
   11/0 seed beads
350 black 12/0
   three-cut seed beads
One 1 3/4" x 2"
   gold-tone oval frame
Sewing thread
One gold-tone pin back
Jewelry glue

Beading:

Transfer the design to the card. Trace the opening in the frame, and cut it out of the tracing paper. Center the frame around the traced floral spray design so that it is pleasing, and make an outline of the template to indicate the outer edge of the background beads.

Following the directions for surface beading found in the General Instructions on page 101, sew on the pearls, 6/0 seed beads, and metallic gold 11/0 beads. Fill in the background with black 12/0 beads using black sewing thread. The background of the piece may need to be colored in after the pearls have been stitched on to create a solid black appearance behind the black beads.

When the background is complete, carefully trim away the excess card. Avoid cutting any beading threads.

Glue the beaded piece into the frame. Glue the pin back to the center back of the pin.

If necessary, refer to the photograph.

131

cosmic leather pin

Materials:

2" x 2" piece of pink leather
1 1/2" x 1 1/2" piece of
  turquoise leather
1" x 1" inch piece of blue leather
Five freshwater pearls
Eleven metallic gold 6/0 seed beads
Forty-three pink hex beads
One 6x12mm turquoise tube
Two side-drilled large
  turquoise chips
One gold-tone 2" eyepin
Five gold-tone 3" headpins
One gold-tone pin back
Jewelry glue

Beading:

Use the templates to cut the leather pieces to the correct size and shape. Glue the leather pieces together to form one three-layer unit.

Using a suitable sharp object, such as a darning needle, pierce the leather. The holes should be large enough to accommodate the diameter of the eyepin. Insert the eyepin through the holes until the loop is flush with the first hole. Trim the other end to 3/8", and form a loop with the trimmed end. Bend the eyepin slightly to allow the leather to lay nearly flat. The assembled pin will never lay entirely flat, and do not attempt to make it do so.

Following the directions for assembling beaded connectors found in the General Instructions on page 98, assemble the headpin drops and trim the lengths to 3/8" excess. Refer to the photograph. Form loops with the trimmed ends, and close the loops around the eyepin and in the end loops of the eyepins.

Glue the pin back to the top center back of the pin.

If necessary, refer to the photograph.

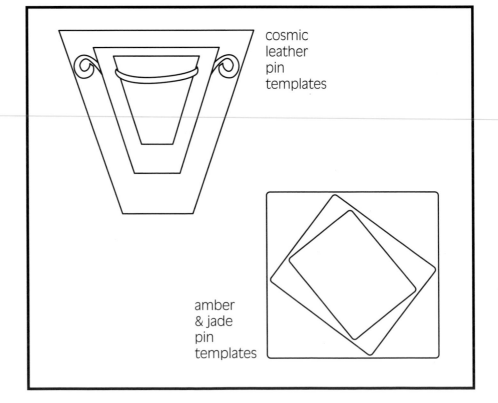

cosmic leather pin templates

amber & jade pin templates

amber & jade pin

Materials:

2" x 2" piece of bronze leather
2" x 2" piece of green leather
4" x 4" piece of rust suede
2" x 2" piece of fusing web
Four 10mm Chinese
    new jade beads
Four side-drilled amber chips
Eight gold 11/0 seed beads
Eight gold-tone headpins
Pin back
Jewelry glue

Beading:

Use the templates to cut the leather pieces to the correct size and shape. Cut two of the largest pieces, and fuse them together with fusing web to strengthen the base square. Glue the remaining leather pieces together to form one three-layer unit.

Following the directions for assembling beaded connectors found in the General Instructions on page 98, assemble the headpin drops. Glue the drops onto the assembled leather piece.

Glue the pin back to the top center back of the pin.

If necessary, refer to the photograph.

dangle charm pin

Materials:

Pin with loops
Chains
Seventeen to 20 charms or beads
Jump rings
Needle-nose pliers

Beading:

Using the needle-nose pliers, attach uneven lengths of chain to the pin loops using the jump rings. The chain lengths should range from 1 to 3 inches.

Using additional jump rings, attach the charms or beads to the bottom of the chains.

If necessary, refer to the photograph.

petit flower pins

... pansy

Beading:

Transfer the design to the card. Following the directions for surface beading found in the General Instructions on page 101, sew the seed beads onto the card. Backtrack the outer rows.

Following the directions for fusing fabric found in the General Instructions on page 99, fuse the fabric to the back of the stitched beadwork. Carefully trim around the edges with nail scissors.

Glue the pin back to the center back of the pin.

If necessary, refer to the photograph.

Materials:

Card stock paper
11/0 seed beads:
    12 yellow
    2 orange
    3 dark green
    57 medium purple
    200 light lavender
    57 dark purple iris
    23 medium orchid
One gold-tone pin back
Fusing web and backing fabric
Jewelry glue

... daisy

Materials:

Card stock paper
11/0 seed beads:
   18 bronze
   100 light orange
   112 medium yellow
   205 pale yellow
   27 light green
   30 medium green
One gold-tone pin back
Fusing web and backing fabric
Jewelry glue

... tulip

Materials:

Card stock paper
11/0 seed beads:
   27 dark purple
   58 medium purple
   56 light purple
   134 white
   17 dark green
   48 light green
One gold-tone pin back
Fusing web and backing fabric
Jewelry glue

... posy

Materials:

Card stock paper
One freshwater pearl
11/0 seed beads:
   60 red
   50 medium pink
   155 pale pink
   36 medium green
   28 light green
One gold-tone pin back
Fusing web and backing fabric
Jewelry glue

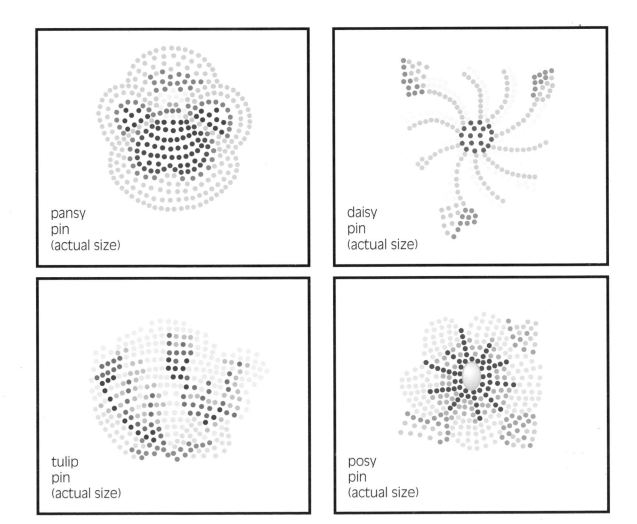

pansy
pin
(actual size)

daisy
pin
(actual size)

tulip
pin
(actual size)

posy
pin
(actual size)

blue diamond barrette

Materials:

11/0 seed beads:
   113 dark sapphire rainbow
   176 light sapphire rainbow
   96 metallic silver
One 3" barrette
Double-sided tape

Beading:

Following the directions for needle-weaving found in the General Instructions on page 100, weave the pattern as diagrammed.

Trim the double-sided tape to fit the barrette blank, and press it into place. Stretch the woven beadwork so that it fits the barrette, and press it into place. Press down firmly until the entire tape surface is in contact with the woven beadwork.

If necessary, refer to the photograph.

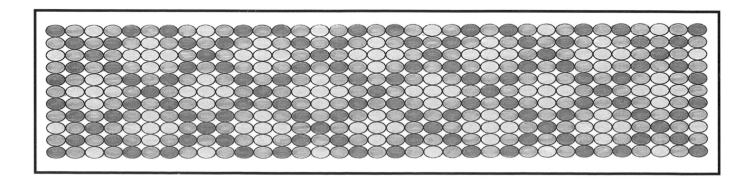

purple diamond barrette

Materials:

11/0 seed beads:
   91 amethyst color-lined
   16 salmon color-lined
   98 lavender
One 2" barrette
Double-sided tape

Beading:

Following the directions for brick-stitching found in the General Instructions on page 99, weave the pattern as diagrammed.

Trim the double-sided tape to fit the barrette blank, and press it into place. Stretch the woven beadwork so that it fits the barrette, and press it into place. Press down firmly until the entire tape surface is in contact with the woven beadwork.

If necessary, refer to the photograph.

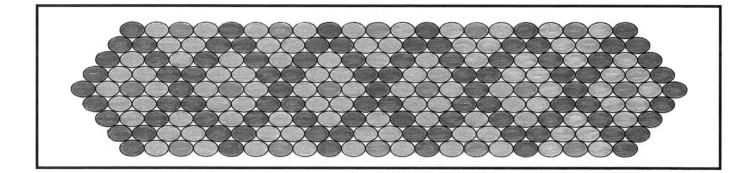

floral barrette

Materials:

11/0 seed beads:
   43 dark green
   60 light green
   36 purple
   12 gold
   90 light blue
   142 white
One 3" barrette
Double-sided tape

Beading:

Following the directions for needle-weaving found in the General Instructions on page 100, weave the pattern as diagrammed.

Trim the double-sided tape to fit the barrette blank, and press it into place. Stretch the woven beadwork so that it fits the barrette, and press it into place. Press down firmly until the entire tape surface is in contact with the woven beadwork.

If necessary, refer to the photograph.

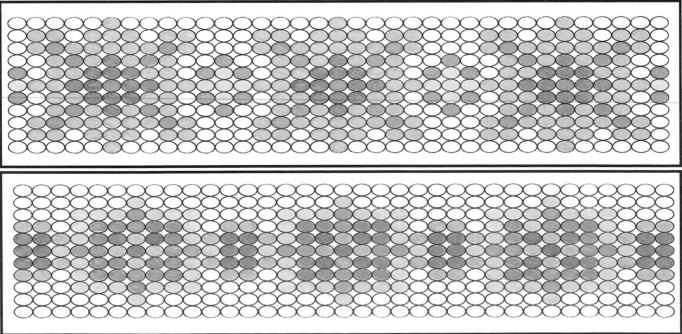

Try another floral design. Use bead colors of your choice.

tortoise shell barrette

Materials:

Thirty-six #2 iris bugle beads
Twenty-eight gold
   11/0 seed beads
Nine iris 6/0 seed beads
One 3 1/2" tortoise shell barrette
Jewelry glue

Beading:

Glue the beads onto the barrette. Starting in the middle, work your way out to each end. Refer to the photograph.

velvet rose ribbon barrette

Materials:

One velvet rose barrette
Fifteen to 20 assorted beads
Beading thread

Beading:

Thread the beads onto the beading thread, and randomly sew the lengths onto the back of the velvet rose(s) barrette.

If necessary, refer to the photograph.

celtic
weave
comb

Materials:

11/0 seed beads:
    138 butterscotch color-lined
    71 off-white
One gold-tone 2" hair comb
Double-sided tape

Beading:

Following the directions for brick-stitching found in the General Instructions on page 99, weave the pattern as diagrammed.

Trim the double-sided tape to fit the comb blank, and press it into place. Stretch the woven beadwork so that it fits the comb, and press it into place. Press down firmly until the entire tape surface is in contact with the woven beadwork.

If necessary, refer to the photograph.

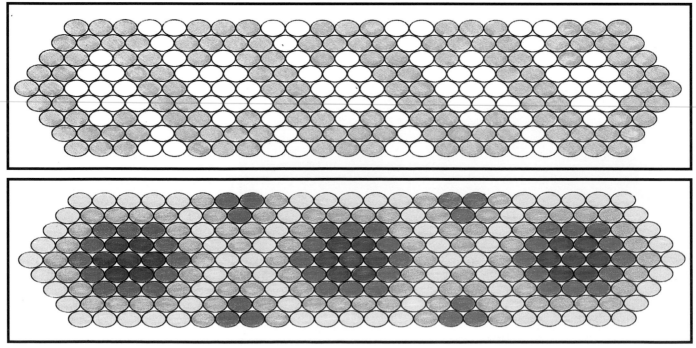

Try another celtic design. Use bead colors of your choice.

clinch combs

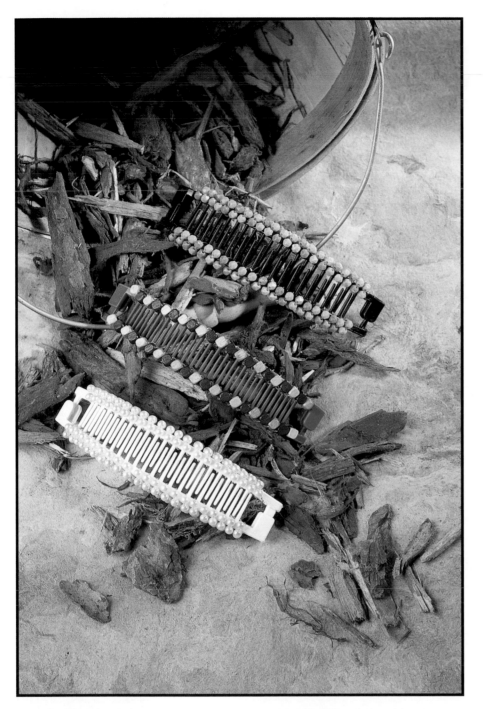

Beading:

Starting at the top of one side, thread the crimp onto the fishing line. Wrap around the side piece just above the first tooth of the comb.

Insert the end of the fishing line through the crimp and pull tight. Squeeze with pliers to flatten the crimp. Adjust the loop so that the crimp is at the back of the comb.

Thread on the beads, and wrap the fishing line around the back of the comb, catching the loose end in each wrap, then coming up between the next two teeth of the comb. Continue to add beads and wrap the fishing line around the comb so that one strand of the fishing line lands between each tooth, adjusting beads as necessary so they land on the top and outer sides of the comb.

Finish by threading on a crimp, winding the fishing line around one more time and putting the end through the crimp. Squeeze with pliers, trim off the excess fishing line, and repeat on the other side.

If necessary, refer to the photograph.

... multi-color

Materials:

Eighty-four pink 4mm English cuts
Eighty-four aqua 4mm English cuts
Eighty-four periwinkle blue
   4mm English cuts
Four crimps
Two yards of 25 lb.
   test nylon fishing line
One black clinch comb

... square beads

Materials:

Twenty-two aqua
   square wood beads
Twenty grape
   square wood beads
Four crimps
Two yards of 25 lb.
   test nylon fishing line
One purple clinch comb

... pink pearl

Materials:

Approximately 130
   4mm pink pearls
Four crimps
Two yards of 25 lb.
   test nylon fishing line
One white clinch comb

141

black lace collar

Materials:

One lace collar
4mm gold beads
Gold leaf-shaped beads
7mm black beads
Gold seed beads
Black seed beads
Black sewing thread

Beading:

Starting at the center front of the collar, hand-stitch each group of beads in place spacing them evenly around the collar. Work from the center of the collar to the sides. Make sure that each side of the design is even.

If necessary, refer to the photograph.

frosted amber pocket embellishment

Materials:

Shirt with pocket
Six freshwater pearls
One bronze 8mm crystal
Nineteen amber 6/0 seed beads
Four amethyst 6/0 seed beads
Eight amethyst 8/0 seed beads
One 20x25mm oval
   frosted amber cabochon
400 metallic gold
   11/0 seed beads
Leather
Fusing web

Beading:

Using the template, cut one octagonal piece each of the leather and the fusing web. Cut the center out of the leather as shown in the diagram, leaving the fusing web intact. Position the fusing web on the bead card, then position the leather over it with gold side up.

Following the directions for surface beading found in the General Instructions on page 101,

bring knotted thread up from any number on the outer edge of the card, and thread on metallic gold beads until the beaded thread reaches the same number inside the circle. Repeat all around. Outline interior oval and outer octagon with metallic gold beads. As shown, sew the pearls and the large seed beads (anchored with small gold seed beads) directly over the leather using a small needle.

Attach hangers at the base of the embellishment. Position the oval cabochon in the center of the open oval space. Backtrack seed beads around the cabochon and outer edge. Fuse together according to manufacturer's directions. Melted fusing web will hold the cabochon in place. Be sure to hold hangers aside when trimming the excess from the bead card.

If necessary, refer to the photograph.

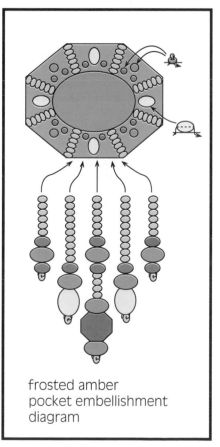

frosted amber
pocket embellishment
diagram

beaded collar & pockets

Beading:

Using the technique shown below, sew the beads to the collar and the pockets of the shirt or blouse.

Space the beads 3/8" to 1/2" apart. Bury the finished thread inside the collar or pocket flap. Clip close, being careful not to cut the fabric.

If necessary, refer to the photograph.

Materials:

Shirt or blouse with
   collar and pockets
Approximately 100
   4mm English cut or
   6/0 seed beads
   in a coordinating color
Approximately 100
   11/0 seed beads
   in a coordinating color
Sewing thread

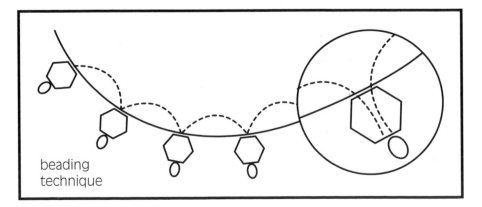

beading
technique

144

blazer cuffs & pocket

Materials:

Bugle beads in
assorted sizes and colors
Seed beads in
assorted sizes and colors
Sewing thread
Large beads, optional

Beading:

Starting at the top of the blazer pocket, randomly sew on the assorted bugle and seed beads close together. Allow the beads to become more sparse and uneven as you sew. This will give the beads the look of "falling snow."

If desired, replace the buttons on the blazer with large beads.

If necessary, refer to the photograph.

coin dress

Materials:

One dress
Seventy-five to 80
    1" coin beads
Sewing thread
Straight pin

Beading:

Begin by marking the center of the neck on the dress with a straight pin.

Starting at the center of the neck and working out toward the shoulder seam, securely sew the coin beads on 3/4" apart in an even, consistent row around the neck opening. Repeat the process for the other side.

Repeat the process on the second row going only half way to the shoulder seams.

Repeat the process on the sleeve cuffs.

If necessary, refer to the photograph.

gloves

Materials:

One pair of gloves
An assortment of beads
Nylon beading thread or
 industrial strength glue

Beading:

Plan out the desired design with the assortment of beads. Following the directions for surface beading found in the General Instructions on page 101, sew the beads on the gloves. If preferred, the beads can be glued into position.

If you choose to use the designs shown in the models, refer to the photograph.

house magnet

Materials:

Sky blue polymer clay
#2 bugle beads:
   24 matte light topaz
   18 opaque white
   47 matte dark topaz
   19 satin green
   28 silver-lined light blue
Fifty-one matte green
   11/0 seed beads
Self-adhesive magnet strips
Varnish, if desired

Beading:

Following the directions for working with polymer clay found in the General Instructions on page 100, condition the clay and roll it out in a thin layer. Make a tracing of the design template, and use it to lightly outline the pattern onto the rolled clay.

Press the beads into the clay referring to the pattern shown. Do not press the beads too deep into the clay or they will disappear.

Bake according to the General Instructions, and coat with varnish, if desired.

Apply the magnet strips to the back of the piece.

If necessary, refer to the photograph.

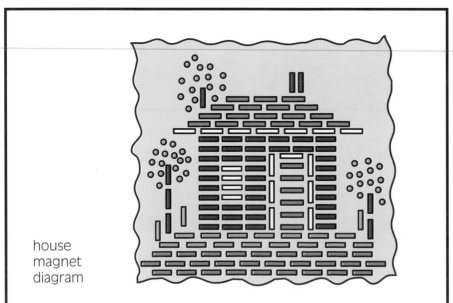

house
magnet
diagram

beehive stationery box & note cards

Materials:

Cardboard box with
   flip-up top
Note cards and envelopes
One permanent black
   fine-point marker
Assorted beads
Assorted charms
Industrial strength glue

Beading:

Draw a design on the top of the cardboard box and the note cards with a permanent black fine-point marker.

Glue the assorted beads and charms to the top of the cardboard box and note cards, embellishing the designs.

If necessary, refer to the photograph.

butterfly stationery box

Materials:

Fabric covered
   cardboard box with lid
Two butterfly gift tags
An assortment of rhinestones
Industrial strength glue

Beading:

Glue the butterfly gift tags to the top of the cardboard box. Embellish the butterfly gift tags by randomly gluing on the rhinestones. Add additional rhinestones if desired.

149

vase

Materials:

One glass vase
An assortment of rhinestones
Toothpick
Industrial strength glue

Beading:

Lay the vase on a table and arrange the rhinestones into a desired design.

Starting at the top edge, glue on the rhinestones one at a time. Use the toothpick to apply the glue.

To achieve a straight line, an envelope or folded sheet of paper can be used. Make sure any excess glue is wiped off the vase.

If necessary, refer to the photograph.

cabochon & crystal votive cup

Materials:

One 2"-diameter votive candle cup
Eleven 10x15mm
    acrylic cabochons
275 crystal AB 11/0 seed beads
Industrial strength glue

Beading:

Glue the cabochons around the candle cup, adjusting them for even spacing before the glue dries — the cabochons will not lay perfectly flat. Allow the glue to dry thoroughly.

Run a thin bead of glue around each cabochon, and place the 11/0 seed beads with the holes perpendicular to the surface — complete each one before gluing the next. Adjust the beads before the glue dries. Allow the glue to dry thoroughly.

If necessary, refer to the photograph.

frosted votive cups

Materials:

Frosted votive candle cups
An assortment of beads
Wire or string

Beading:

String the beads onto the wire or string as desired, and tightly wrap the wire or string around the top of the votive cup under the rim. If desired, some of the wire or string with beads can be pulled down around the votive cup. Glue can be used to help tack the wire or string into place.

If necessary, refer to the photograph.

suncatchers

Materials for one suncatcher:

.021 gauge wire
An assortment of beads
Two fishing swivels
An assortment of crystals
An assortment of small charms
Industrial strength glue

Beading:

String the beads onto the wire, leaving 1 1/2" at the top to form a loop.

Add one fishing swivel, then an assortment of crystals. Hook the remaining fishing swivel to the top of the 15" length of wire, and string on additional beads under the swivel. Add small charms occasionally.

Bend the wire into a spiral shape as the beads are added. Tie the wire around the last bead, and secure it with glue.

If necessary, refer to the photograph.

Beading options:

Ornamental jewelry pieces often make the main focal point or base when making suncatchers.

Start with the base and create from there, stacking beads and attaching crystals as desired onto fishing line or thin wire. Use beads that are different shapes and sizes.

Antique crystals, chandelier crystals, and charms work great.

153

clear crystal napkin rings

Materials:

Metal napkin rings
An assortment of clear crystals
Gold-tone .021 gauge wire

Beading:

Randomly place the clear crystals on the wire, and wrap the wire around each metal napkin ring.

The rings do not have to be identical — the placement of the crystals adds a unique touch to each ring!

If necessary, refer to the photograph.

large round bead napkin rings

Materials:

Five large round beads of
   identical size in either
   the same color or, if
   desired, different colors
   for each ring
Gold-tone wire

Beading:

String the five large round beads onto the wire. Then, using the wire, randomly wrap the wire around the beads and in between the beads.

If necessary, refer to the photograph.

candles

Materials:

Two decorator candles,
   4" in diameter
An assortment of studs
   and rhinestones
Industrial strength glue

Beading:

   Plan a design before beginning. Reference points can be marked on the candle by poking a pin into the wax.

   Push the studs into the candle as desired. Glue on the rhinestones. Let the glue dry thoroughly.

   If necessary, refer to the photograph.

pre-strung beaded candle shade

Materials:

One wire lamp shade form
Pre-strung glass beads
Industrial strength glue

Beading:

Starting at the top, glue the pre-strung beads around the lamp shade form.

The beads should be glued closely together as they are wrapped around the lamp shade form.

If necessary, refer to the photograph.

victorian candle shade

Materials:

One lamp shade
An assortment of beads
An assortment of silk flowers
Antique beaded glass fringe
Industrial strength glue

Beading:

Glue the silk flowers and the beads to the lamp shade, as desired.

Hand-sew the beaded fringe to the lower edge of the lamp shade.

If necessary, refer to the photograph.

blue metal drawer knobs

Materials:

Metal drawer knobs
    with holes or loops
Blue acrylic paint
An assortment of beads,
    charms, or crystals
Several jump rings or wire

Beading:

The number of drawer knobs needed will depend on the item to which you will be attaching them.

Paint the metal drawer knobs, or leave them with their original finish.

Using jump rings or wire, attach an assortment of beads, charms, or crystals to the holes or loops on the knobs. Follow the directions for embellishing simple objects found in the General Instructions on page 99.

If necessary, refer to the photograph.

Drawer knobs can also be embellished with beads by simply gluing the beads onto them.

sun face knobs

Materials:

Round wooden drawer knobs
Gold-tone face charms
Acrylic paints:
    Navy blue
    Gold
    Metallic Gold
    White
Industrial strength glue
Clear gloss acrylic spray

Beading:

Paint the drawer knobs with navy blue acrylic paint.

Cut the loops off the charms if necessary and glue the charms to the drawer knobs in the bottom left hand corner.

At random, paint sun rays with gold and metallic gold acrylic paints coming out from the sun's face.

If desired, speckle the rays with white acrylic paint dots.

Let the paint dry thoroughly and spray with clear gloss acrylic spray.

If necessary, refer to the photograph.

golden egg

Materials:

One 2 3/4" craft paper egg
Gold acrylic paint
Fifteen freshwater pearls
Eighty blue #2 bugle beads
125 pink #2 bugle beads
155 green #2 bugle beads
Jump ring or split ring
Industrial strength glue

Beading:

Paint the craft paper egg with the gold acrylic paint. Measure around the egg, and divide the circumference into five equal sections. Mark the dividing points with a light pencil mark. The beads will be glued over the line later, so it will not show.

Begin the gluing on the row of pink bugle bead peaks, then add the blue and green rows. Decrease the number of beads in each row as you work from pink to green to accommodate the curve of the egg.

Add the floral patterns as shown in the diagram below.

It may help to draw the pattern on the egg before gluing on the beads.

If necessary, refer to the photograph.

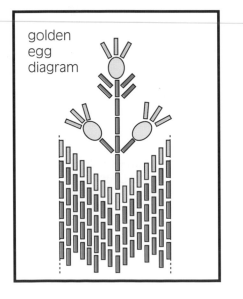

golden egg diagram

christmas egg

Materials:

One 2 3/4" craft paper egg
Sixty gold 15mm bugle beads
130 red 6/0 seed beads
200 gold #2 bugle beads
130 green #2 bugle beads
150 metallic green
    11/0 seed beads
Jump ring or split ring
Industrial strength glue

Beading:

Glue the band of 15mm bugle beads around the center of the egg, shifting the position of the beads as needed to make the pattern fit evenly.

Glue a band of red 6/0 seed beads and green #2 bugle beads above and below the center band. Outside each of these bands, glue on a row of metallic green 11/0 beads with the sides up so the holes are not visible.

Fill in the remainder of the upper and lower spaces with gold #2 bugle beads. Work in horizontal rows, decreasing the number of beads in each row to accommodate the curve of the egg.

If necessary, refer to the photograph.

heart ornament

Materials:

Dark red polymer clay
Dark red matte rainbow beads:
    Approximately 200
        11/0 seed beads
    Approximately thirty
        6/0 seed beads
    Approximately thirty
        #2 bugle beads
Small wire loop
Varnish, if desired

Beading:

Following the directions for working with polymer clay found in the General Instructions on page 100, condition the clay and roll it out in a thin layer.

Using the heart template, cut out the shape using a knife.

Following the diagram, press the beads into the surface of the clay.

After all the beads have been placed, trim away excess clay. Insert the wire loop for hanging and bake.

If necessary, refer to the photograph.

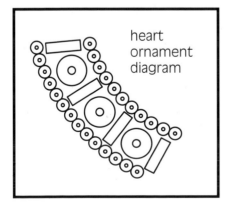

heart
ornament
diagram

heart
ornament
template

wooden tray

Materials:

One wooden tray
One piece of wrapping paper
An assortment of
　small rhinestones
Decoupage
Brush
Industrial strength glue

Beading:

Cut and arrange the wrapping paper on the wooden tray. Decoupage the wrapping paper onto the wooden tray following manufacturer's instructions. Let the decoupage dry thoroughly.

Using an assortment of small rhinestones, embellish the design on the wrapping paper by gluing them to the tray.

If necessary, refer to the photograph.

safety-pin basket

Materials:

Eighty-one size 1 safety pins,
   gold- or silver-tone finish
303 faceted crystal beads (8mm)
25-gauge gold wire
Needle-nose pliers

Beading:

Add two beads to each safety pin. To create the bottom of the basket, start by threading one safety pin (through the bottom hole) and one bead onto a piece of wire. Continue this pattern until 18 safety pins and 18 beads have been used.

After each layer, form the beaded length into a circle, and, using needle-nose pliers, twist the wire ends tightly together. Trim the ends. A new piece of wire is used for each layer.

The next layer will be threaded in the following order: one bead, one safety pin (through the top hole), one safety pin (through the bottom hole), one safety pin (through the top hole), and one bead. Refer to the diagram. Continue this pattern until nine new safety pins and nine beads have been used.

The third layer will be threaded in the following order: one bead, one safety pin (through the bottom hole), one safety pin (through the top hole), one safety pin (through the bottom hole), and one bead. Refer to the diagram. Continue this pattern until 18 new safety pins and nine beads have been used.

The top layer will be threaded in the same order as the third layer. Continue this pattern until 36 new safety pins and 18 beads have been used.

The top, scalloped row will be threaded in the following order: one bead, one safety pin (through the top hole), two

beads, and one safety pin (through the top hole). Continue this pattern until 54 beads have been used.

Shape the top of the basket. The handle is made from three loops, each made up of 11 beads.

Beading options:

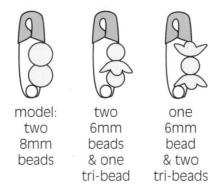

model:
two
8mm
beads

two
6mm
beads
& one
tri-bead

one
6mm
bead
& two
tri-beads

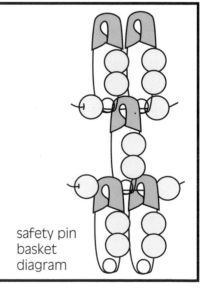

safety pin
basket
diagram

victorian ornaments

Materials for each ornament:

About ten grams of
    metallic gold 11/0 seed beads
About twenty grams of ivory or
    cream 11/0 seed beads
Sewing thread
4" x 4" piece of card stock
Photographic or painted image
    to fit in frame opening
10" length of narrow red ribbon
10" length of narrow
    green ribbon
3" circle of self-adhesive
    gold metallic paper
    for backing

Beading:

Following the directions for
surface beading found in the
General Instructions on page 101,
transfer the beading patterns
onto the card stock. Following
the diagrams, sew the beads
onto the card stock.

Using the templates, cut the
images to be mounted, and glue
them into the openings in the
center of the beadwork. Apply
the self-adhesive gold backing to
the backs of the beadwork, and
press carefully so all the threads
are in close contact with the gold
backing. Carefully trim away the
excess card and gold backing.

Form a loop and bow using
the red and green ribbons. Trim
the ends, and sew or glue the
bows to the center tops.

victorian ornaments templates (enlarge 142%)

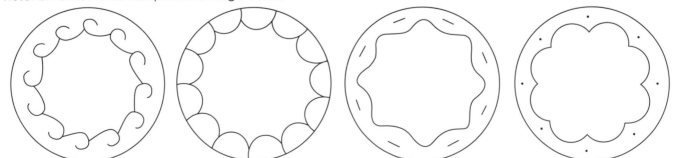

Two-Hour Cross-Stitch Projects

General Instructions

Carrying Floss

To carry floss, weave floss under the previously worked stitches on the back. Do not carry floss across any fabric that is not, or will not be, stitched. Loose threads, especially dark ones, will show through the fabric.

Centering the Design

Fold the fabric in half horizontally, then vertically. Place a pin in the fold point to mark the center. Begin stitching all designs at the center point of the graph and the fabric.

Cleaning Completed Work

When stitching is complete, soak in cold water with a mild soap for five to ten minutes. Rinse well and roll in a towel to remove excess water. Do not wring. Place work face down on a dry towel and iron on warm setting until dry.

Codes

The code indicates the brand of thread and color number used for stitching. Cross-stitches are indicated by a solid block of color with or without a symbol. Cross-stitches are labeled "X st." Back-stitches are indicated by a colored straight line. Back-stitches are labeled "BS." French Knots are indicated by a colored circle. French Knots are labeled "FK." Any other stitches or special instructions are noted at the end of the code.

Graphs

Each color on the graph represents a different color of floss. Make one stitch for each colored square, referring to the code to verify which stitch to use.

Fabrics

Counted cross-stitch is usually worked on even-weave fabrics. These fabrics are manufactured specifically for counted-thread embroidery and are woven with the same number of vertical as horizontal threads per inch. Because the number of threads in the fabric is equal in each direction, each stitch will be the same size. It is the number of threads per inch in even-weave fabrics that determines the size of a finished design.

Finished Design Size

To determine size of finished design, divide stitch count by number of threads per inch of fabric. When design is stitched over two threads, divide stitch count by half the threads per inch.

Floss

All numbers are for DMC brand floss. Use 18" lengths of floss. For best coverage, separate strands. Dampen with wet sponge. Then put back together the number of strands appropriate for fabric.

Needles

Needles should slip easily through fabric holes without piercing fabric threads. For fabric with 11 or fewer threads per inch, use needle size 24; for 14 threads per inch, use needle size 24 or 26; for 18 or more threads per inch, use needle size 26. Never leave needle in design area of fabric. It may leave rust or permanent impression on fabric.

Number of Strands

The number of strands used per stitch varies depending on the fabric used. Generally, the rule to follow for cross-stitching is 3 strands on Aida 11, 2 strands on Aida 14, 1 or 2 strands on Aida 18 (depending on desired thickness of stitches) and 1 strand on hardanger 22. For back-stitching, use 1 strand on all fabrics. When completing a french knot, use 2 strands and 1 wrap on all fabrics.

Preparing Fabric

Cut fabric at least 3" larger on all sides than finished design size. A 3" margin is the minimum amount of space that allows for comfortably working the edges of the design. To prevent fraying, whipstitch or machine-zigzag along raw edges or apply liquid fray preventative.

Securing the Floss

Insert needle up from the underside of the fabric at starting point. Hold 1" of thread behind the fabric and stitch over it, securing with the first few stitches. To finish thread, turn under four or more stitches on the back of the design. Never knot floss unless working on clothing. Another method of securing floss is the waste knot. Knot floss and insert needle from the right side of the fabric about 1" from design area. Work several stitches over the thread to secure. Cut off the knot later.

Stitches

Backstitch

Complete all cross-stitching before working backstitches or other accent stitches. Working from left to right with one strand of floss (unless designated otherwise on code), bring needle and thread up at A, down at B, and up again at C. Continue in this manner.

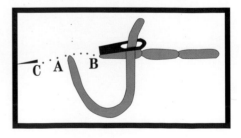

General Instructions

Cross-Stitch

Make one cross-stitch for each colored square and/or symbol on chart.
(1) Bring needle up at A, down at B. Bring needle up at C, down at D.
(2) For rows, stitch across fabric from left to right to make half-crosses, then stitch back to complete stitches.

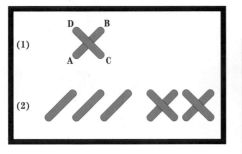

Criss-Cross Stitch

A criss-cross stitch is stitched in the same manner as the cross-stitch with two colors of thread.
With one color of thread, stitch all required stitches going in one direction. Bring needle up at A, down at B; up at C, down at D.
With the other color of thread cross all stitches. Bring needle up at 1, down at 2; up at 3, down at 4.

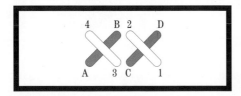

French Knot

(1) Bring needle up through fabric at A; smoothly wrap floss once around needle.
(2) Hold floss securely off to one side and push needle down through fabric beside the starting point (B).
(3) Completed French Knots.

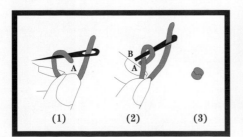

Lazy Daisy

(1) Bring the needle up at A. Put the needle down through fabric at B and back up through at C, keeping the floss under the needle to form a loop. Pull the floss through. To hold the loop in place, go down on other side of floss near C, forming a straight stitch over loop.
(2) Completed Lazy Daisy.

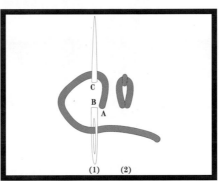

Three-Quarter Stitch

(1) Three-quarter stitches are indicated on the graph when half a square if filled with color and/or a symbol. If working over 1 thread, the short stitch will pierce fabric area. If working over 2 threads, it will slip through the hole between 2 threads. In each case, the long stitch is the overstitch, even though in some cases this may violate the rule that all stitches should be worked from left to right and back again.
(2) When two symbols occupy a single square on the graph, make a three-quarter stitch and a quarter stitch to fill the square. Which color applies to which stitch depends on the line you want to emphasize. Use the three-quarter stitch to express dominant line or color.

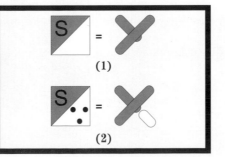

Satin Stitch

Satin Stitch consists of a series of straight stitches done next to each other to cover an area.
(1) Bring the needle up at A. Go down at B. Come up at C, next to A, to start the next stitch. Continue in the same manner as the first stitch.
(2) Completed area of Satin Stitch.

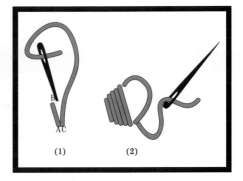

Stitching Method

For smooth stitches, use the push-and-pull method. Starting on wrong side of fabric, push needle straight up, pulling floss completely through to right side. Reinsert needle and bring it back straight down, pulling needle and floss completely through to back of fabric. Keep floss flat but do not pull thread tight. For even stitches, tension should be consistent throughout.

Twisted Floss

If floss is twisted, drop the needle and allow the floss to unwind itself. Floss will cover best when lying flat. Use thread no longer than 18" because it will tend to twist and knot.

In the Garden

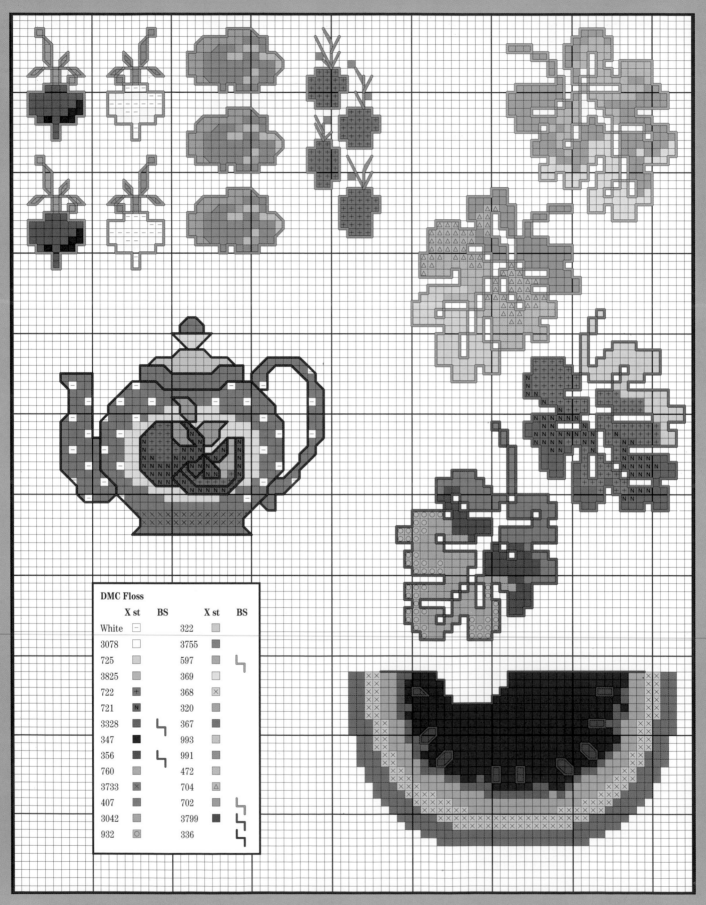

DMC Floss

	X st	BS		X st	BS
White			322		
3078			3755		
725			597		⌐
3825			369		
722	+		368	⊠	
721	N		320		
3328		⌐	367		
347			993		
356		⌐	991		
760			472		
3733	⊠		704	△	
407			702		⌐
3042			3799		⌐
932	⊙		336		⌐

In the Garden

DMC Floss

	X st		X st	BS	FK		X st	BS	FK
White	·	321	■	⌐	●	702	■	⌐	
743		208	■			3818	■		
729		3755				947	■		
407		334	N			3776	★		
946		798	■			420	■		
335		958				632	■		
309	■	704				310	■	⌐	●

DMC Floss

	X st		X st	BS
White	·	3348		
743		3347		
741		3345		
740		890	N	
498		3778		
341		355		
340		436	+	
333		434	B	
792		801		⌐
823		938	K	

In the Garden

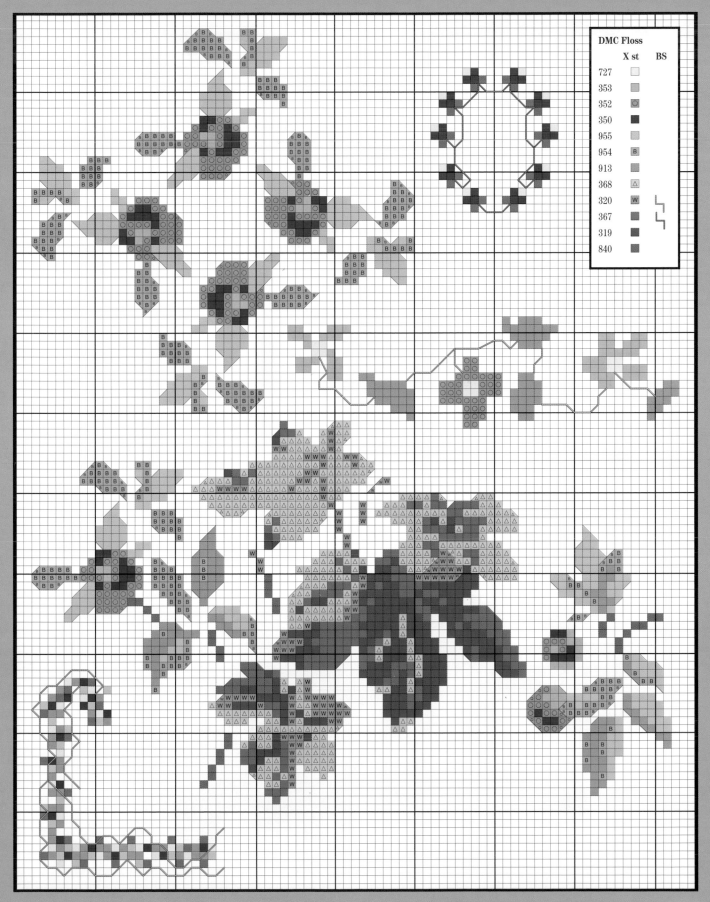

DMC Floss

	X st	BS
727		
353		
352	○	
350		
955		
954	B	
913		
368	△	
320	W	
367		
319		
840		

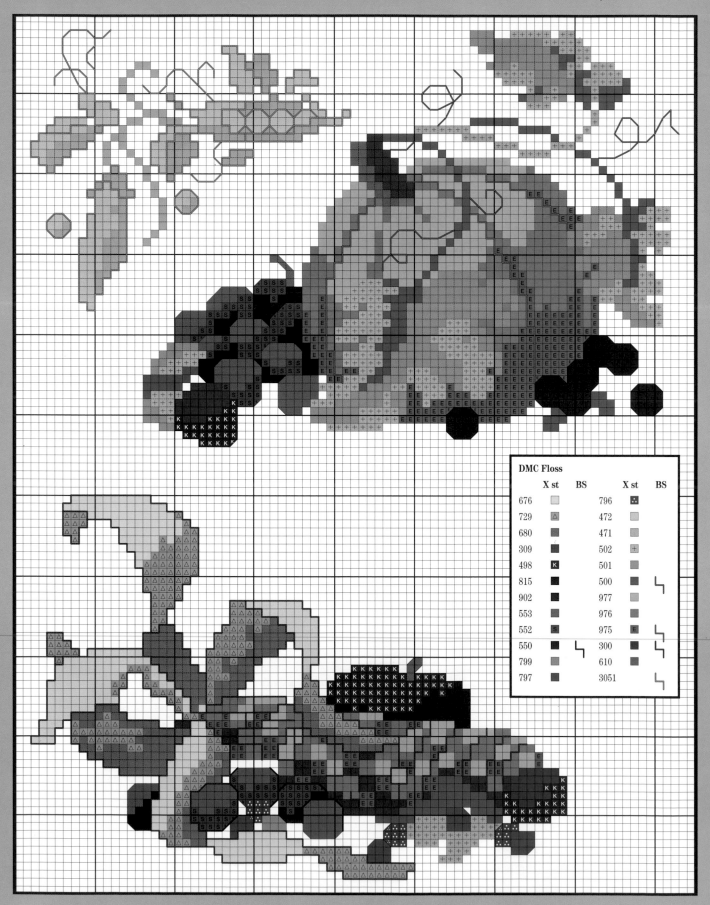

DMC Floss

	X st	BS		X st	BS
676			796		
729			472		
680			471		
309			502		
498	K		501		
815			500		
902			977		
553			976		
552	S		975	E	
550			300		
799			610		
797			3051		

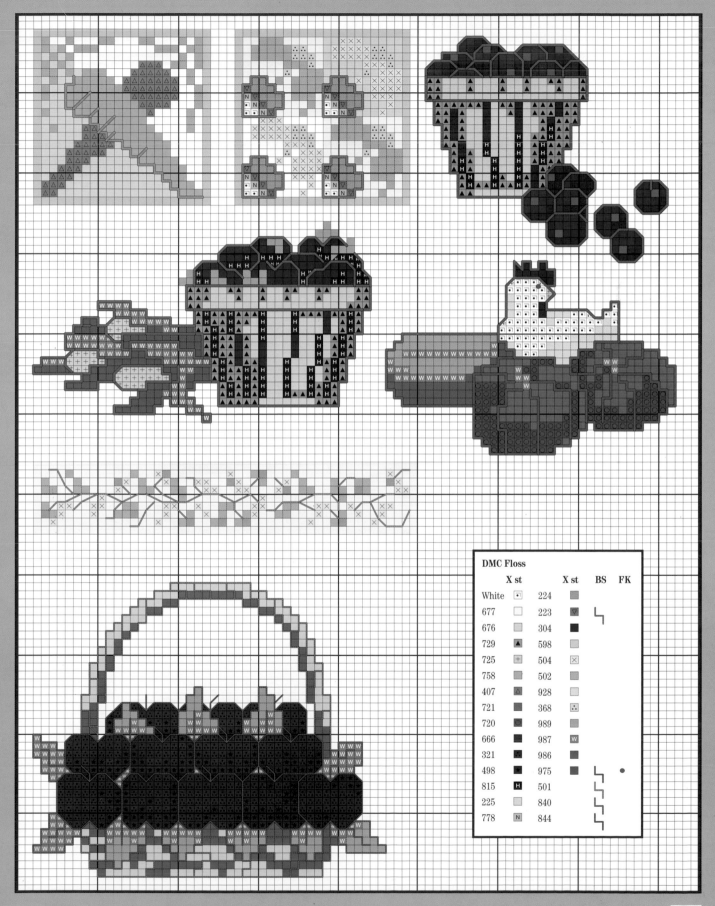

DMC Floss

	X st		X st	BS	FK
White	⊡	224			
677		223	▽	⌐	
676		304			
729	▲	598			
725	+	504	⊠		
758		502			
407	△	928			
721		368	⊡		
720	◉	989			
666		987	W		
321		986			
498	✶	975		⌐	●
815	H	501		⌐	
225		840		⌐	
778	N	844		⌐	

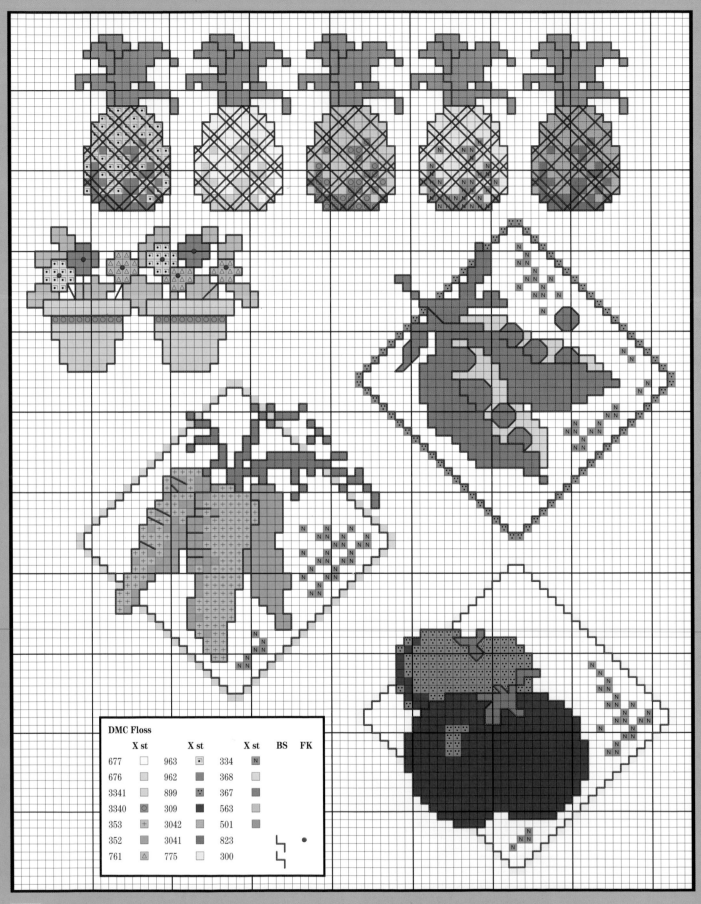

DMC Floss

	X st		X st		X st	BS	FK
677		963		334			
676		962		368			
3341		899		367			
3340		309		563			
353		3042		501			
352		3041		823			
761		775		300			●

In the Garden

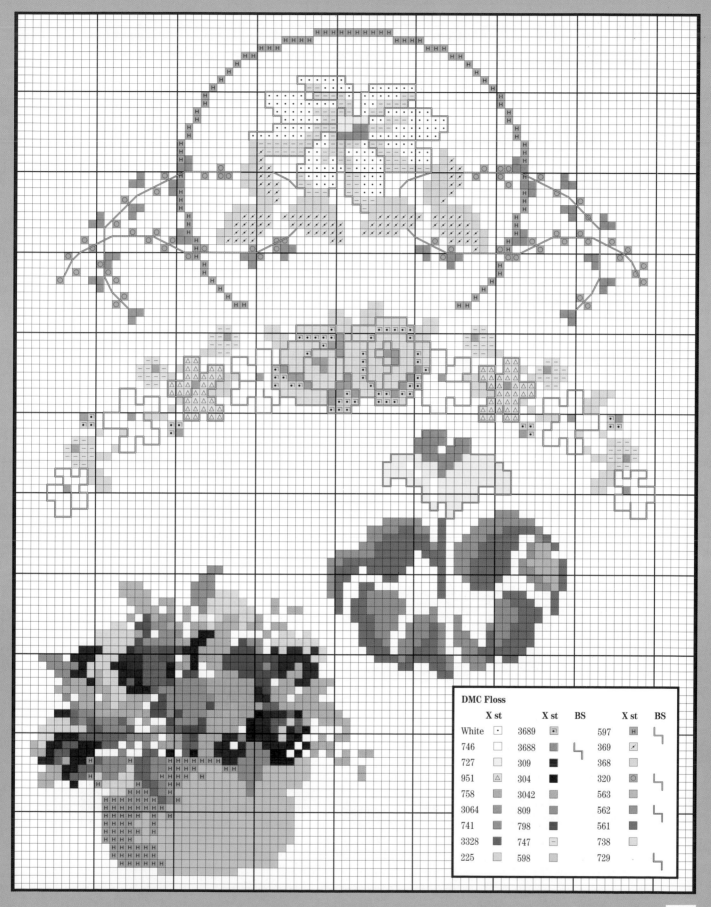

DMC Floss

	X st		X st	BS		X st	BS
White	·	3689	⊡		597	H	
746		3688		⌐	369	◪	
727		309			368		
951	△	304			320	◎	⌐
758		3042			563		
3064		809			562		⌐
741		798			561		
3328		747	−		738		
225		598			729	·	⌐

DMC Floss

	X st	BS		X st	BS
Ecru	+		550	★	
676			796		
948	○		3348		
754			3347		
722			320		
3328			319		⌐
353			501		
760	✕	⌐	500		⌐
321			739		
498			435		
815			839		⌐
902			986		⌐
333			844		⌐

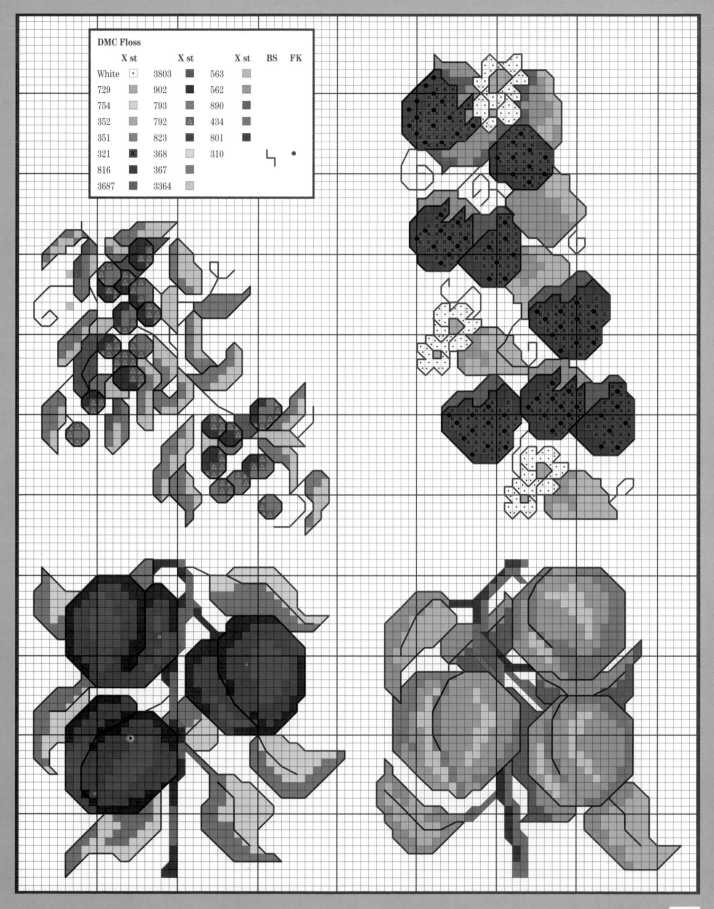

DMC Floss

	X st		X st		X st	BS	FK
White	·	3803		563			
729		902		562			
754		793		890			
352		792		434	△		
351		823		801			
321	K	368		310			
816		367					•
3687		3364					

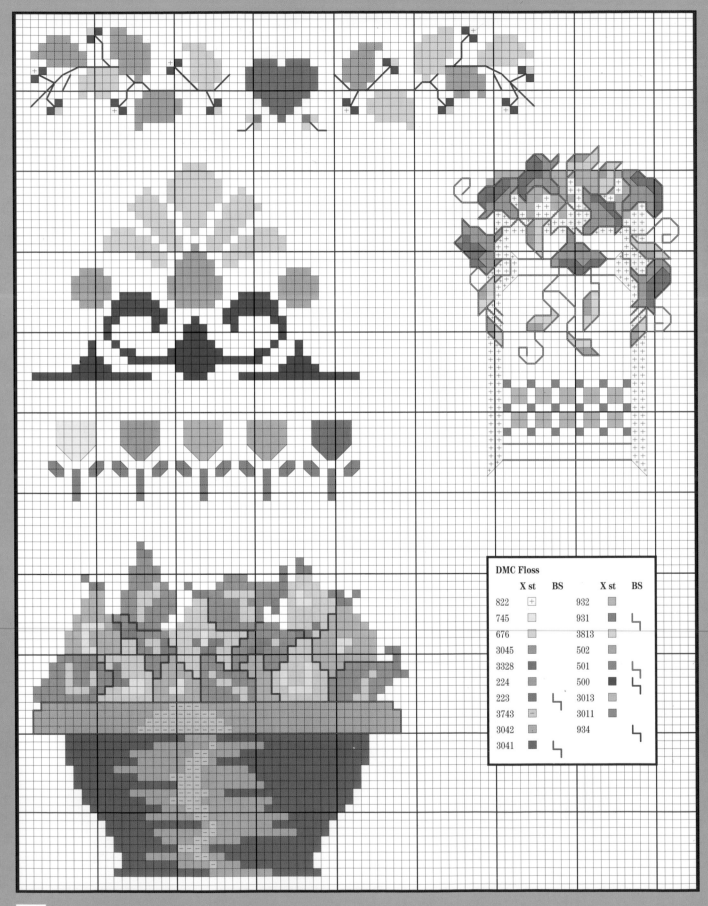

DMC Floss

	X st	BS		X st	BS
822	+		932		
745			931		⌐
676			3813		
3045			502		
3328			501		⌐
224			500		⌐
223		⌐	3013		
3743	–		3011		
3042			934		⌐
3041		⌐			

In the Garden

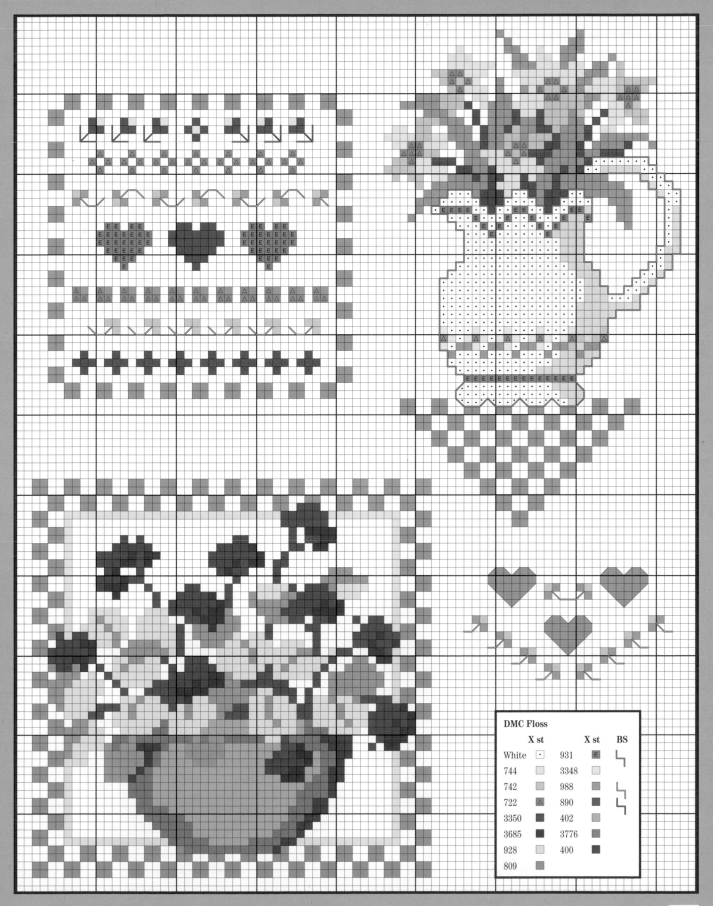

DMC Floss

	X st		X st	BS
White	·	931	E	⌐
744		3348		
742		988		⌐
722	△	890		⌐
3350		402		
3685		3776		
928		400		
809				

In the Garden

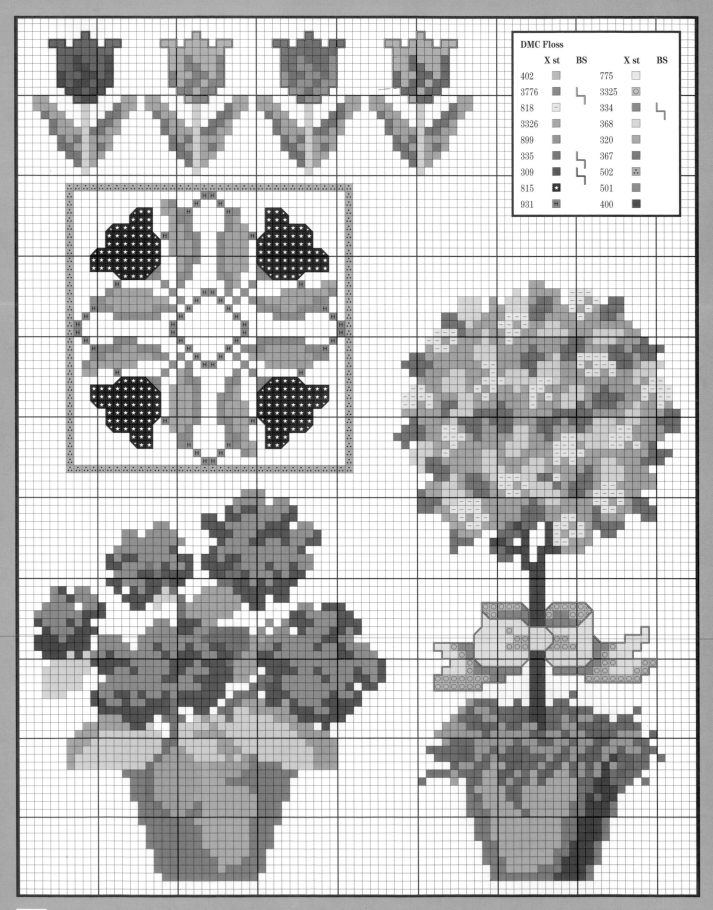

In the Garden

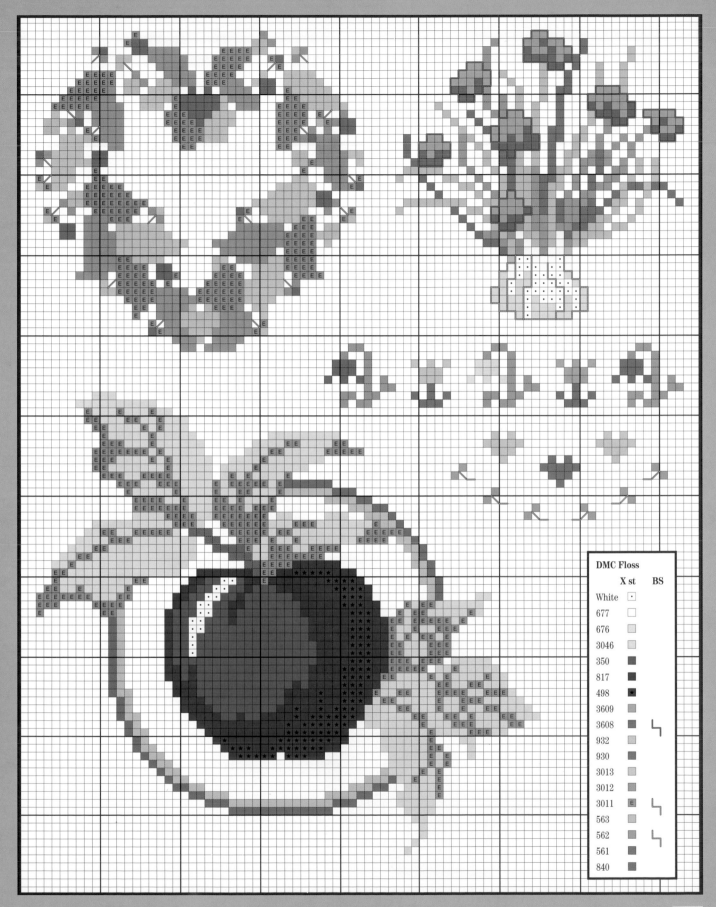

DMC Floss		
	X st	BS
White	·	
677		
676		
3046		
350		
817		
498	★	
3609		
3608		⌐
932		
930		
3013		
3012		
3011	E	⌐
563		
562		⌐
561		
840		

In the Garden

DMC Floss

X st

743	
818	
605	R
604	
603	
3325	
334	
312	
368	
320	
367	

Buttons

In the Garden

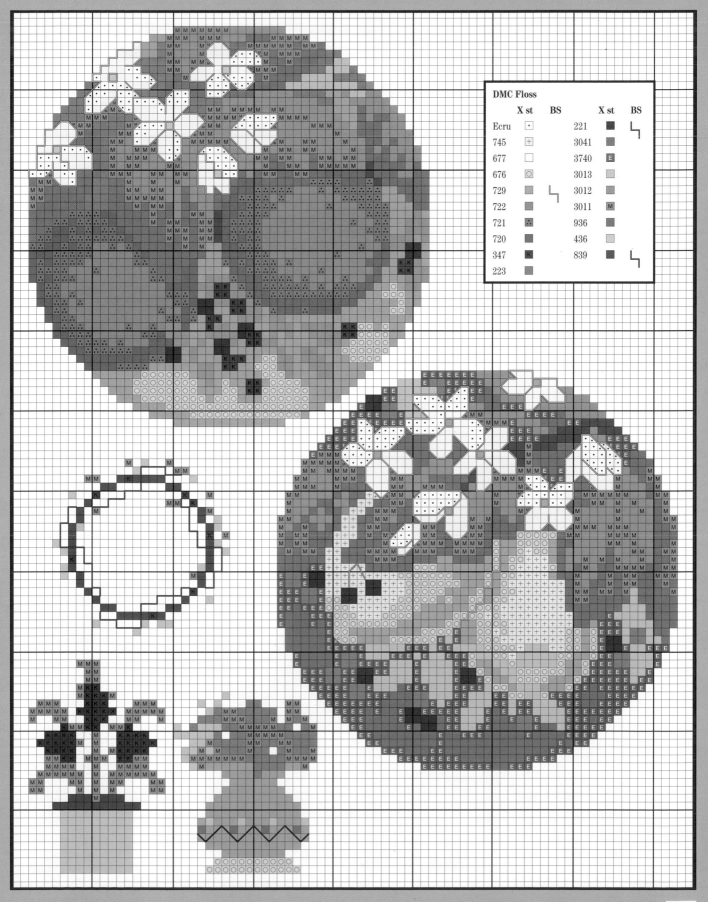

DMC Floss

	X st	BS		X st	BS
Ecru	·		221	■	⌐
745	+		3041	▨	
677	□		3740	E	
676	◎		3013	▨	
729	▨	⌐	3012	▨	
722	▨		3011	M	
721	▨		936	■	
720	▨		436	▨	
347	K		839	■	⌐
223	▨				

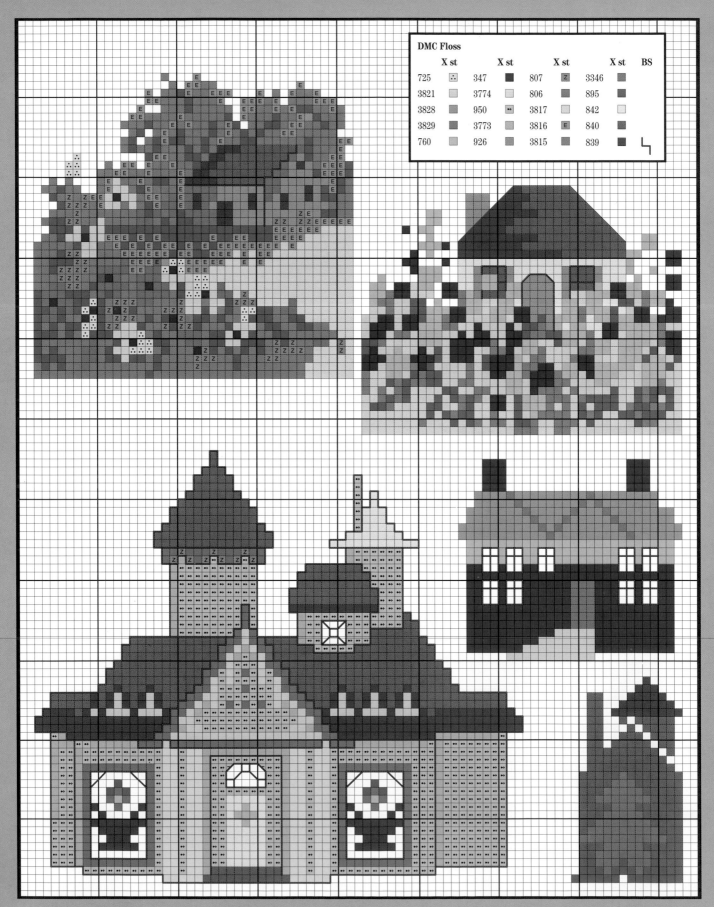

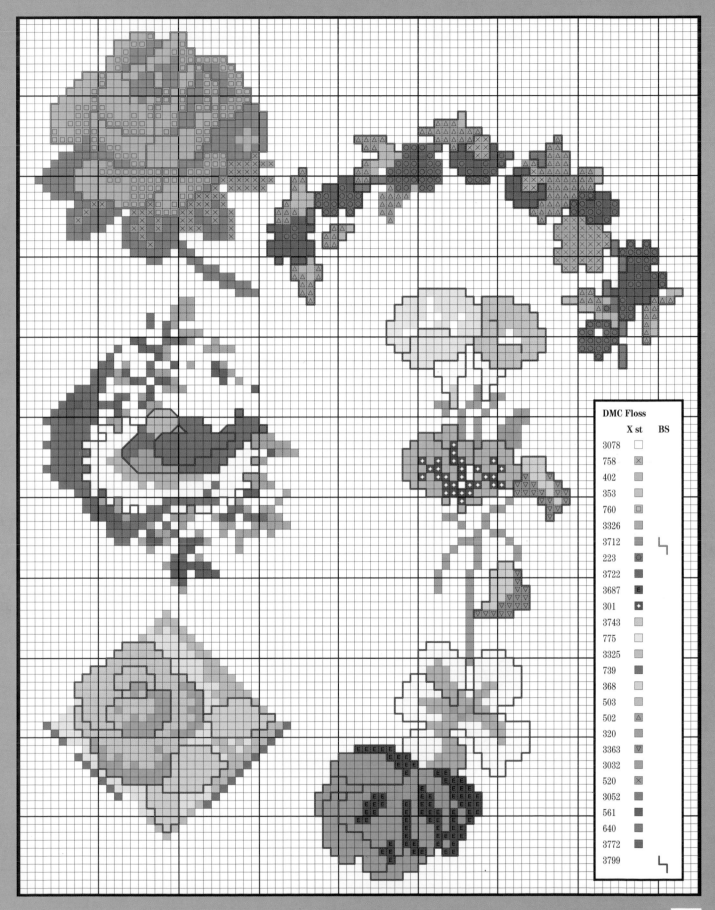

DMC Floss		
	X st	BS
3078	☐	
758	⊠	
402	▨	
353	▨	
760	☐	
3326	▨	
3712	▨	⌐
223	⊙	
3722	▨	
3687	E	
301	✦	
3743	▨	
775	☐	
3325	▨	
739	▨	
368	▨	
503	▨	
502	△	
320	▨	
3363	▽	
3032	▨	
520	⊠	
3052	▨	
561	▨	
640	▨	
3772	▨	
3799		⌐

In the Garden

DMC Floss

	X st	BS
677		
3825		
778		
316	B	
315		
3042	○	
3041		⌐
932		⌐
931		
823		⌐
927		
926		⌐
924		⌐
3053		⌐
3051	∴	⌐
934		⌐
950		⌐
407		⌐
632	N	⌐
610		⌐
640		⌐
317		⌐

In the Garden

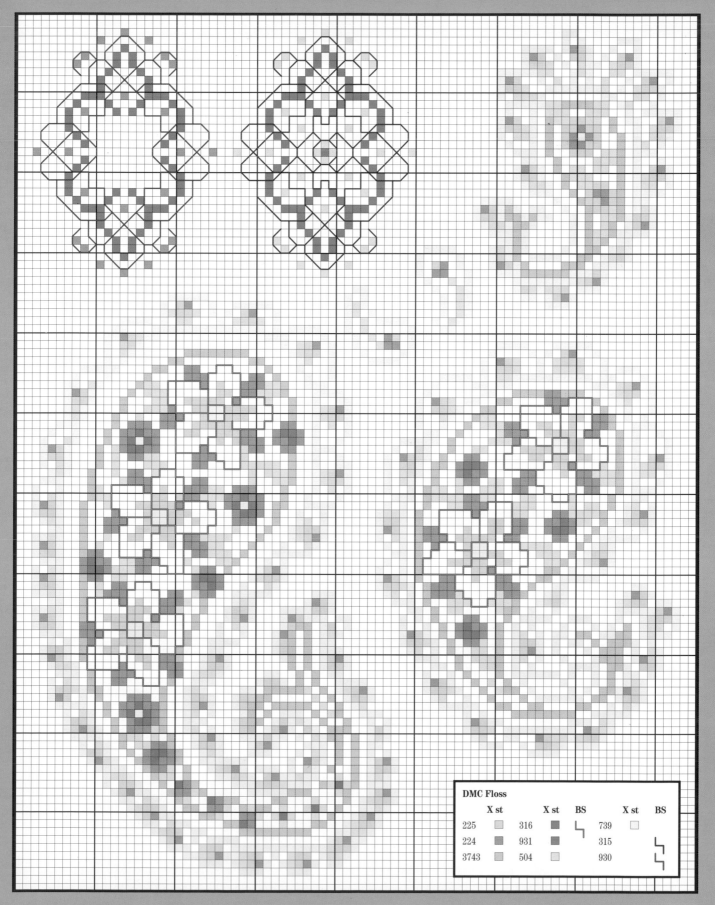

DMC Floss

	X st		X st	BS		X st	BS
225		316		739			
224		931		315			
3743		504		930			

For All Seasons

For All Seasons

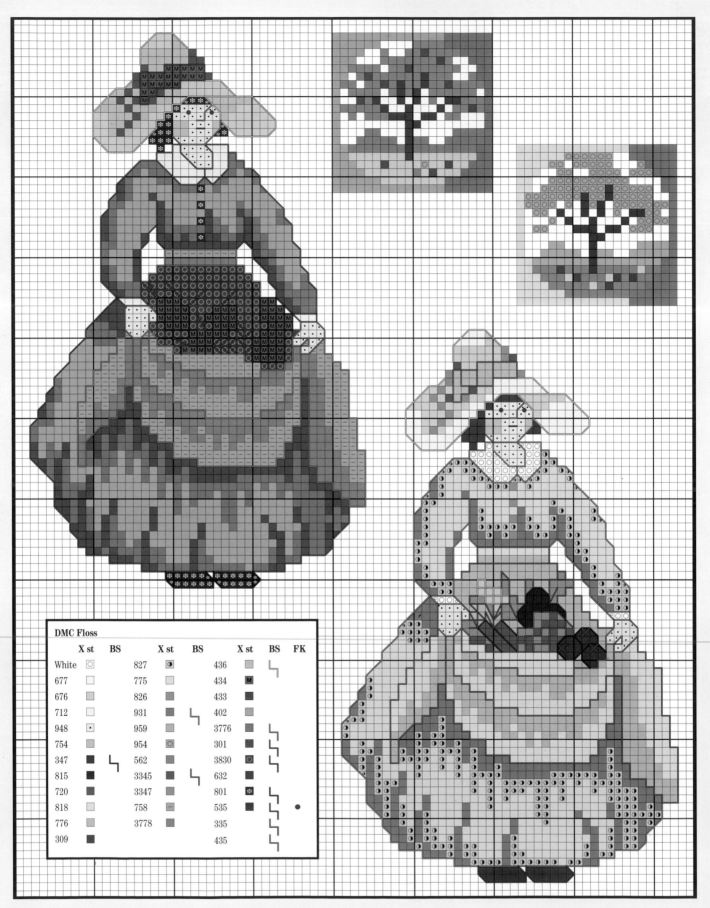

DMC Floss

	X st	BS		X st	BS		X st	BS	FK
White	○		827	◑		436		⌐	
677			775			434	M		
676			826			433			
712			931		⌐	402			
948	·		959			3776		⌐	
754			954	○		301		⌐	
347		⌐	562			3830	○	⌐	
815			3345		⌐	632		⌐	
720			3347			801	❋	⌐	
818			758	—		535		⌐	●
776			3778			335		⌐	
309						435		⌐	

For All Seasons

DMC Floss

	X st	BS		X st	BS		X st	BS	FK
White	◎		326	■		959	▨		
3823	☐		815	■		3817	▨		
745	☐		433	△	⌐	3816	⊠		
743	☐		224	▨		3815	■		
729	▨	⌐	223	▨		367	■		
948	⊡		3721	■		500	⊞		
712	▨		3806	■		632	▨	⌐	
754	▨		554	■		535	■	⌐	●
721	▨		3807	■		221	■	⌐	
435	■	⌐	772	☐		553	■	⌐	

For All Seasons

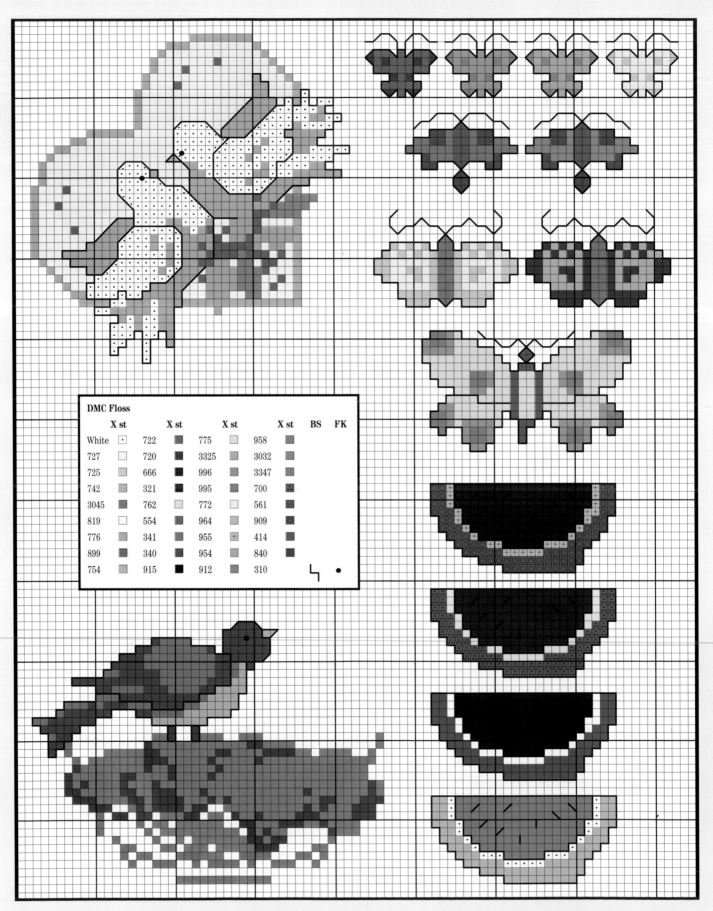

DMC Floss

	X st		X st		X st		X st	BS	FK
White	·	722		775		958			
727		720		3325		3032			
725		666		996		3347			
742		321		995		700			
3045		762		772		561			
819		554		964		909			
776		341		955	+	414			
899		340		954		840			
754		915		912		310			●

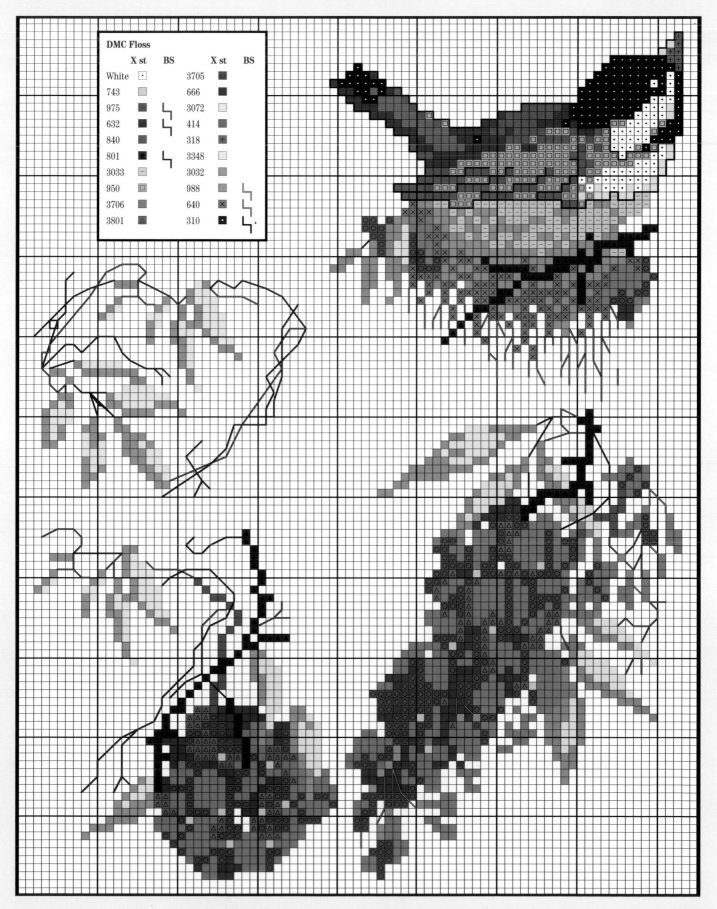

DMC Floss

	X st	BS		X st	BS
White	·		3705		
743			666		
975		⌐	3072		
632		⌐	414		
840			318	+	
801		⌐	3348		
3033	–	⌐	3032		
950			988		⌐
3706			640	×	⌐
3801	△		310		⌐

For All Seasons

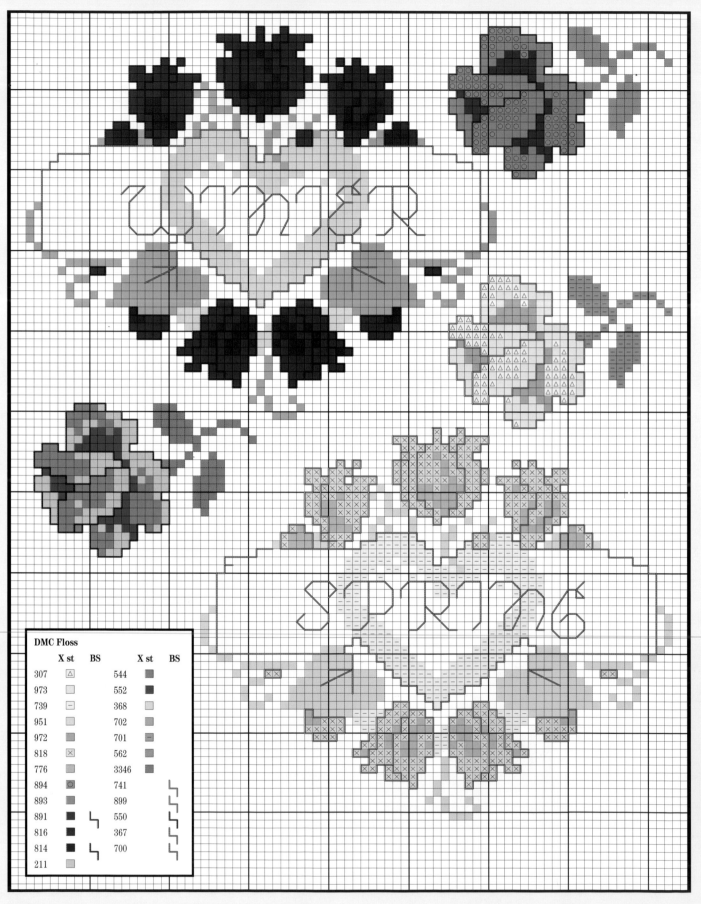

DMC Floss

	X st	BS		X st	BS
307	△		544	■	
973			552	■	
739	−		368		
951			702		
972	■		701	−	
818	✕		562	■	
776			3346	■	
894	◎		741		
893	■		899		
891	■	⌐	550		⌐
816	■		367		⌐
814	■	⌐	700		⌐
211					

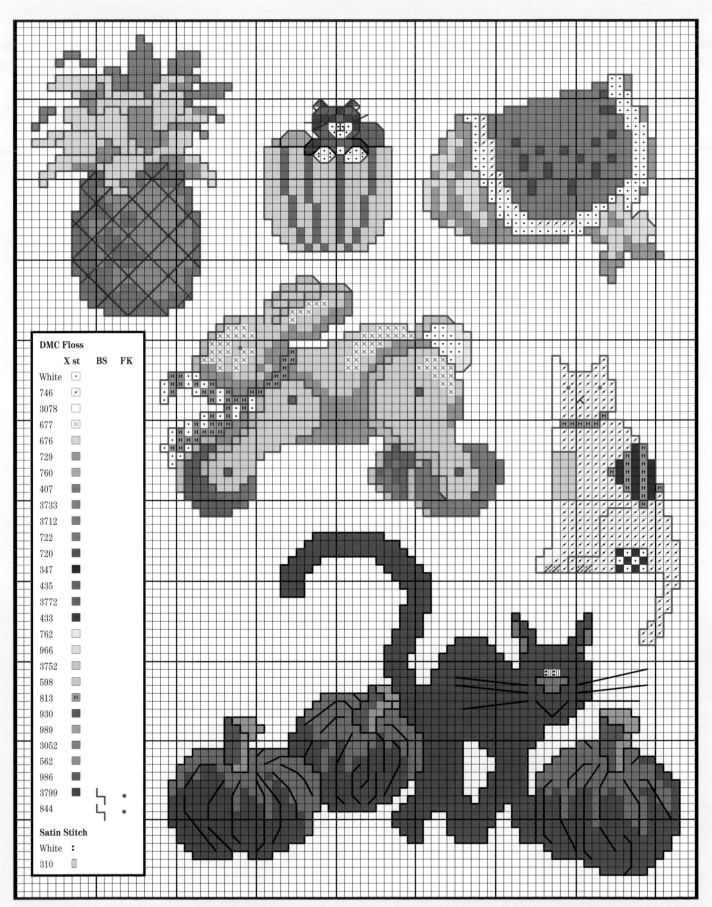

DMC Floss

	X st	BS	FK
White	·		
746	✗		
3078	☐		
677	⊠		
676			
729			
760			
407			
3733			
3712			
722			
720			
347			
435			
3772			
433			
762			
966			
3752			
598			
813	H		
930			
989			
3052			
562			
986			
3799			
844			

Satin Stitch

White	⦂
310	▯

For All Seasons

DMC Floss

	X st		X st		X st	BS
Ecru	△	351	■	611	■	■
727	□	350	■	3021	J	⌐
722	■	341	■	3033	□	
721	△	340	■	841	■	
818	□	772	□	610	⊡	
353	△	3364	■	840	■	
3326	■	3032	■	720	■	⌐
899	+	988	■			

DMC Floss

	X st	BS
677		
745	○	
744		
725		
676	M	
729		
977		
740		
921		
347	V	⌐
326		
355		
816		⌐
353		
327		
3756	·	
800		
824		
311		⌐
371	U	⌐
3052		
910		
3345		
890	✳	
844		⌐
986		⌐
435		⌐

For All Seasons

DMC Floss

	X st	BS
White	·	
725		
743		
948		
754		
976		⌐
666		
347		
301	△	
326	✳	
553		
3041		
928		
930		⌐
502		
912		
501		⌐
3053		
703		
701	✕	
699	◇	⌐
841		
840		⌐
415		
414		⌐

For All Seasons

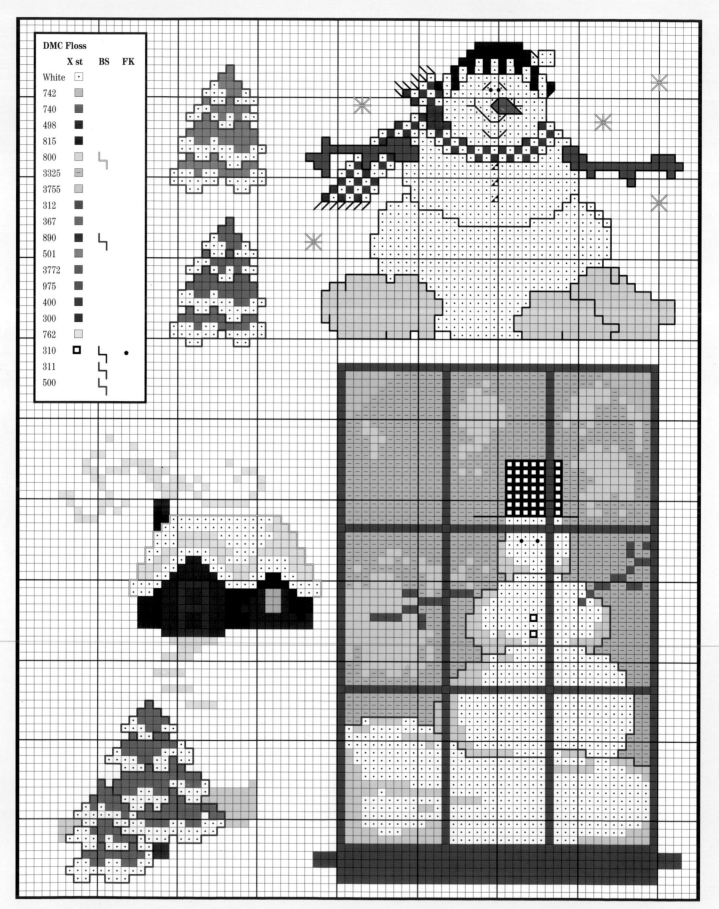

DMC Floss

	X st	BS	FK
White	·		
742			
740			
498			
815			
800		⌐	
3325	−		
3755			
312			
367			
890		⌐	
501			
3772			
975			
400			
300			
762			
310	□	⌐	•
311			
500			

DMC Floss

	X st	BS	FK
White	·		
725		⌐	
783			
721			
976			
975			
224			
223	◉		
221		⌐	
605			
3806	M		
3804			
3803		⌐	
932	▨		
800			
320	▣		
367			
319			
910	✕		
842			
841	▨		
840	K	⌐	•
400			
839		⌐	
928			
927		⌐	
930			
3799		⌐	
890		⌐	
898		⌐	
3371		⌐	•

Criss Cross

605 & 3803	✕

Step 1: Cross-stitch (2 strands)

DMC

−	725
∴	721
●	347
△	327
×	334
□	562
▲	839

Step 2: Backstitch (1 strand)

⌐ 310

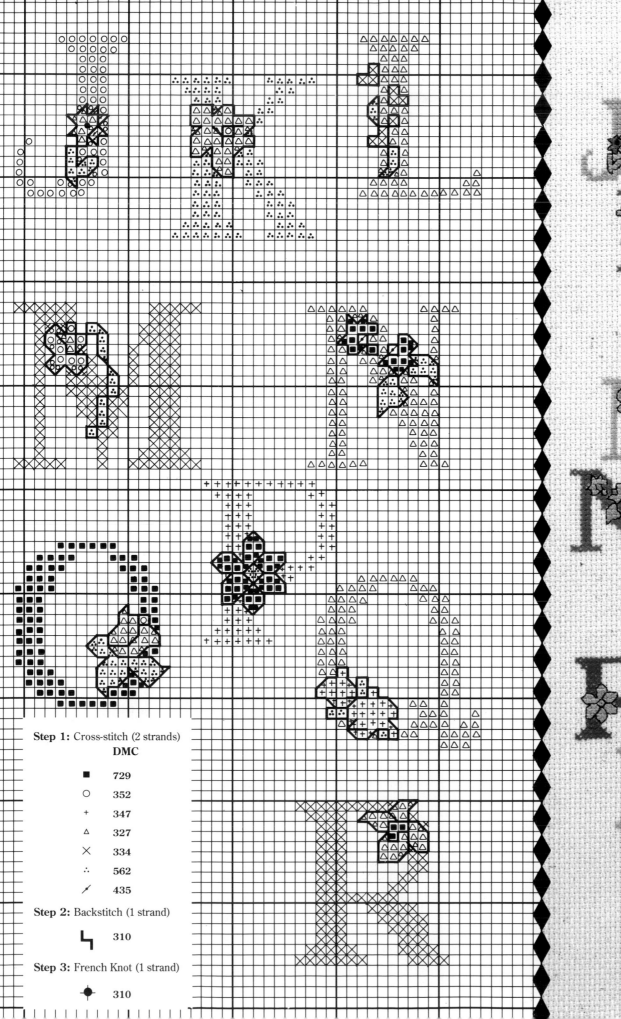

Step 1: Cross-stitch (2 strands)

DMC

■	729
○	352
+	347
△	327
✕	334
∴	562
╱	435

Step 2: Backstitch (1 strand)

⌐	310

Step 3: French Knot (1 strand)

✦	310

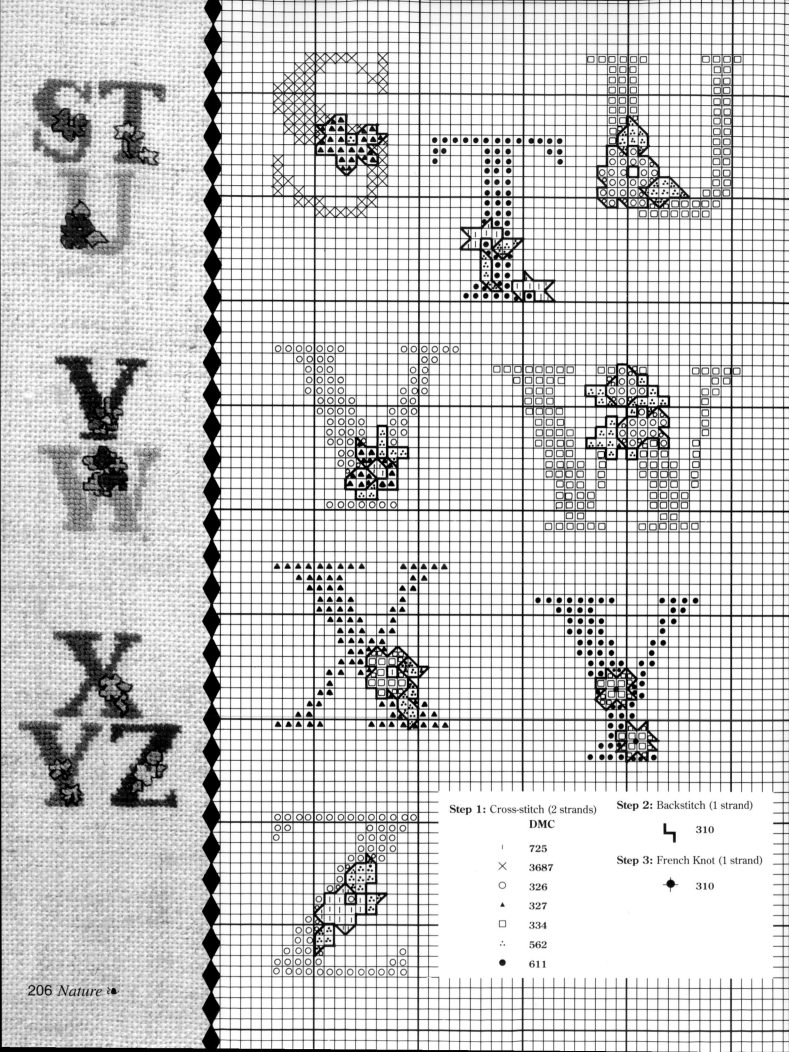

Step 1: Cross-stitch (2 strands)

DMC

	725
×	3687
○	326
▲	327
□	334
∴	562
●	611

Step 2: Backstitch (1 strand)

⌐ 310

Step 3: French Knot (1 strand)

✦ 310

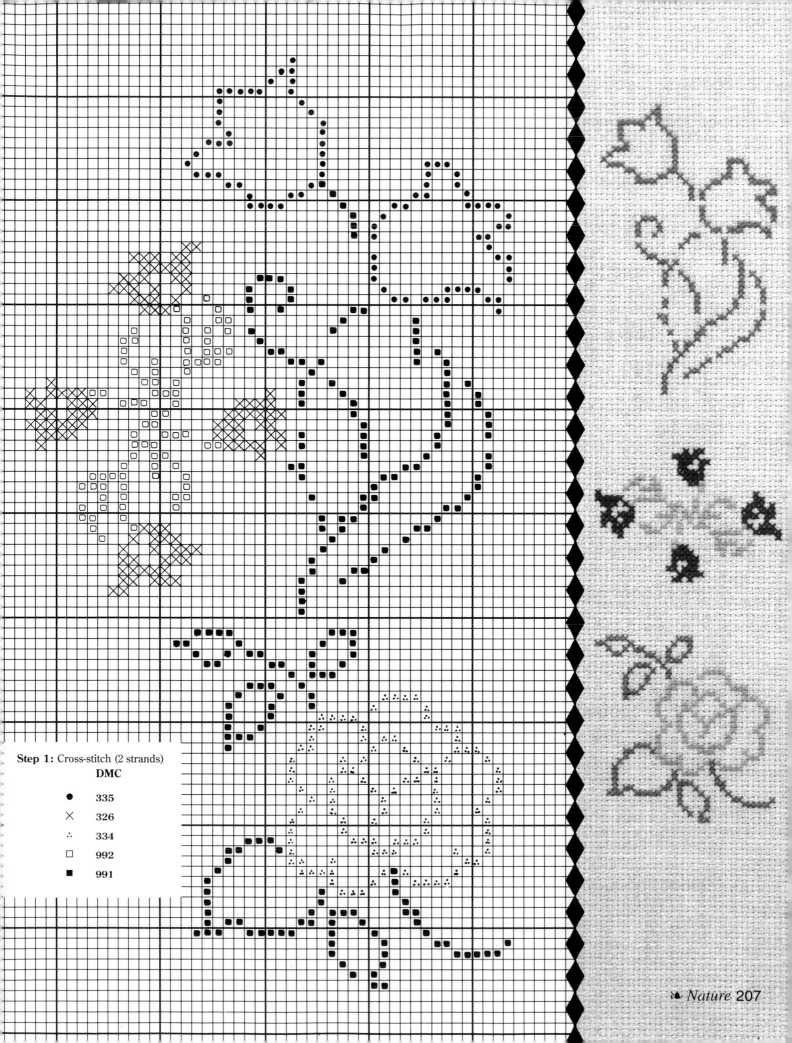

Nature **207**

Step 1: Cross-stitch (2 strands)

DMC

	3716
O	351
X	341
●	3746
△	334
∴	988
■	986
▲	3799

Step 2: Backstitch (1 strand)

⌐ 3799

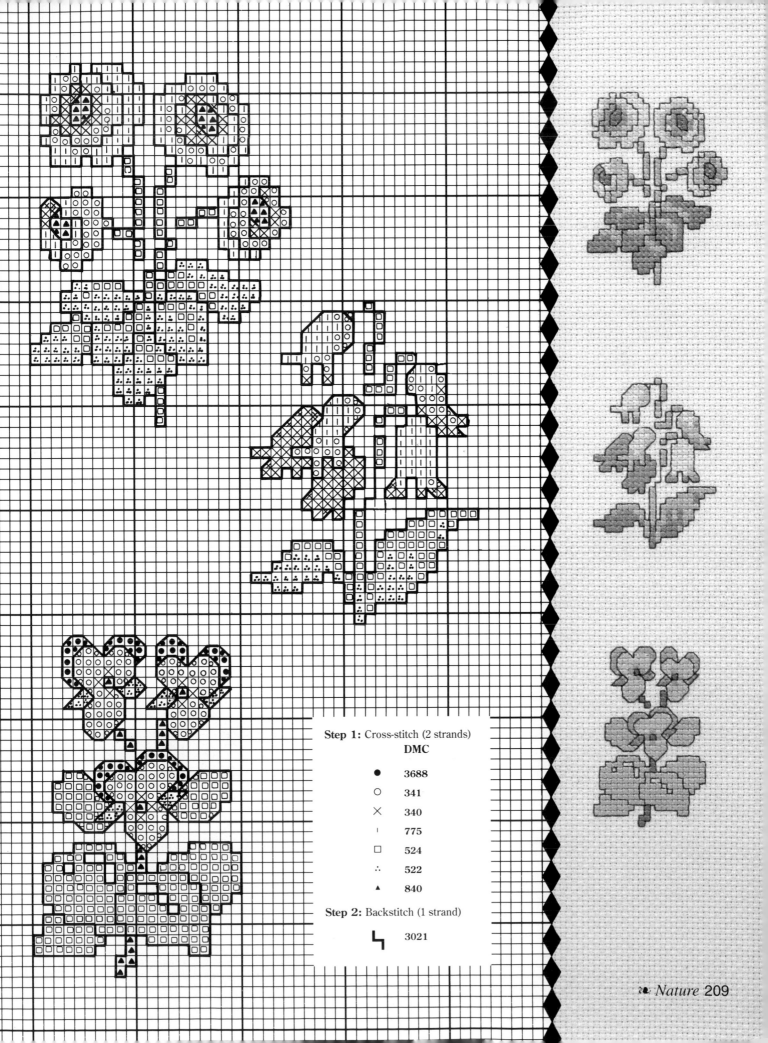

Step 1: Cross-stitch (2 strands)

DMC

●	3688
○	341
✕	340
ı	775
□	524
∴	522
▲	840

Step 2: Backstitch (1 strand)

⌐	3021

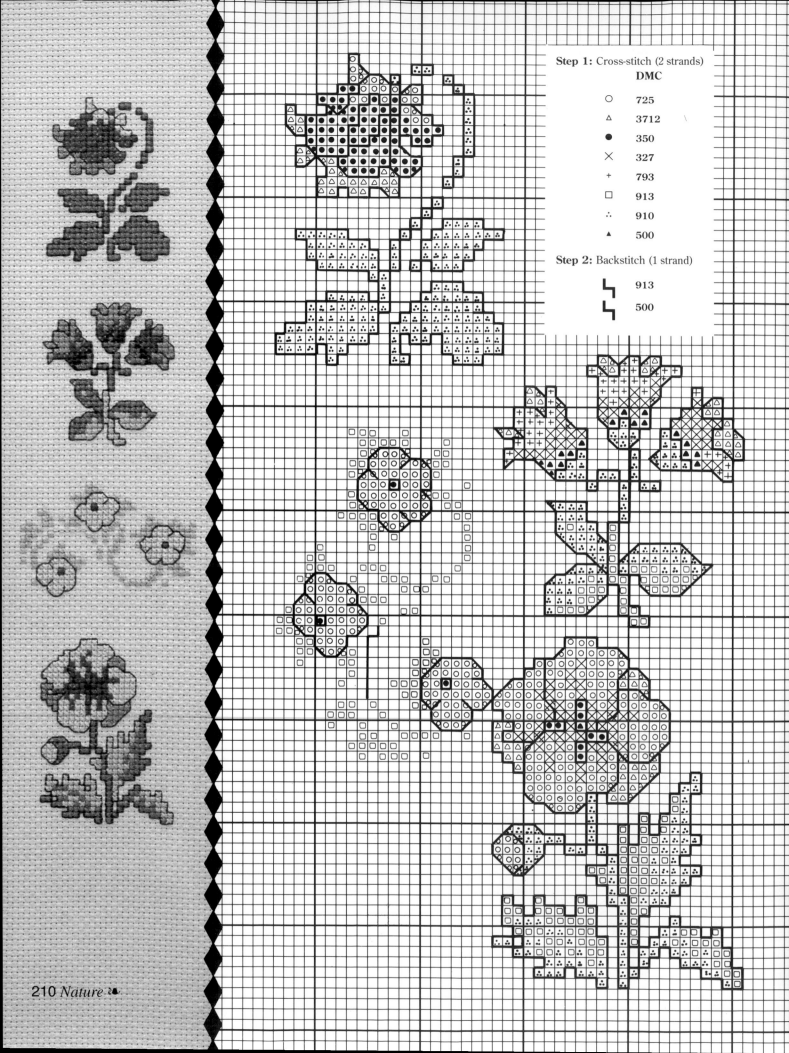

Step 1: Cross-stitch (2 strands)

DMC

○ 725
△ 3712
● 350
✕ 327
+ 793
□ 913
∴ 910
▲ 500

Step 2: Backstitch (1 strand)

⌐ 913
⌐ 500

Step 1: Cross-stitch (2 strands)

DMC

+	725
∴	722
○	900
●	817
✕	3347
△	3346
▲	986

Step 2: Backstitch (1 strand)

⌐	3799

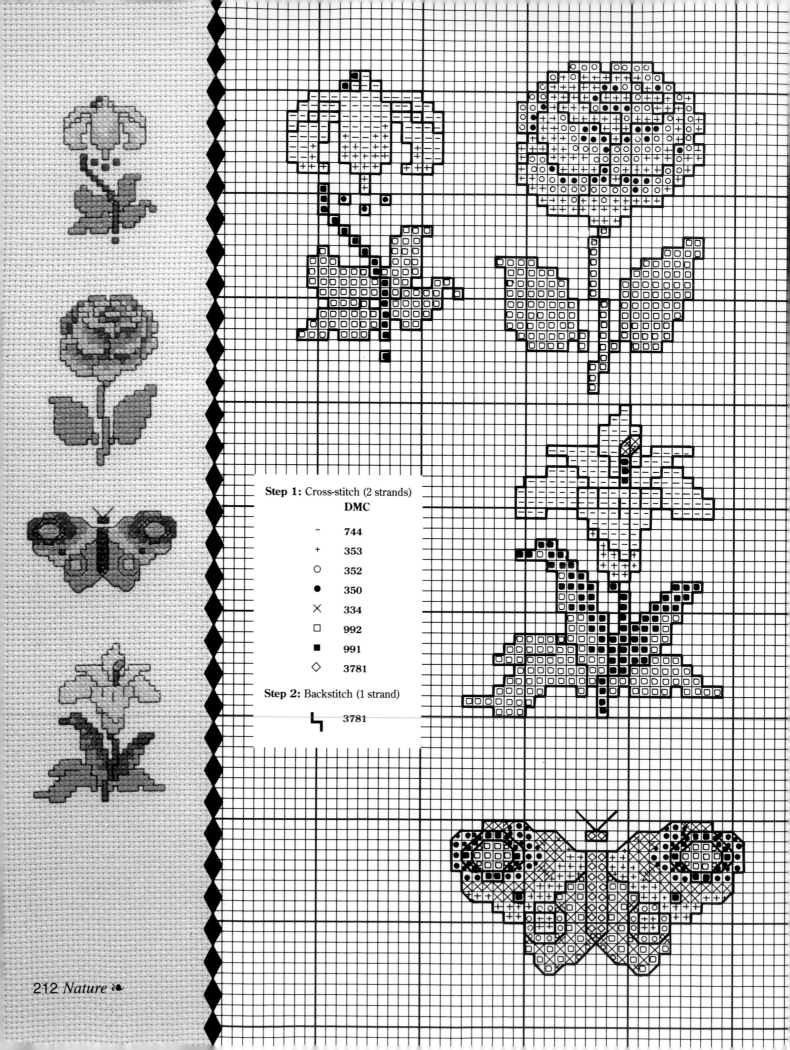

Step 1: Cross-stitch (2 strands)

DMC

-    744
+   353
○   352
●   350
✕   334
□   992
■   991
◇   3781

Step 2: Backstitch (1 strand)

└ 3781

Step 1: Cross-stitch (2 strands)

DMC

I	676
○	402
△	961
▲	3685
∴	209
□	966
✕	562

Step 2: Backstitch (1 strand)

⌐	562
⌐	3371

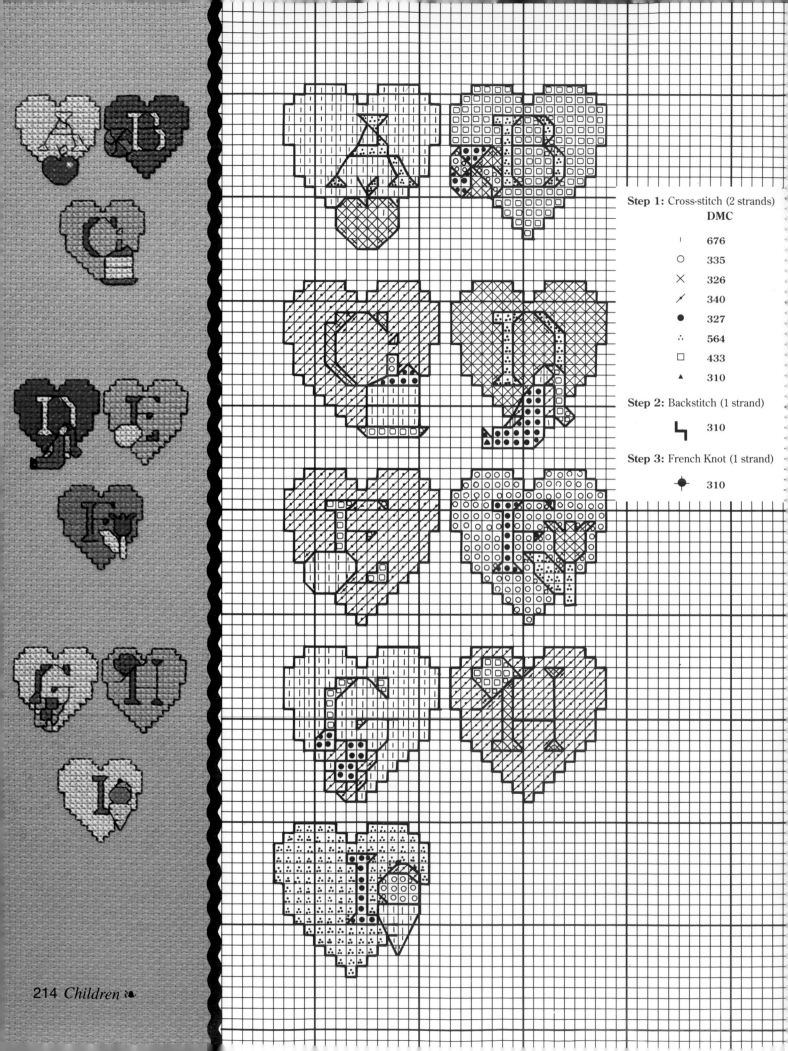

Step 1: Cross-stitch (2 strands)
DMC

| | 676
O 335
X 326
/ 340
● 327
∴ 564
□ 433
▲ 310

Step 2: Backstitch (1 strand)

⌐ 310

Step 3: French Knot (1 strand)

● 310

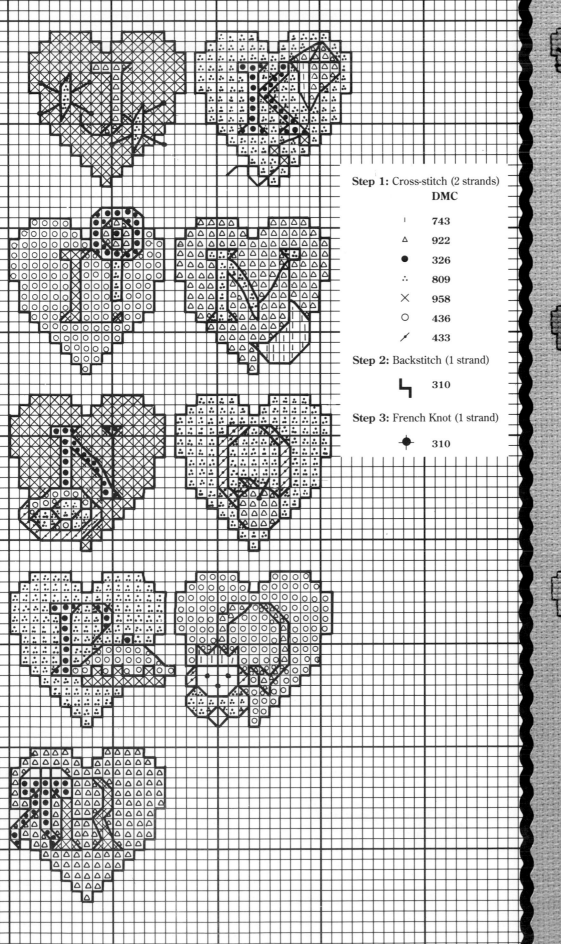

Step 1: Cross-stitch (2 strands)

DMC

I	743
△	922
●	326
∴	809
✕	958
○	436
⟋	433

Step 2: Backstitch (1 strand)

⌐	310

Step 3: French Knot (1 strand)

◆	310

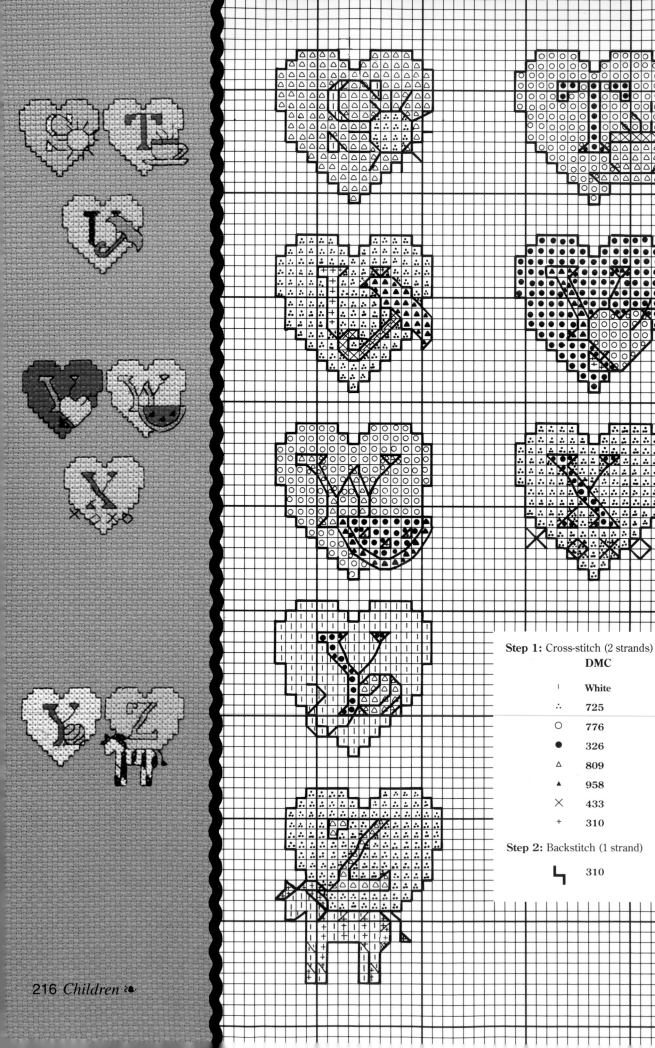

Step 1: Cross-stitch (2 strands)
DMC

I	White
∴	725
○	776
●	326
△	809
▲	958
✕	433
+	310

Step 2: Backstitch (1 strand)

⌐	310

Step 1: Cross-stitch (2 strands)

DMC

+	963
○	962
●	3350
✕	340
▲	824
☐	959
■	434

Step 2: Backstitch (1 strand)

⌐ 3750

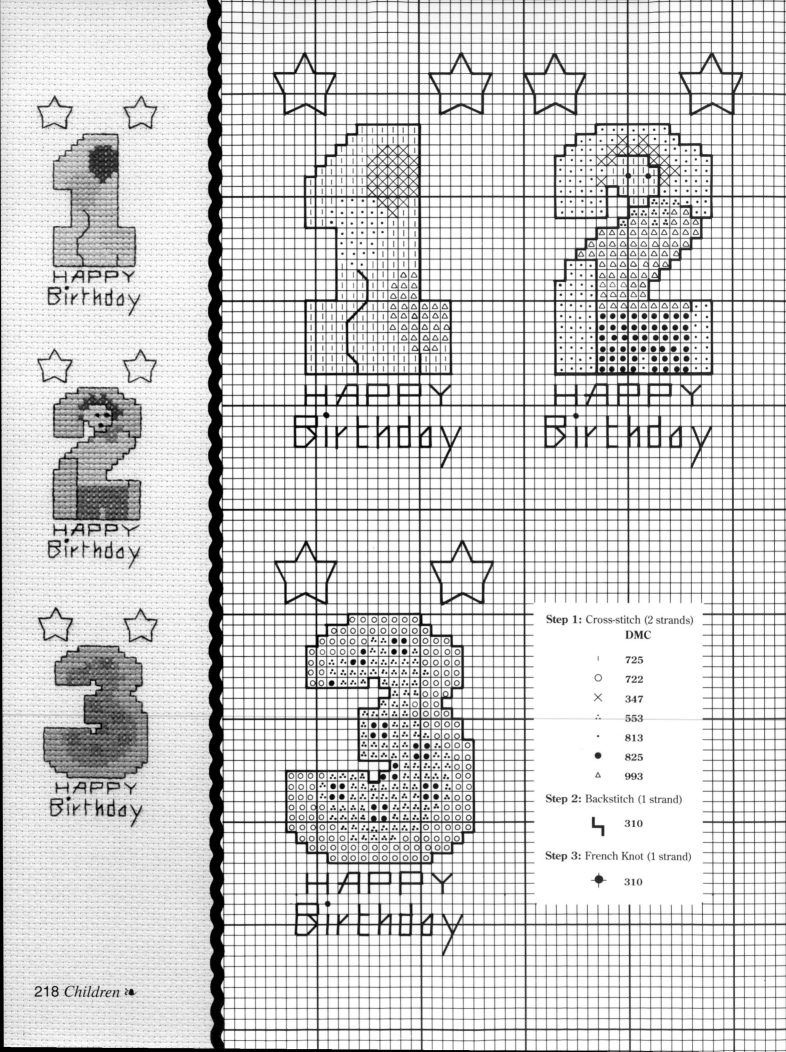

Step 1: Cross-stitch (2 strands)

DMC

⌶	725
○	722
✕	347
∴	553
·	813
●	825
△	993

Step 2: Backstitch (1 strand)

⌐ 310

Step 3: French Knot (1 strand)

✦ 310

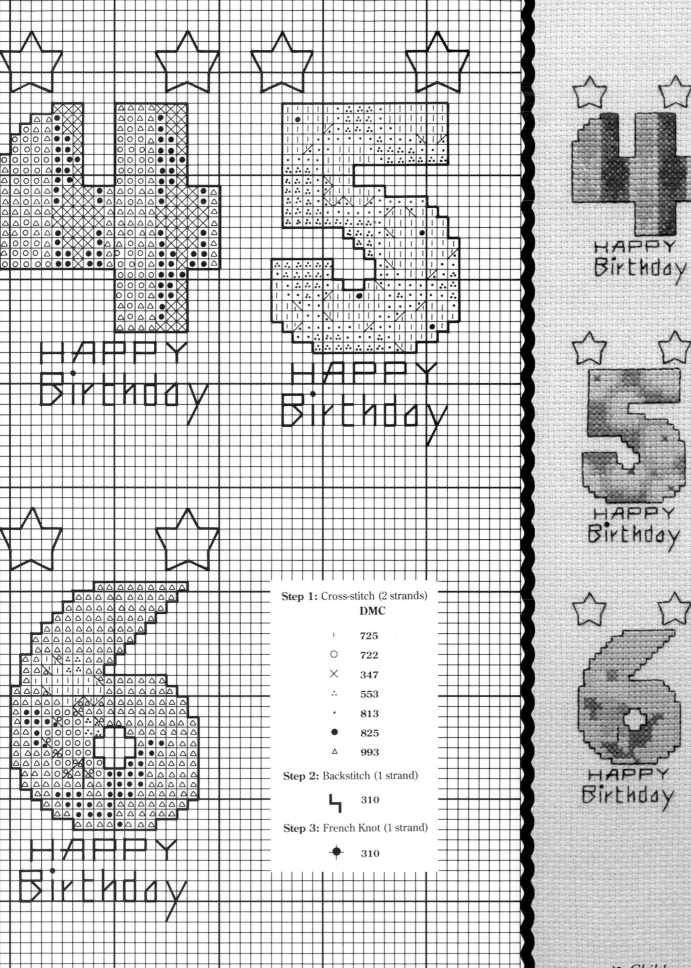

Step 1: Cross-stitch (2 strands)

DMC

I	725
O	722
X	347
∴	553
•	813
●	825
△	993

Step 2: Backstitch (1 strand)

⌐ 310

Step 3: French Knot (1 strand)

✦ 310

HAPPY
Birthday

HAPPY
Birthday

HAPPY
Birthday

HAPPY
Birthday

HAPPY
Birthday

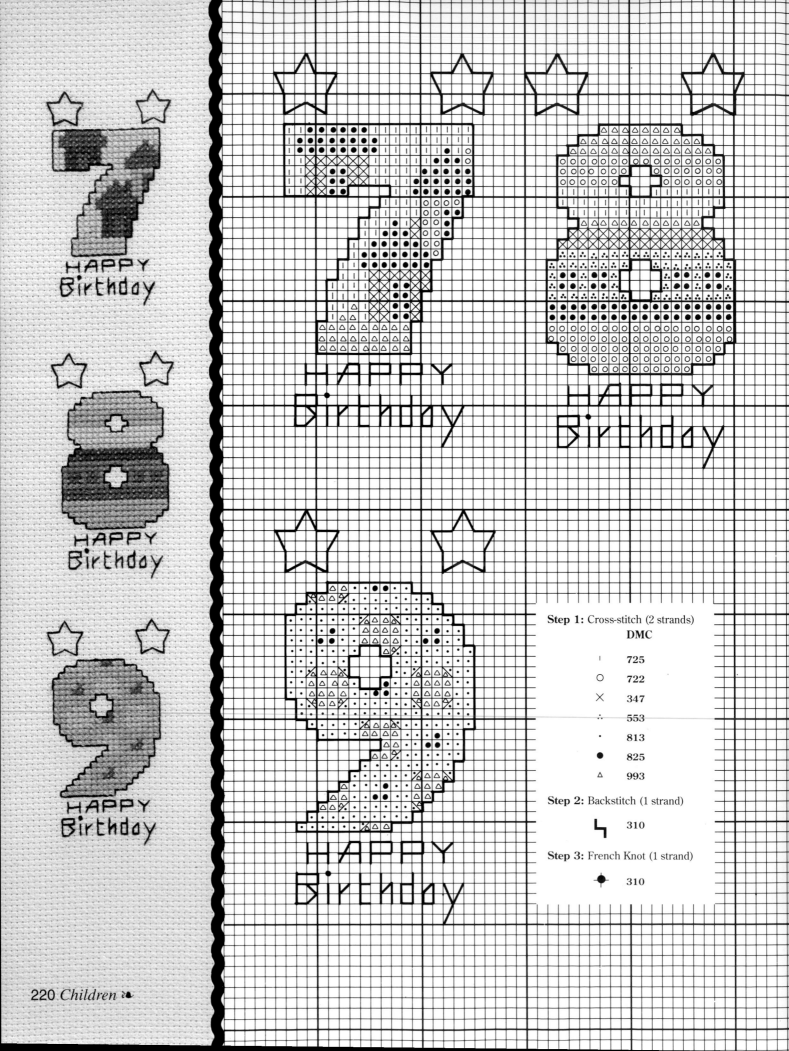

Step 1: Cross-stitch (2 strands)

DMC

I	725
O	722
X	347
∴	553
•	813
●	825
△	993

Step 2: Backstitch (1 strand)

⌐	310

Step 3: French Knot (1 strand)

◆	310

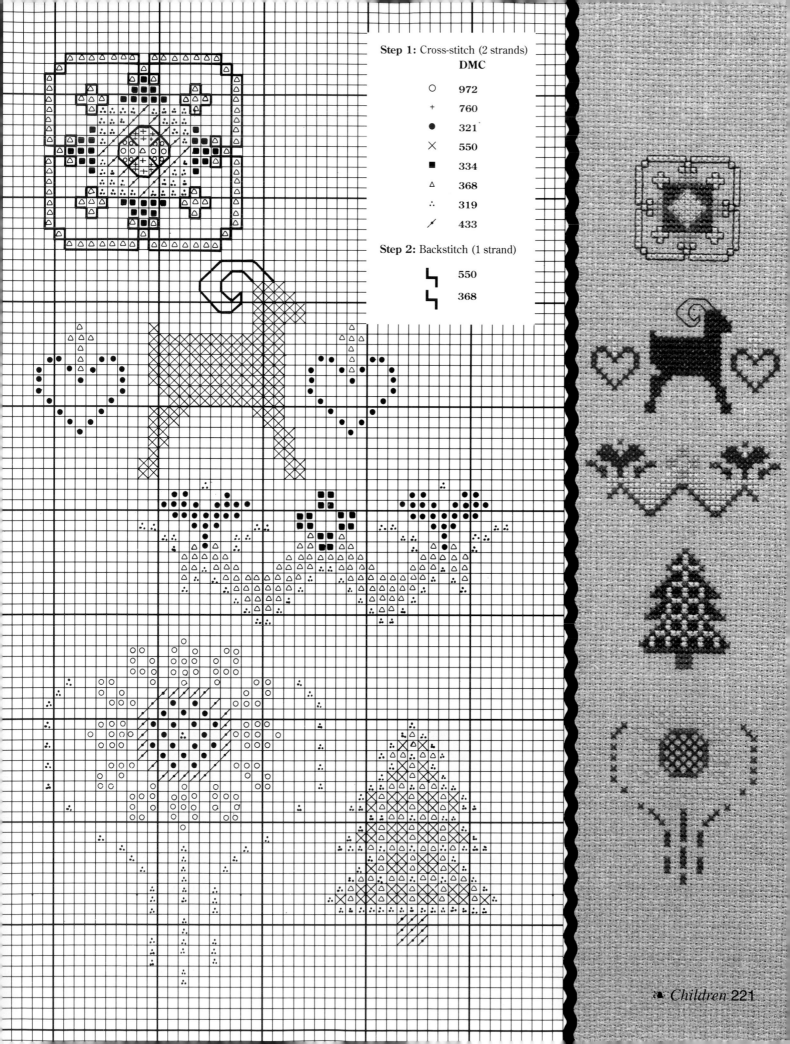

Step 1: Cross-stitch (2 strands)

DMC

○	972
+	760
●	321
✕	550
■	334
△	368
⸪	319
╱	433

Step 2: Backstitch (1 strand)

⌐	550
⌐	368

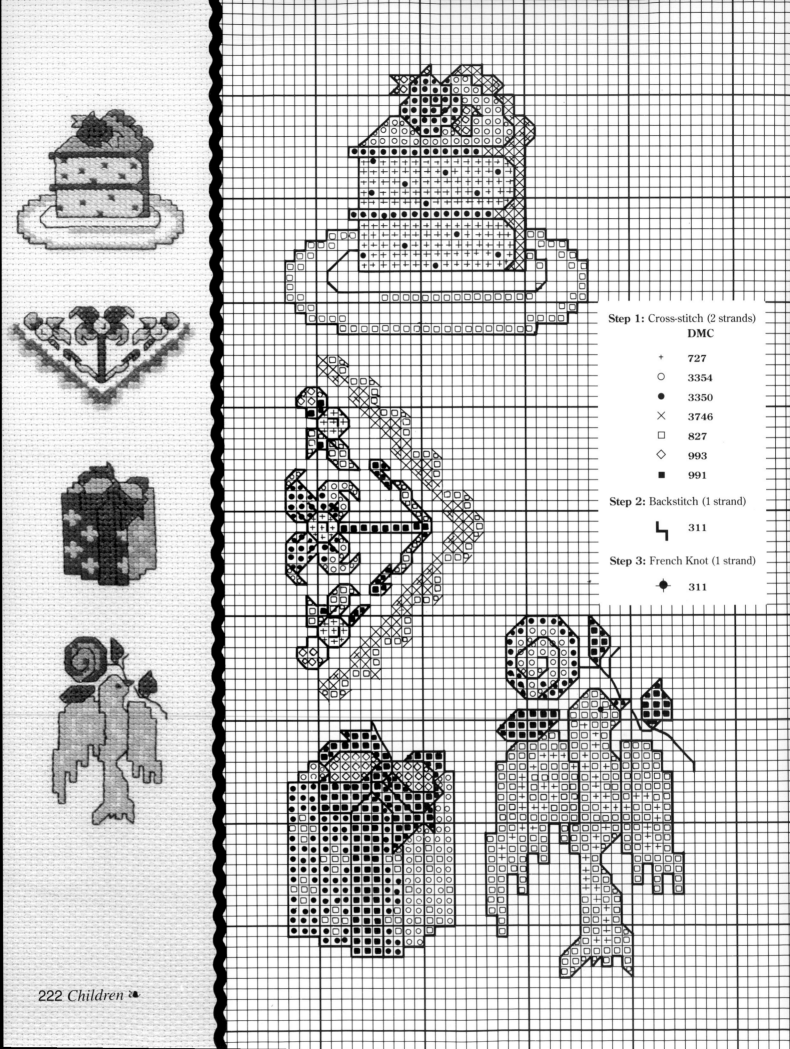

Step 1: Cross-stitch (2 strands)

DMC

+	**727**
○	**3354**
●	**3350**
✕	**3746**
□	**827**
◇	**993**
■	**991**

Step 2: Backstitch (1 strand)

⌐ **311**

Step 3: French Knot (1 strand)

◆ **311**

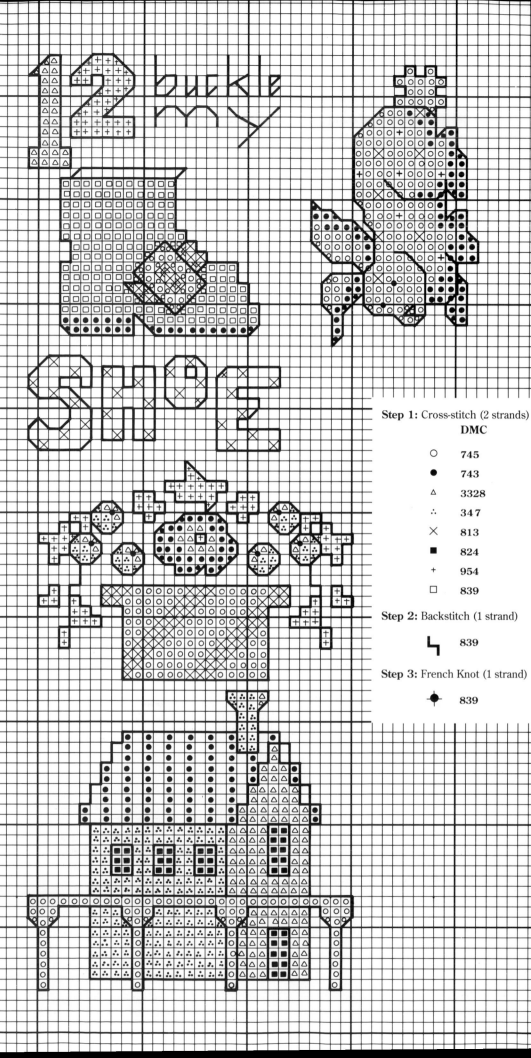

Step 1: Cross-stitch (2 strands)
DMC

○	**745**
●	**743**
△	**3328**
∴	**347**
✕	**813**
■	**824**
+	**954**
□	**839**

Step 2: Backstitch (1 strand)

⌐ **839**

Step 3: French Knot (1 strand)

◆ **839**

Step 1: Cross-stitch (2 strands)

DMC

−	3770
○	743
∴	722
✕	961
●	553
△	322
□	3347
■	938

Step 2: Backstitch (1 strand)

961

553

938

Step 3: French Knot (1 strand)

3347

938

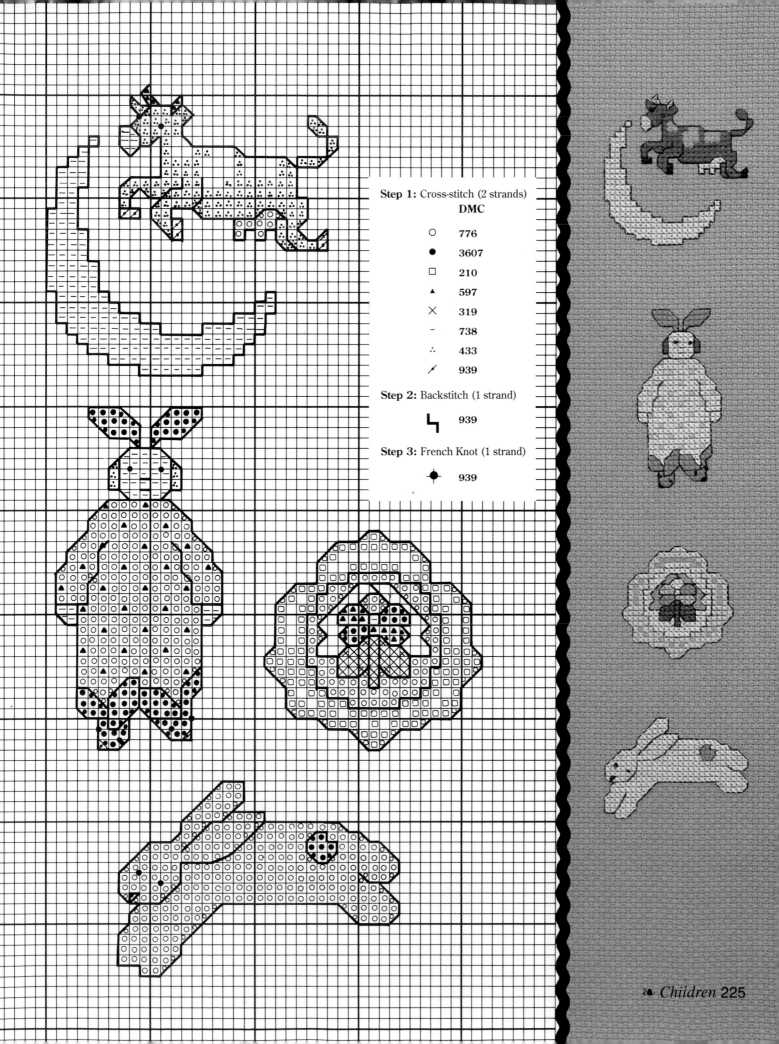

Step 1: Cross-stitch (2 strands)

DMC

○	776
●	3607
□	210
▲	597
✕	319
–	738
∴	433
⟋	939

Step 2: Backstitch (1 strand)

⌐ 939

Step 3: French Knot (1 strand)

● 939

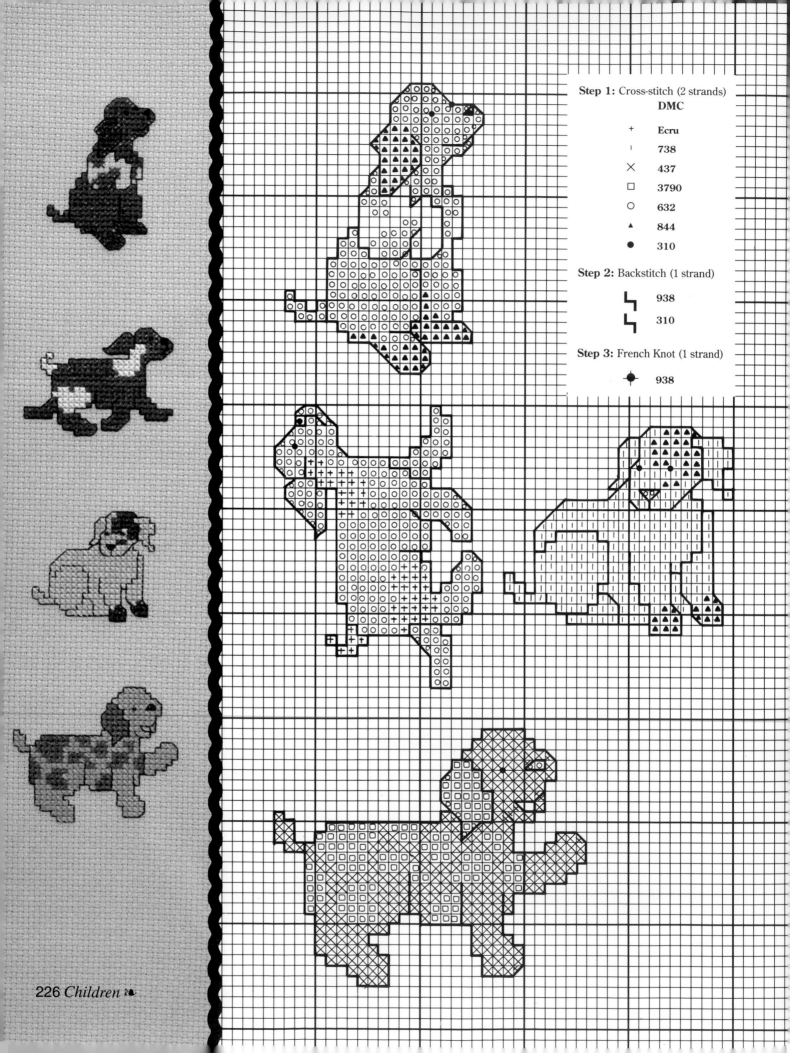

Step 1: Cross-stitch (2 strands)

DMC

+	Ecru
I	738
×	437
□	3790
○	632
▲	844
●	310

Step 2: Backstitch (1 strand)

⌐	938
L	310

Step 3: French Knot (1 strand)

◆	938

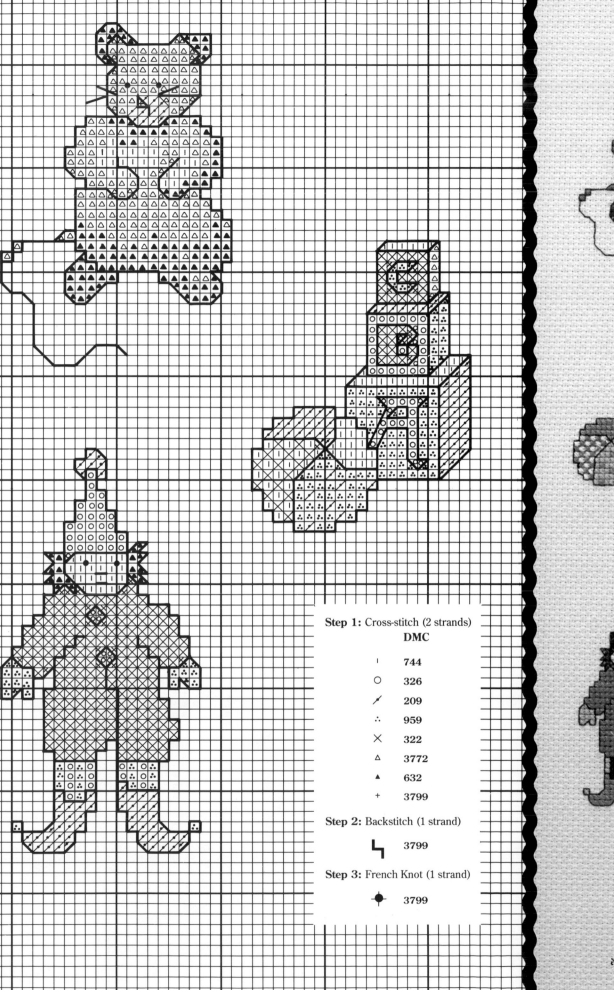

Step 1: Cross-stitch (2 strands)

DMC

I	744	
O	326	
✗	209	
∴	959	
✕	322	
△	3772	
▲	632	
+	3799	

Step 2: Backstitch (1 strand)

⌐ 3799

Step 3: French Knot (1 strand)

◆ 3799

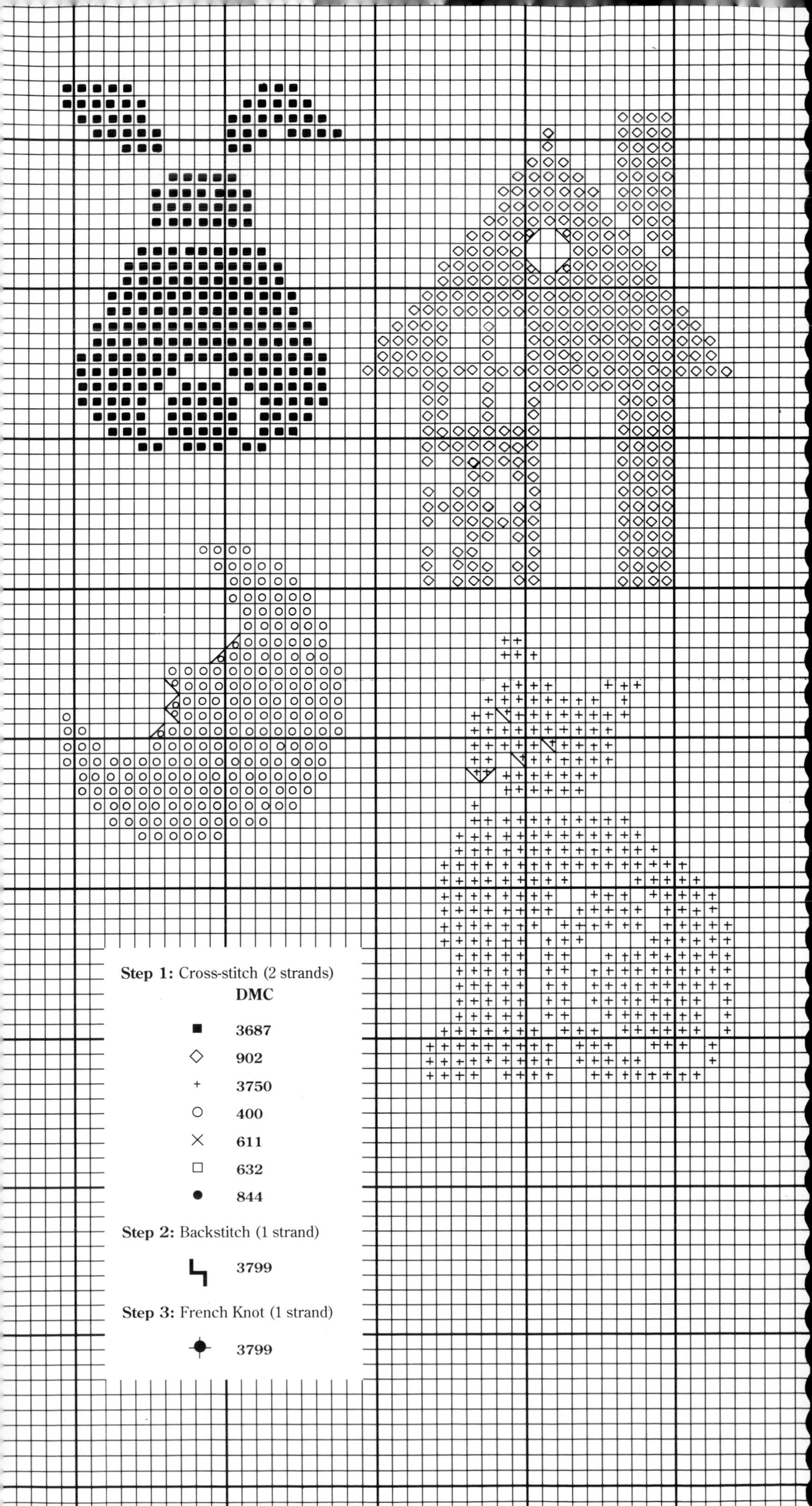

Step 1: Cross-stitch (2 strands)
DMC

■	3687
◇	902
+	3750
○	400
×	611
□	632
●	844

Step 2: Backstitch (1 strand)

└ 3799

Step 3: French Knot (1 strand)

● 3799

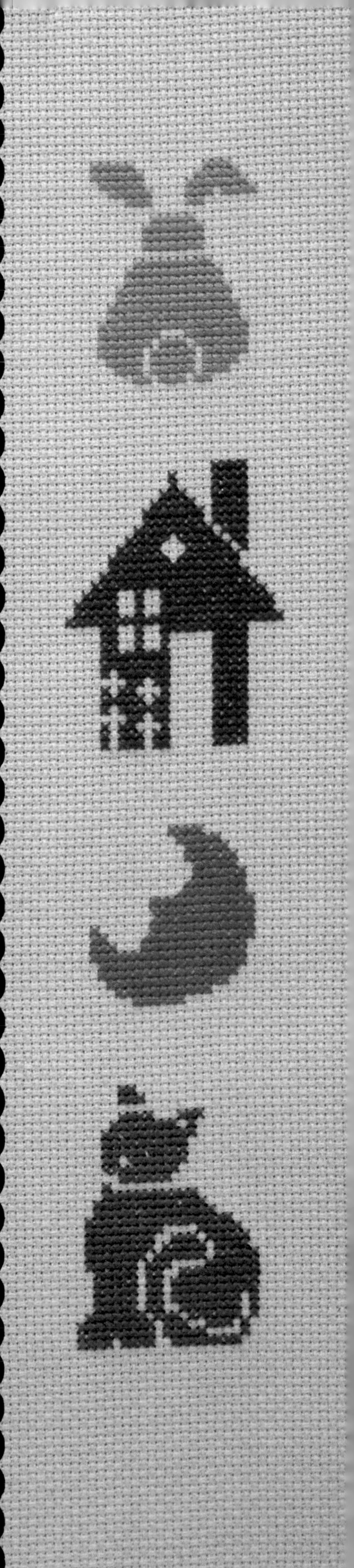

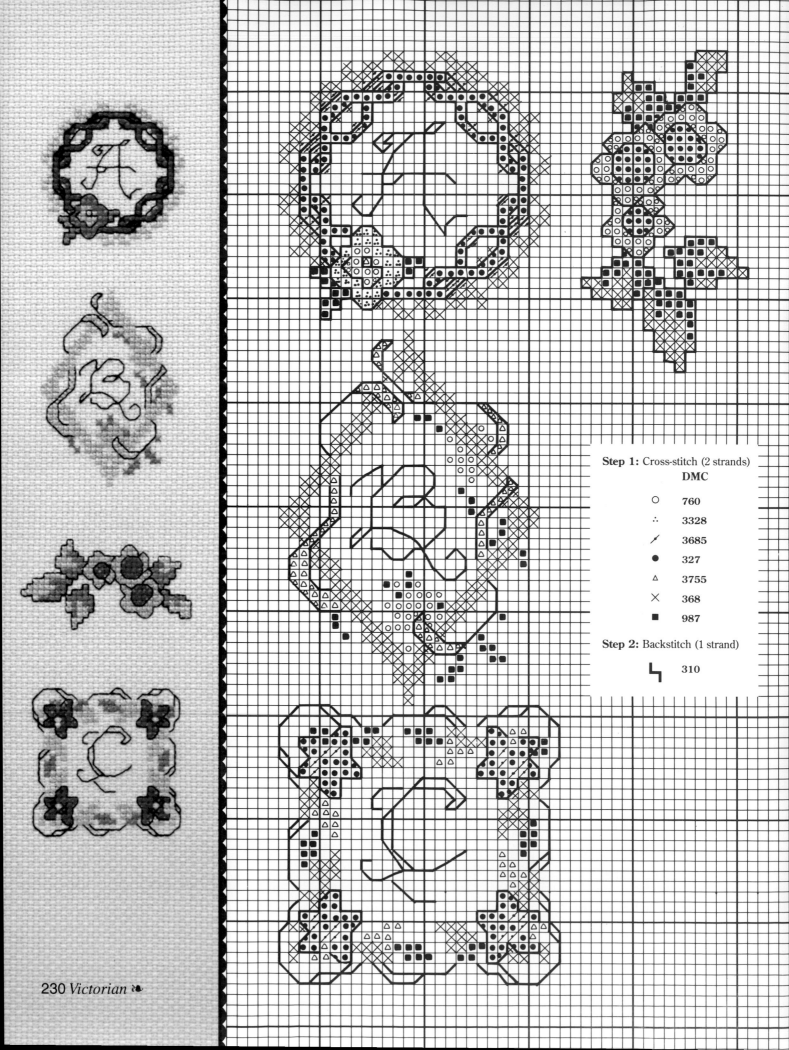

Step 1: Cross-stitch (2 strands)

DMC

○	760
∴	3328
✗	3685
●	327
△	3755
✕	368
■	987

Step 2: Backstitch (1 strand)

⌐	310

Step 1: Cross-stitch (2 strands)

DMC

+	760
○	3328
●	3731
◇	3685
✕	518
∴	989
□	986

Step 2: Backstitch (1 strand)

⌐ 310

Step 3: French Knot (1 strand)

● 310

Step 1: Cross-stitch (2 strands)

DMC

○ 676
∴ 3328
■ 816
△ 3325
∕ 927
✕ 993
● 936

Step 2: Backstitch (1 strand)

⌐ 310

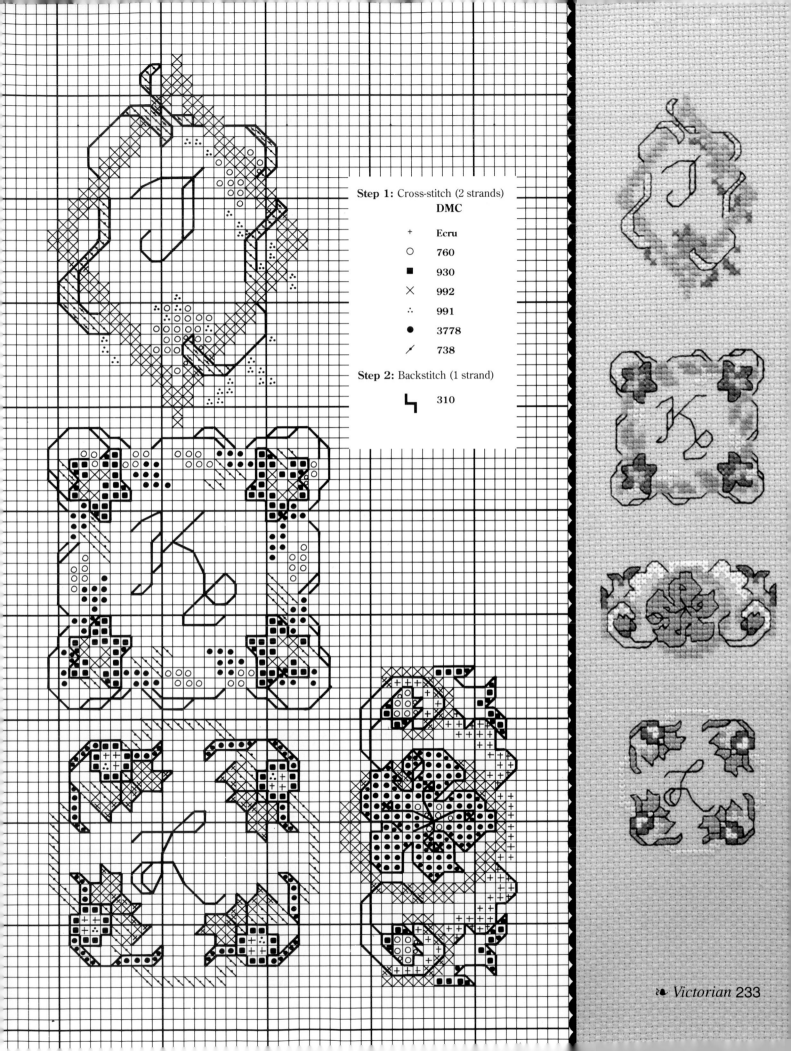

Step 1: Cross-stitch (2 strands)

DMC

+	**Ecru**
○	**760**
■	**930**
✕	**992**
∴	**991**
●	**3778**
✗	**738**

Step 2: Backstitch (1 strand)

⌐ **310**

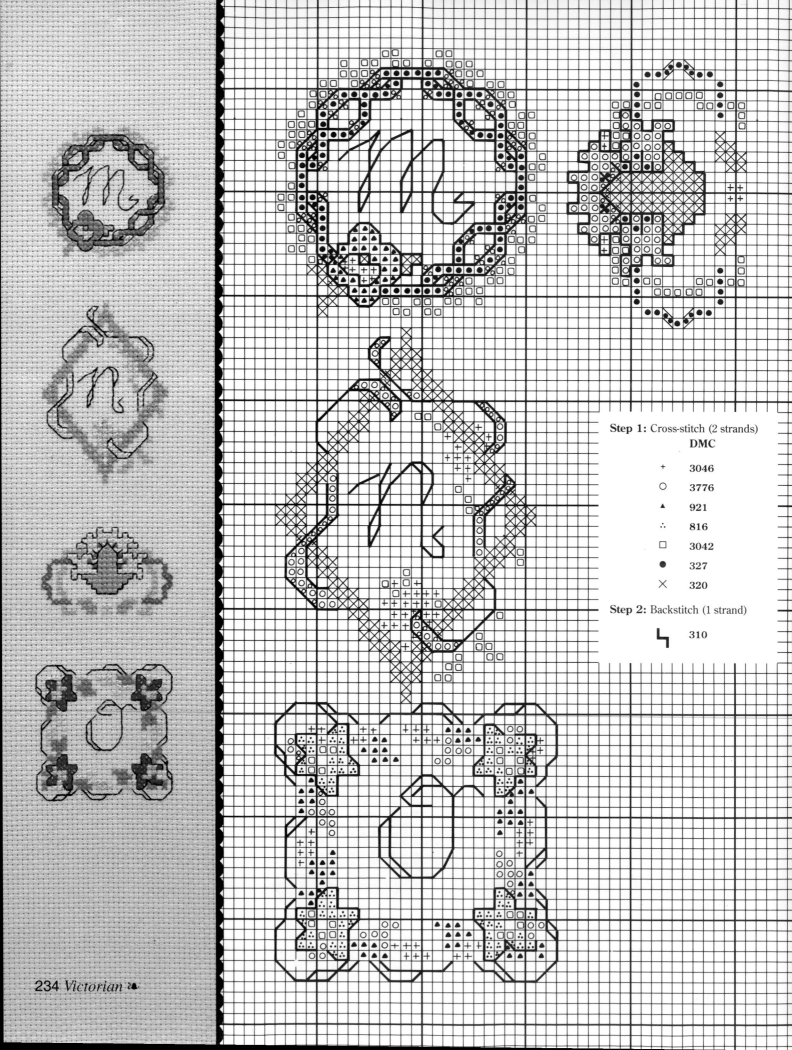

Step 1: Cross-stitch (2 strands)

DMC

+	3046
○	3776
▲	921
∴	816
□	3042
●	327
✕	320

Step 2: Backstitch (1 strand)

⌐	310

Step 1: Cross-stitch (2 strands)

DMC

+	676
○	760
●	3328
╱	221
∴	3740
✕	3364
☐	987

Step 2: Backstitch (1 strand)

⌐ 310

Step 3: French Knot (1 strand)

✦ 310

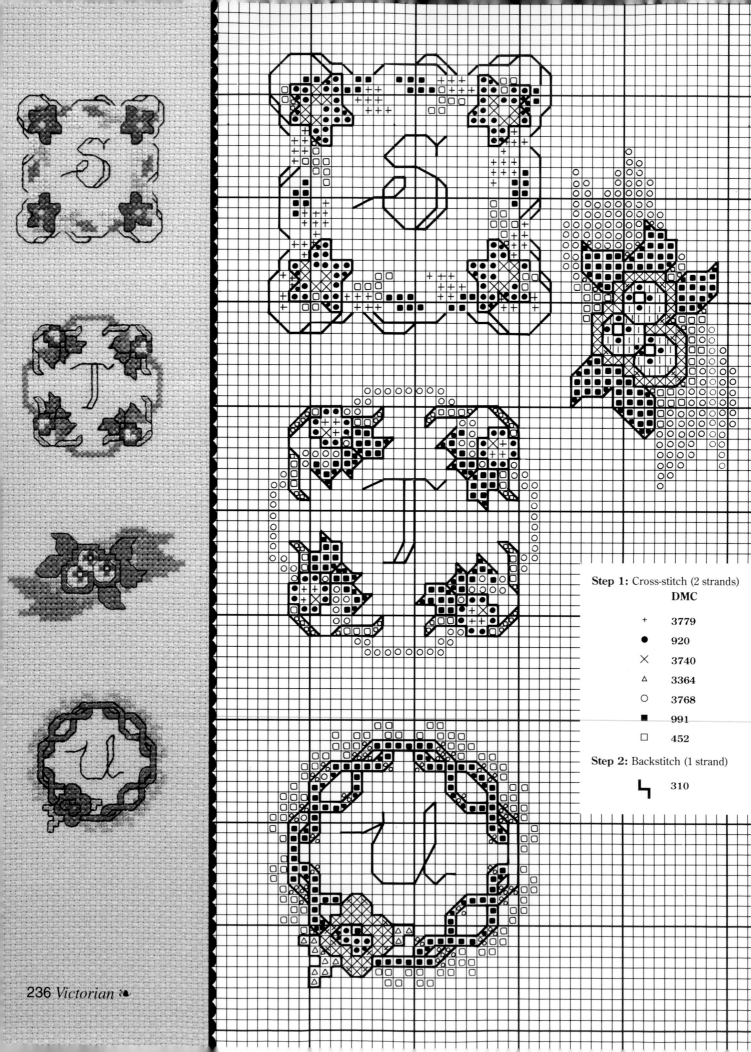

Step 1: Cross-stitch (2 strands)

DMC

+	3779
●	920
✕	3740
△	3364
○	3768
■	991
□	452

Step 2: Backstitch (1 strand)

⌐	310

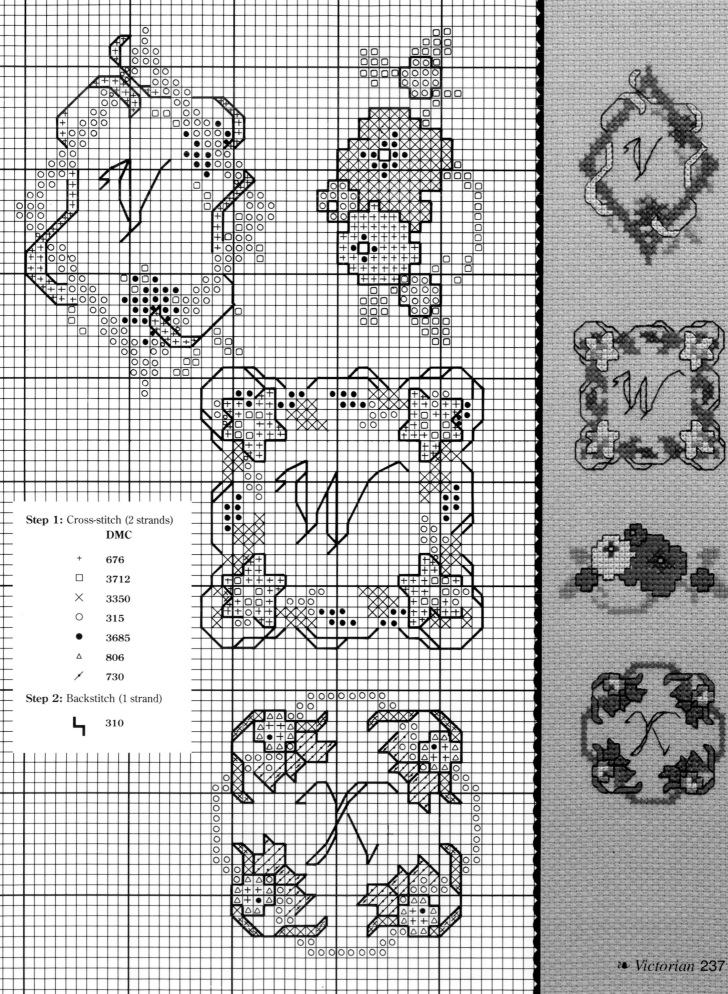

Step 1: Cross-stitch (2 strands)

DMC

+	676
□	3712
✕	3350
○	315
●	3685
△	806
╱	730

Step 2: Backstitch (1 strand)

⌐	310

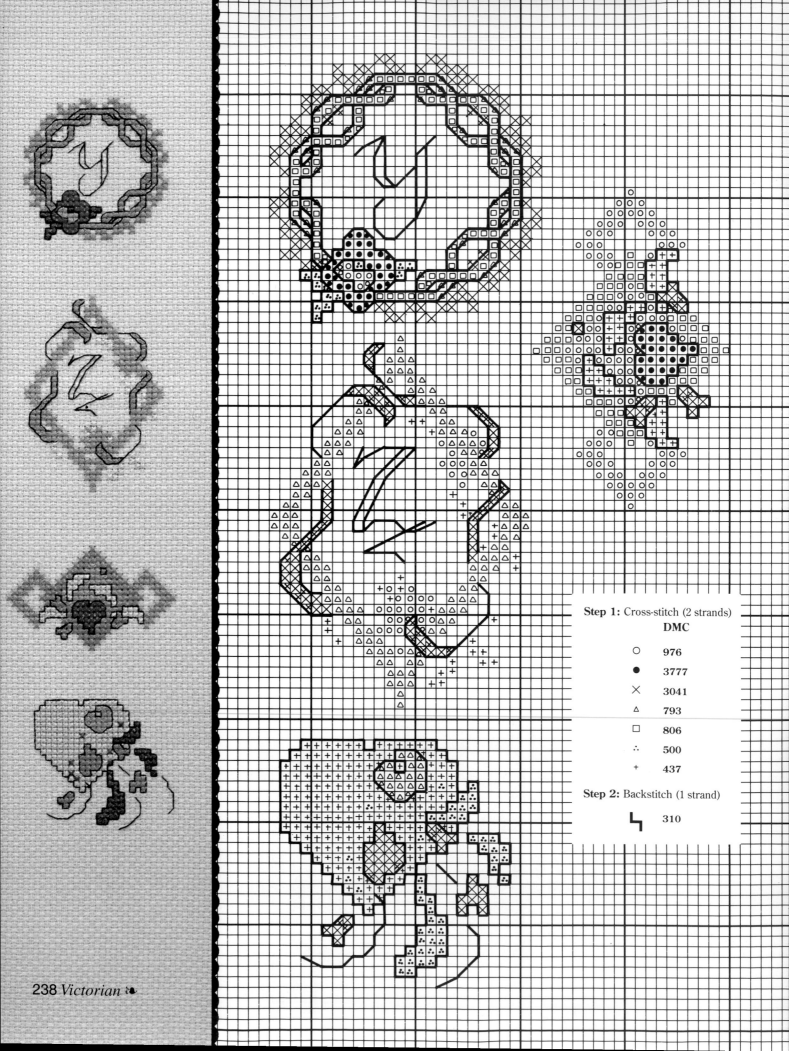

Step 1: Cross-stitch (2 strands)

DMC

○	**976**
●	**3777**
✕	**3041**
△	**793**
□	**806**
∴	**500**
+	**437**

Step 2: Backstitch (1 strand)

⌐	**310**

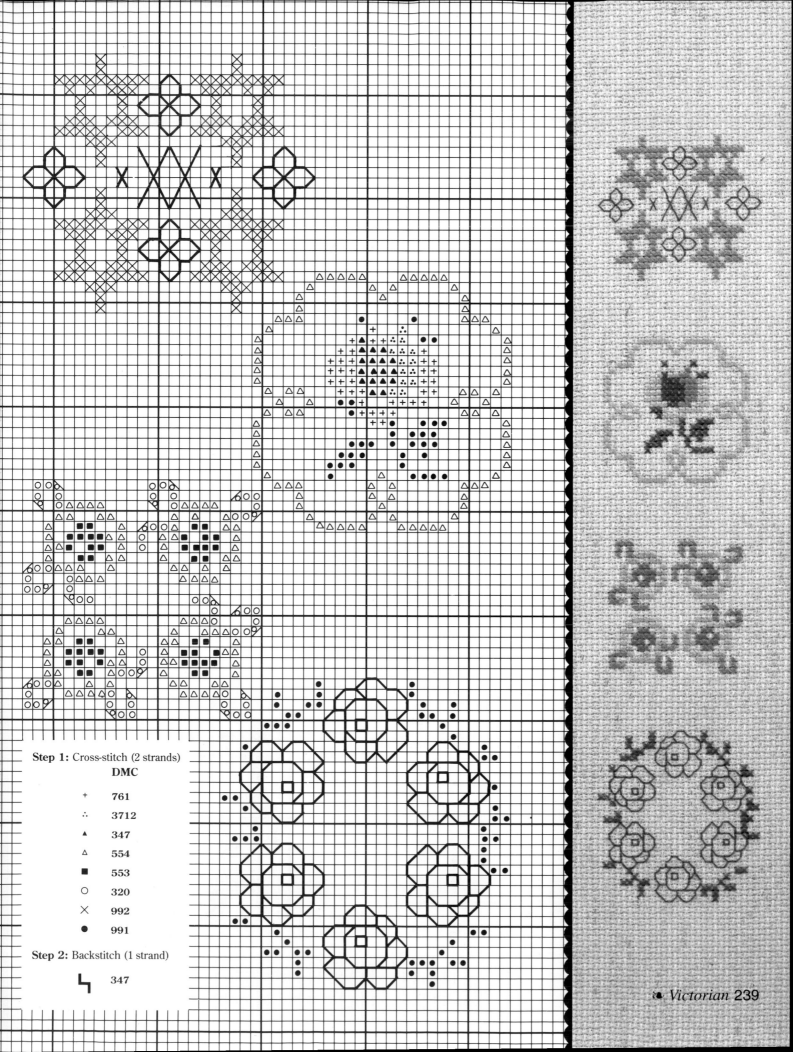

Step 1: Cross-stitch (2 strands)

DMC

+	761
∴	3712
▲	347
△	554
■	553
○	320
✕	992
●	991

Step 2: Backstitch (1 strand)

⌐	347

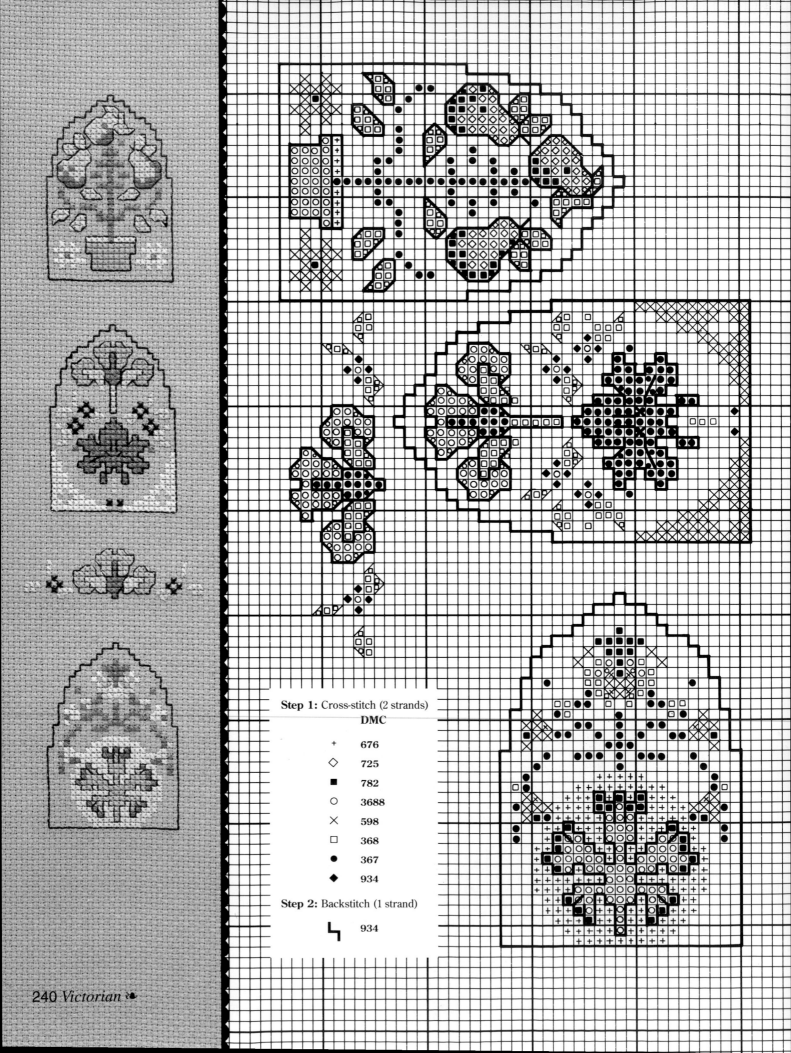

Step 1: Cross-stitch (2 strands)

DMC

+	676
◇	725
■	782
○	3688
✕	598
□	368
●	367
◆	934

Step 2: Backstitch (1 strand)

⌐	934

Step 1: Cross-stitch (2 strands)

DMC

✕	3045
○	223
□	326
+	340
■	333
●	924
∴	472
◆	934

Step 2: Backstitch (1 strand)

⌐	934

Step 1: Cross-stitch (2 strands)   Step 2: Backstitch (1 st

DMC

−	745
□	335
✕	341
∴	334
+	926
▲	311
○	368
●	310

311
310

Step 3: French Knot (1

311

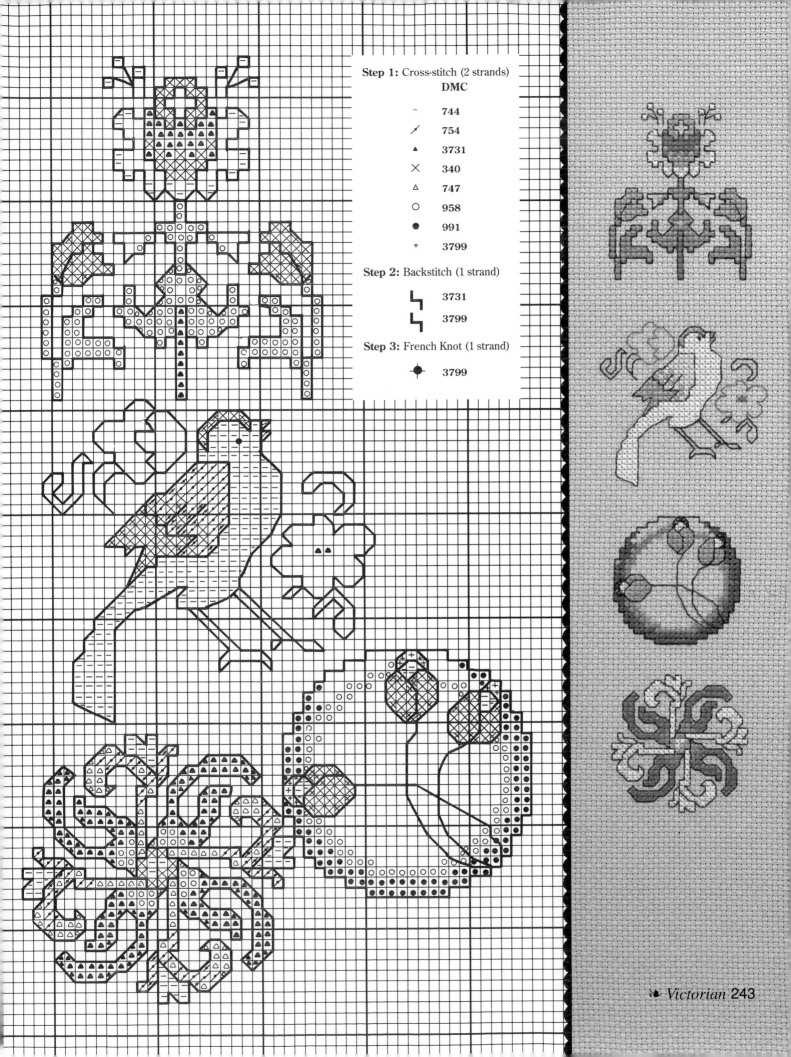

Step 1: Cross-stitch (2 strands)

DMC

–	744
╱	754
▲	3731
✕	340
△	747
○	958
●	991
+	3799

Step 2: Backstitch (1 strand)

⌐	3731
⌐	3799

Step 3: French Knot (1 strand)

●	3799

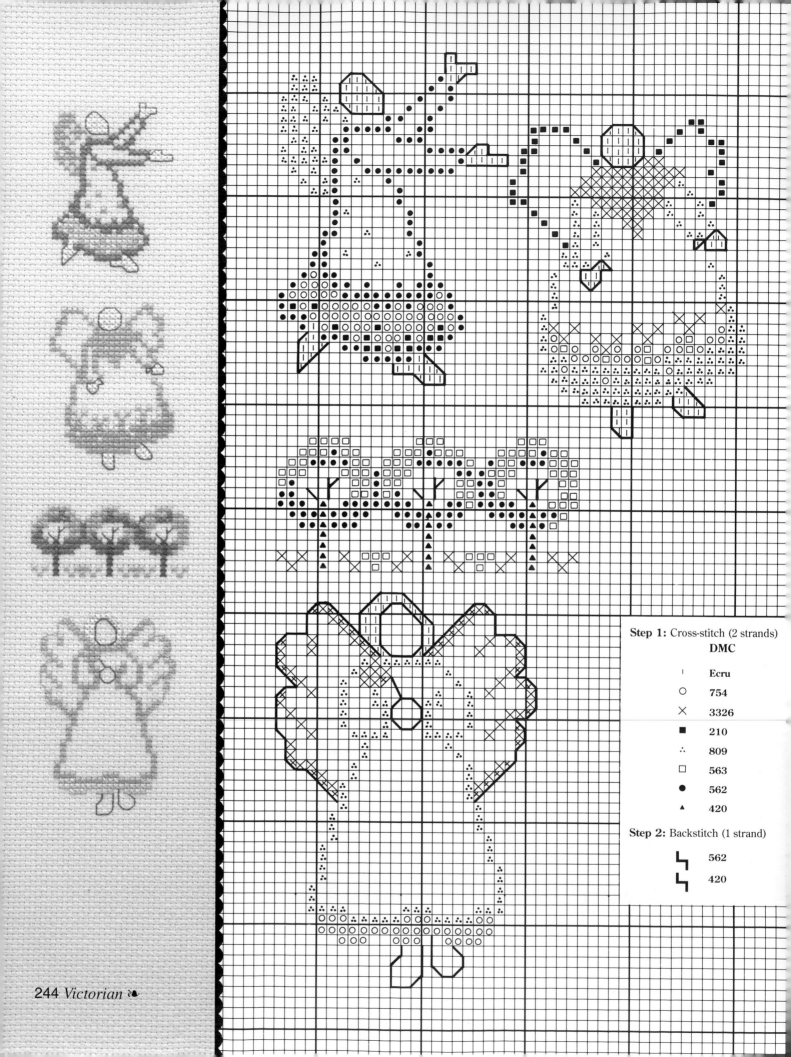

Step 1: Cross-stitch (2 strands)

DMC

ı	Ecru
○	754
✕	3326
■	210
∴	809
□	563
●	562
▲	420

Step 2: Backstitch (1 strand)

⌐	562
⌐	420

Step 1: Cross-stitch (2 strands)

DMC

-	3770
○	3078
∴	899
✗	3747
△	3325
▲	826
✕	964

Step 2: Backstitch (1 strand)

⌐	3799

Step 3: French Knot (1 strand)

●	3799

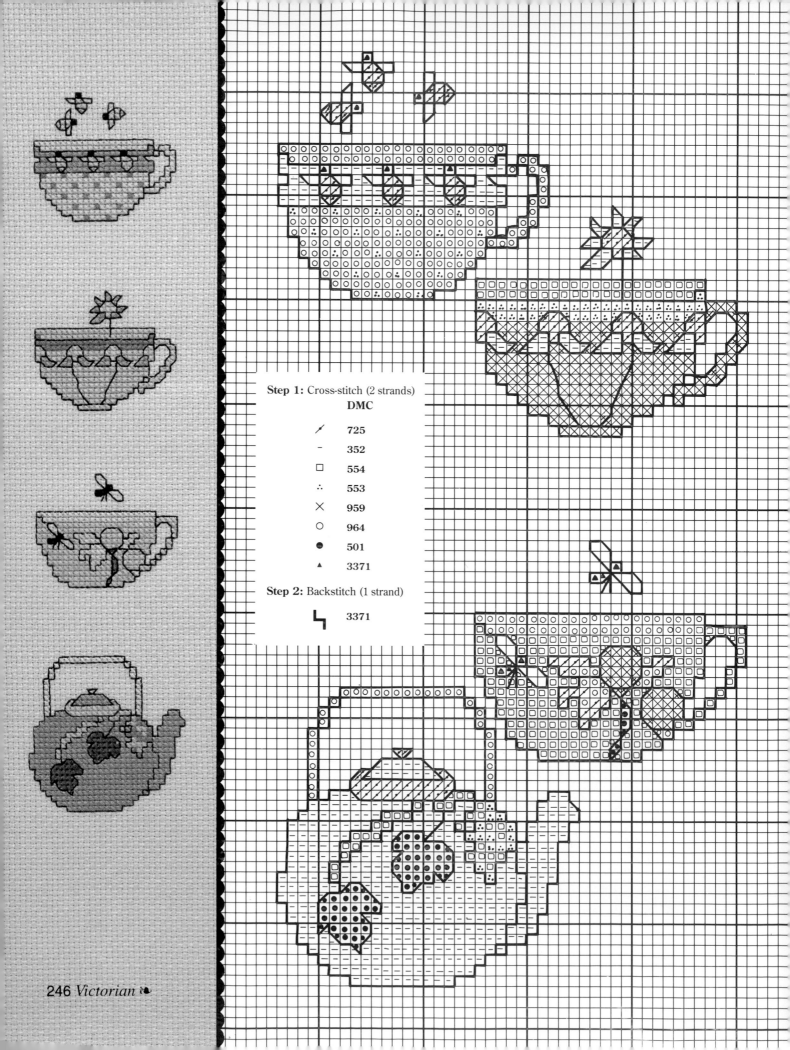

Step 1: Cross-stitch (2 strands)

DMC

✎	**725**
−	**352**
□	**554**
∴	**553**
×	**959**
○	**964**
●	**501**
▲	**3371**

Step 2: Backstitch (1 strand)

⌐	**3371**

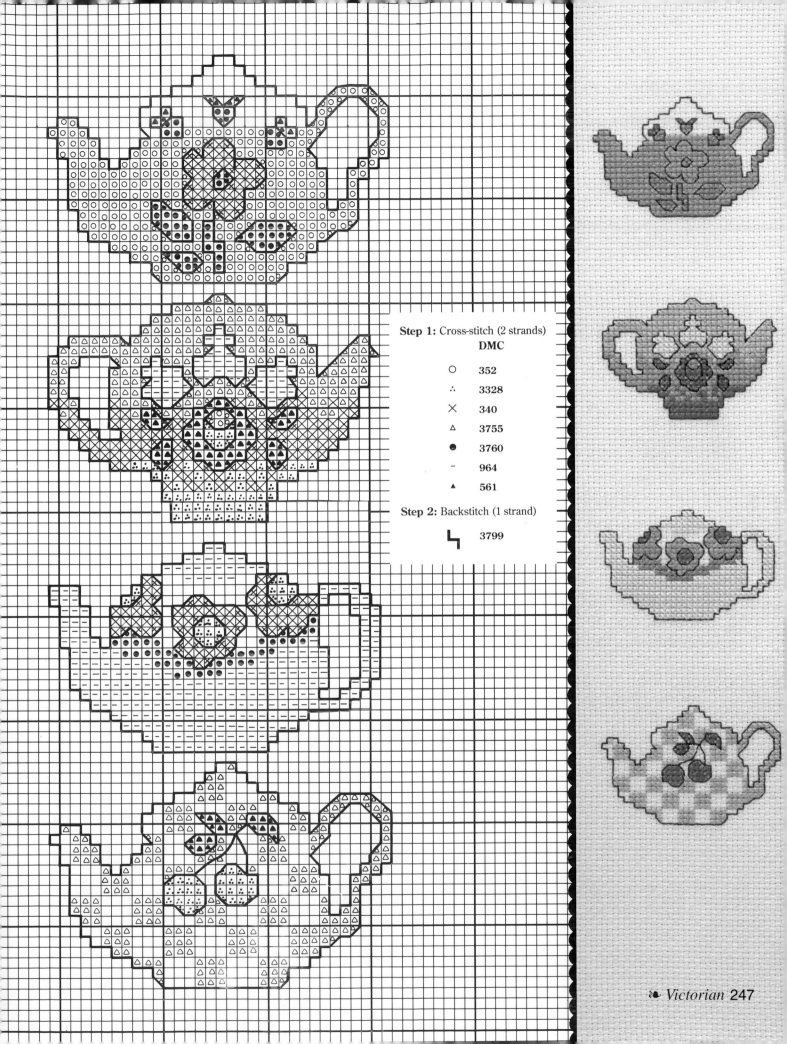

Step 1: Cross-stitch (2 strands)

DMC

○	352
∴	3328
✕	340
△	3755
●	3760
—	964
▲	561

Step 2: Backstitch (1 strand)

⌐	3799

Step 1: Cross-stitch (2 strands)

DMC

▲	725
○	335
✕	340
ı	3761
●	3766
△	989
✗	986

Step 2: Backstitch (1 strand)

| ⌐ | 3750 |

Two-Hour Mini-Quilt Projects

This section explains the techniques and general definitions to be used to create the projects in this book. The basic construction, additional techniques, and embroidery stitches used are thoroughly detailed and diagrammed on pages 252 - 256, and are referenced at the beginning of each project for ease in determining which techniques will be used on individual projects throughout this book. General definitions are provided on page 257.

Each photographed project has been created so it can be reproduced exactly from the designer's model. However, each project can be finished in many ways to create a more personalized piece. There are several additional project ideas at the end of each designer's section; they also have been designed to be used as actual pattern pieces.

The colors that have been used in the diagrams are suggestions only. Remember, a design can look completely different simply by changing fabric texture, color, and print.

Before Beginning

Gathering Tools

The following is a list of the most commonly used tools for quilting and appliquéing, and hints on when and how they should be used. Be sure to read the manufacturer's instructions carefully before beginning a project and take care to follow those directions exactly.

Hand-stitching may be done on all projects that require sewing, but sometimes a sewing machine makes it easier and quicker when adding borders, hanging straps, mitering corners, or making yo-yos.

Marking Tools

Test the marking tool on the fabric first to make certain the marks can be removed easily. Always use a light hand when marking with any marking tool.

To mark around cardboard templates on light-colored fabrics, use a sharp #2 lead pencil. On dark-colored fabrics, use a sharp white dressmaker's pencil, a sliver of soap, or a silver or yellow fabric marking pencil. Chalk pencils or chalk-wheel markers also make clear marks on fabric. Also, disappearing ink pens may be used when marking.

Needles

Needles come in many sizes and lengths. When purchasing needles, remember that the larger the number, the finer the needle. Having a variety of needles on hand is recommended.

Sharps are fine, strong needles with round eyes. They are good for mending and hand-sewing.

Embroidery or crewel needles are sharp needles with long, oval eyes. They are used to stitch fine to medium surfaces. Common sizes are 1 to 10.

Darning needles are long, strong needles with large eyes. They are good for basting and work best when stitching with heavy threads. Keep an assortment of sizes 14 to 18.

Betweens are round-eyed needles, but are shorter than sharps. Common sizes are 5 to 12.

Chenille needles are long-eyed needles with a sharp point. They are good for stitching with heavy threads. Common sizes are 18 to 24.

Scissors & Pinking Shears

Fabric scissors are used for cutting fabric and should be designated for that purpose only. Using fabric scissors to cut other materials will dull the blades and make them less effective.

Craft scissors are essential for cutting cardboard, paper, and plastic templates. They are very strong and have a very refined cutting edge, which makes it possible to get into tight areas.

Embroidery scissors are generally only used for cutting threads.

Pinking shears have notched or serrated blades. They are used to cut edges of fabric with a zig-zag pattern for decorative purposes and are often used to prevent edges of fabric from fraying.

Choosing Fabrics, Threads & Battings

The following is a list of the most commonly used fabrics, threads, and battings for quilting and appliquéing and hints on when and how they should be used:

Fabrics

Fabrics will need to be selected for backing, for backgrounds, and for each motif. The texture, color, and print of fabrics to be used should depend on the desired look of the finished project, as well as the skill of the crafter. Each fabric chosen should be appropriate for the use of the finished project — a piece that needs to be laundered frequently should not be made from non-washable fabrics. Also, keep in mind how easily a particular fabric frays. A fabric that frays very easily will be hard to work with and the edges will have to be secured in some way. Raw edges can generally be cut with pinking shears to prevent fraying.

Quilting fabrics include calico, muslin, and broadcloths. They are medium-weight fabrics made from 100% cotton. Calico and other printed fabrics are available in a variety of patterns and colors. Muslin is white or off-white and is usually used for the background in a pieced design. Broadcloth is a plain weave fabric and is generally a solid color.

Threads

The considerations for fabric choice also apply to thread choice. The type of thread used should be appropriate for the style and use of the finished piece. Another consideration in choosing thread is the type of fabric(s) being used. Like threads should go with like fabrics — natural threads with natural fabrics and synthetic threads with synthetic fabrics.

Embroidery threads of all kind can be used. The color and character of thread are usually subservient to the fabric used, but not always. Sometimes contrasting stitching adds as much to the design as the material itself.

Battings

Batting is used as the middle layer of a quilt. Bonded cotton batting gives a flat, natural appearance and comes in different thicknesses. Polyester batting gives a puffy appearance. Felt may be substituted and renders the same appearance as the bonded cotton batting.

Preparing Fabrics

Before marking and/or cutting, make certain the fabrics have been laundered, dried, and pressed. If the finished piece will be laundered, make certain the fabrics used are preshrunk and colorfast.

Basic Construction

Enlarging Motif Pattern Pieces & Placement Diagrams

All patterns are a reduction of the original size unless specified otherwise. Enlarge patterns to the indicated percentage using a photocopy machine. It is best to use a professional copy center.

If it is desired that the finished project be larger or smaller than the one photographed, adjust enlargements or reductions as needed.

Tracing Motif Pattern Pieces & Placement Diagrams onto Tracing Paper

Lay a sheet of tracing paper on top of enlarged motif pattern pieces and placement diagram. Trace the designs to make a template or full-scale outlined drawing for all pattern pieces.

Preparing & Cutting Out Motifs

When cutting out motifs, be certain to add seam allowances when necessary. Always cut out on a flat surface so fabrics do not pucker.

Preparing Motifs for Hand-Sewing

Mark and pin the traced designs on the motif fabrics. Then cut out allowing a small margin around the traced lines.

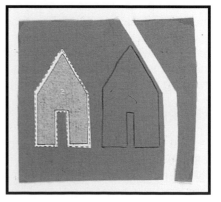

Preparing Motifs with Fusible Web

1. Trace pattern from book.

2. Enlarge as necessary.

3. Trace pattern onto translucent tracing paper.

4. Turn tracing paper over so pattern is visible in reverse.

5. Place fusible web on top of reverse pattern, paper side up.

6. Trace pattern on paper side of fusible web.

7. Cut out pattern on fusible web leaving a ¼" border around pattern.

8. Follow manufacturer's instructions to fuse the fusible web to the motif fabrics.

9. Cut out pattern following pattern line.

10. Fuse the fabric motifs to project.

Preparing Motifs with Double-Sided Adhesive

Always pre-test double-sided adhesive on fabrics to be used. Peel off paper backing (printed side). Apply sticky side on wrong side of fabrics. Trace patterns on paper backing and cut out motifs on the traced lines.

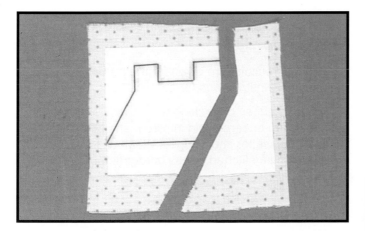

Tracing Placement Diagram onto Background Fabric

Tracing using Tracing Paper

Using the full-sized placement diagrams for positioning, pin the traced placement diagrams to the background fabric. Pin or baste along the traced lines. Tear the tracing paper away. This method is not as accurate as tracing the design directly onto the fabric using transfer paper.

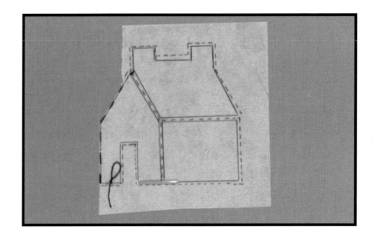

Tracing using Transfer Paper

Since transfer paper comes in many colors, choose a paper that is closest in color and tone to the background fabric being used. However, it must be able to be seen. Be certain to follow the manufacturer's instructions. To reduce the amount of marks on the fabric, trace with dashed lines instead of solid lines.

Place the traced placement diagram to the background fabric and pin it in place. Insert a piece of transfer paper between the diagram and the fabric. Trace over diagram, transferring marks to fabric.

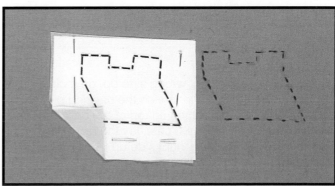

Attaching Motifs

When the design has been transferred to the background, simply place the motifs over the marked outlines.

Attaching Motifs for Hand-Sewing

Hand-stitch motifs as indicated in the assembly instructions for each project.

Attaching Motifs with Fusible Web

Fuse motifs to background fabrics following manufacturer's instructions.

Attaching Motifs with Double-Sided Adhesive

Adhere motifs to background fabrics following manufacturer's instructions.

Layering & Stitching

After cutting the backing and batting, create a "quilt sandwich" in three layers in the following order: backing, batting, and assembled quilt top.

Quilt Top

Batting
Backing

First, lay the backing, wrong side up, on a clean, flat surface. Be careful not to stretch the backing out of shape. Next, lay the batting on top of the backing, smoothing out all wrinkles. Last, lay the assembled quilt top on top of the batting, right side up. Smooth out any wrinkles.

If necessary, pin or baste in place. Finish the mini quilt by stitching around the edges. Use stitches as indicated in the assembly instructions for each project or as desired.

Finishing

Mitering Corners

Lay the first corner to be mitered on the ironing board. Fold under one strip at a 45° angle and adjust so seam lines match perfectly. Press and pin securely.

Fold the fabric diagonally with right sides together, lining up the edges of the border. If necessary, use a ruler to draw a pencil line on the creases to make the line more visible.

Stitch on the pressed crease, sewing from the corner to the outside edge. Press the seam open and trim away excess border strip, leaving a ¼"-wide seam allowance. Repeat for the three remaining corners.

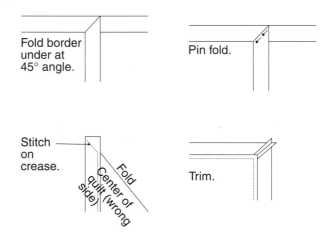

Fold border under at 45° angle.

Pin fold.

Stitch on crease.

Fold Center of quilt (wrong side)

Trim.

Making Borders

Cutting directions are given for the border strips in the assembly instructions for each project.

Fold long edges of backing over edges of assembled quilt top. Turn under ½", pin in place, and blindstitch. Repeat process for short edges. When all four sides have been blindstitched, press border flat.

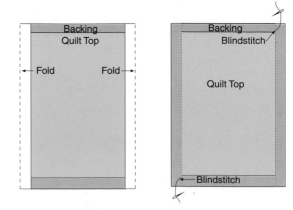

Backing
Quilt Top

Fold   Fold

Backing
Blindstitch

Quilt Top

Blindstitch

Adding A Hanging Strap

A hanging strap must be added if the mini quilt is to be hung. This strap will hold the hanger, whether it be a wooden dowel, a twig, or a cinnamon stick.

Use desired scraps of fabric and cut as indicated in the assembly instructions for each project. Fold the fabric straps in half, wrong sides together. Attach these straps to the back of the project as indicated.

Adding Decorative Accents

Decorative accents range from buttons and beads to charms and personal items. Buttons and beads can be sewn on in the traditional manner. Charms and other objects can be secured in place with fabric or craft glue.

Outline stitching is also considered a decorative accent and should be done with a permanent ink pen. Be careful not to leave the pen on fabric too long or it will run.

Making Yo-Yos

Yo-Yos are the circular-shaped decorative fabric accents that embellish many of the projects in this book. They are often used to replicate flowers.

Cut out a circle in the appropriate size for each yo-yo. A ¼" seam allowance has already been added.

Stitch a gathering stitch ¼" along the circumference of each circle. Draw up the circle and tuck the raw edges into the center of the yo-yo. Press flat with the gathering in the center.

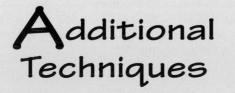

Additional Techniques

Blush Painting

Using a round fabric-dye brush and acrylic paint, dip brush in paint and blot off excess paint onto a paper towel. Very lightly "blush" desired areas.

Gathering

Gathering refers to machine- or hand-stitching two parallel rows of long stitches ¼" to ½" from edge of fabric. Leave ends of thread 2" or 3" long. Pull the two threads and gather fabric to fit required measurement. Long edges may need to be gathered from both ends. Disperse fullness evenly and secure the threads. A heavy thread is recommended; be careful to avoid breaking the threads.

Painting on Fabric

Painting on fabric requires the use of a textile medium. To use a textile medium, pour a small amount of paint onto a palette. Place a few drops of textile medium on the paint. Mix it into the paint. The paint will become more transparent as more textile medium is added.

After the patterns have been traced onto the fabrics, paint in the background colors first. Then, go back and paint the details. It will be similar to coloring in a coloring book — be certain to stay within the traced lines.

Allow the paint to dry thoroughly. Most fabrics painted with textile medium can be heat-set in a dryer or with a warm iron on the reverse side of the fabric.

There are several brands to choose from, but the manufacturer's instructions must be followed for the brand that is being used.

Sponge Painting

Dip a small damp sponge into paint and blot off excess onto a paper towel. Blot the surface of the project, using light or heavy coverage as desired.

Stenciling

Transfer patterns onto a piece of clear acetate or a piece of lightweight cardboard. Use a craft knife or single-edged razor to cut out the portion of the design to be stenciled from the acetate or cardboard. Secure the stencil in place with masking tape.

Load the stencil brush with stencil paint and blot off excess on a paper towel. Too much paint left on the stencil brush will cause the paint to seep underneath the stencil. Bounce the stencil brush up and down across the open portion of the stencil. Remove the stencil and fill in any unwanted spaces.

Embroidery Stitches

Back Stitch

Bring needle up at A; go down at B to the right of A. Come back up at C to the left of A. Repeat B-C, inserting the needle in the same hole.

Blanket Stitch

Similar to the buttonhole stitch, but the stitches are farther apart.

Blind or Slip Stitch

Insert needle in folded edge of fabric for the length of the stitch (⅛" to ¼"). Bring it out and take small stitch through second piece of fabric.

Buttonhole Stitch

Bring needle up at A; go down at B. Bring needle up again at C keeping thread under the needle. For second stitch, go down at D and back up at E.

French Knots

Bring needle up through fabric at A. Smoothly wrap floss around the needle once. Hold floss securely off to one side, push the needle down through the fabric at B.

Herringbone Stitch

Work the stitch from right to left. Bring needle up at A; go down at B. Bring needle up again at C taking a small horizontal backstitch. Continue working, alternating from side to side.

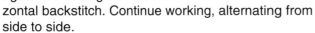

Lazy Daisy Stitch

Bring needle up at A and form a loop. Go down at B as close to A as possible, but not into A. Come up at C and bring the tip of the needle over the thread. Go down at D, making a small anchor stitch.

Running or Whip Stitch

A line of straight stitches with an unstitched area between each stitch. Bring needle up at A; go down at B.

Satin Stitch

Bring needle up at A; go down at B forming a straight stitch. Bring needle up again at C and go down again at D forming another smooth straight stitch that slightly overlaps the first straight stitch. Repeat to fill the design area.

Stem Stitch

Working from left to right, make slightly slanting stitches along the designated line. Bring needle up at A then insert needle through fabric at B. Bring needle back up at C, which is at the midpoint of the previous stitch. Make all stitches the same length. Insert needle through fabric at D and continue on in the same manner.

Straight Stitch

Bring needle up at A; go down at B forming a straight stitch the desired length.

"X" or Cross Stitch

Bring needle up at A; go down at B forming a straight stitch the desired length. Cross the stitch with an equal-sized stitch coming up at C and going down at D.

Definitions

Acrylic: Acrylic or water-based paints work best for fabric painting because they dry quickly and come in a variety of pre-mixed colors. They clean up easily with soap and water when still wet.

Appliqué: The art of applying fabric cutouts or other materials to a background to create a decorative pattern.

Background: Material to which motifs are applied.

Backing: The fabric that forms the bottom or back layer of a quilt.

Basting Stitches: Long running stitches used to hold two or more layers of fabric in place temporarily. To be removed when quilting is finished.

Batting: Layers or sheets of cotton or polyester material used as a filler between the quilt top and the backing.

Border: Plain, pieced, or appliquéd bands of fabric, used to frame the central section of the quilt top.

Crazy Quilting: A piecing technique using small, irregularly shaped pieces of fabric and decorative stitches.

Decorative Stitch: A stitch used to decorate an appliqué design as opposed to a stitch used to secure the motif in place.

Double-sided Adhesive: No-sew, no-iron material used to secure fabric to backing or background fabric.

Fusible Web: Often used to secure a motif to a background before stitching. A web with weak adhesive can easily be removed if desired. Different webs are made for different types of fabric.

Hand-stitched Method: Hand-stitching motifs to a background.

Layering: To create a "quilt sandwich" with three layers: backing, batting, and assembled quilt top.

Machine-stitched Method: Machine-stitching motifs to a background. Good for heavy fabrics that are difficult to hand-stitch or for items that will be used heavily or laundered frequently. Has a sharper appearance than hand-stitched appliqué.

Mitering a Corner: Joining vertical and horizontal strips of fabric at a 45° angle to form a 90° corner.

Mixed-media Appliqué: Use of other materials in combination with fabric to create a design. Can also refer to the use of dying and hand-painting techniques in combination with appliqué.

Motif: A piece of the appliqué design.

Motif Patterns: Pattern pieces to be traced onto tracing paper, then cut out and traced onto motif or background fabrics.

Placement Diagram: A reference drawing of the finished appliqué. It can also be used as a pattern.

Quilting: Sewing layers of fabric and batting together by hand or by using a sewing machine. It is often decorative and is generally the finishing step in appliqué or piecing.

Seam Allowance: The distance between the cut edge of fabric and the stitching line. In quilts, this is usually ¼". However, if the pieces of the quilt are small, ¼" seam allowances may overlap on the back when the quilt is assembled, causing excess bulk. If this occurs, trim seam allowances to ⅛".

Textile Medium: A necessary paint additive used when painting on fabrics. It prevents paints from peeling and helps to permanently adhere them to fabrics.

Tracing Paper: A relatively transparent paper used to trace patterns and placement diagrams.

Transfer Paper: A paper coated on one side with graphite or chalk. When it is pressed by a pencil, it transfers the graphite or chalk to the surface underneath it.

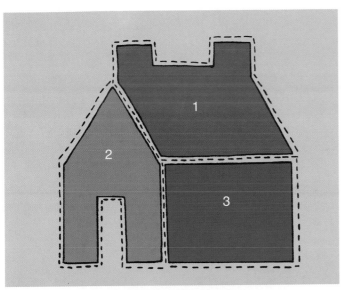

**Placement Diagram
Enlarge 200%**

Materials

Fabric: assorted cottons for motifs and borders
    background: 8¼" x 6¼"
    outside borders: 3½" x 16½" (2); 4½" x 6½" (2)
Cotton batting: thin bonded, 8" x 10"
Fusible web
Iron and ironing board
Straight pins
Thread: coordinating
Sponge
Acrylic paint: desired color
Permanent ink pen
Sandpaper
Scissors
Sewing machine
Tracing paper and marking tool
Frame: pine, 8" x 10"
Cardboard: 7½" x 9½"
Masking tape

Stenciled House

Assembly
¼" seam allowance

1. Sponge-paint frame. Let paint dry thoroughly. Sand edges of frame slightly to distress.

2. Trace, apply fusible web to, and cut out pieces 1–3 according to General Instructions.

3. Pin and sew side borders to background. Pin and sew top and bottom borders to background. See photograph.

4. Fuse pieces 1–3 to background. See Placement Diagram.

5. Outline stitches along border of background and pieces 1–3 using a permanent ink pen.

6. Place assembled quilt top right side down. Place batting on top. Place cardboard on top of batting. Wrap edges of quilt around cardboard. Tape to secure. Mount and secure in frame.

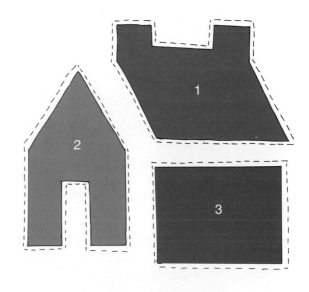

**Motif Patterns
Enlarge 200%**

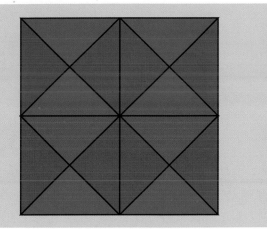

Placement Diagram

Patchwork Pillow

Materials

Fabric:
    polished cotton squares: 4" x 4" (8)
    polished cotton squares to coordinate
      with first cotton squares: 4" x 4" (8)
    polished cotton for backing: 9" square
    polished cotton for ruffle: 84" x 3½"
Needles
Straight pins
Thread: coordinating
Stuffing: polyester
Scissors
Iron and ironing board
Sewing machine

Assembly
¼" seam allowance

1. When cutting squares, cut so each square is exactly 4" x 4".

2. Fold each square in half diagonally. Press flat.

3. Pillow top is assembled in quarter sections. Begin with piece 1, Diagram A. Lay piece 2 on piece 1. Sew along stitch lines in Diagram B. Lay piece 3 on piece 2. Sew along stitch lines in Diagram C. Lay piece 4 on piece 3. Sew along stitch lines in Diagram D. Tuck piece 4 under piece 1. Stitch along last edge, Diagram E.

4. After each quarter section is complete, sew together as a four patch. Alternate colors so center looks like a pinwheel. See Placement Diagram.

5. Cut out ruffle fabric. Make a ⅛" finished hem on one long edge. Gather-stitch other long edge. Sew short edges of ruffle together.

6. Place quilt front, right side up. Place ruffle right side down on quilt fabric with hemmed edge on inside. Adjust gathers to fit. Stitch ruffle to quilt front. Place backing fabric on top of quilt front and ruffle, right side down. Stitch all three layers together on three sides. Turn right side out. Stuff. Blind-stitch opening closed.

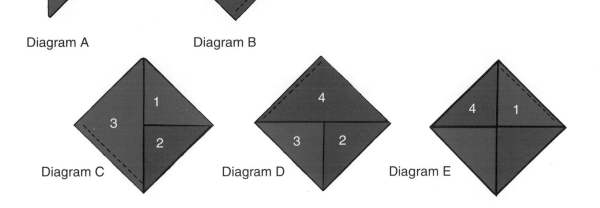

Diagram A   Diagram B

Diagram C   Diagram D   Diagram E

Placement Diagram
Enlarge 200%

Materials

Fabric: assorted cottons for motifs
    backing: 11" x 9",
    background: 9" x 7"
    piece 1: muslin, 6" x 6"
Cotton batting: thin bonded, 9" x 7"
Fusible web
Iron and ironing board
Needles
Straight pins
Thread: coordinating
Embroidery floss: coordinating
Permanent ink pen
Buttons: wood, ⅜"-diameter (2)
Scissors
Tracing paper and marking tool

Motif Patterns
Enlarge 200%

Snowman

Assembly

1. Trace, apply fusible web to, and cut out pieces 1–10 according to General Instructions. Fuse pieces 1–10 to background, following manufacturer's instructions. Sew wood buttons to vest using thread. See Placement Diagram.

2. Layer backing, batting, and assembled background. Pin. Fold backing borders to front of assembled quilt. Miter corners. Secure corners with a stitch in each corner. See photograph.

3. Buttonhole-stitch around the borders of assembled quilt.

4. Outline stitches around snowman's body, nose, bottom of vest, heart, and patch using a permanent ink pen. Make dots for snowman's eyes using a permanent ink pen.

5. Hang as desired.

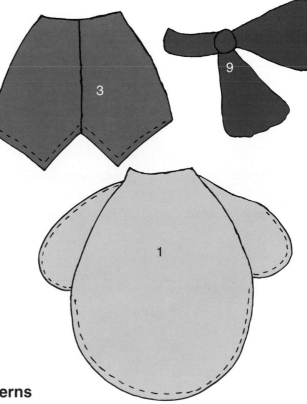

**Placement Diagram
Enlarge 250%**

Materials

Fabric: assorted cottons for motifs
    backing: 9" x 7"
    spools: broadcloth, 8" x 10"
    center patch: muslin, 6¼" x 4½"
    outside borders: 1½" x 4½" (2); 1½" x 6¼" (2)
    squares for outside borders: 1½" x 1½" (4)
Cotton batting: thin bonded, 9" x 7"
Fusible web
Iron and ironing board
Needles
Straight pins
Thread: neutral-colored
Embroidery floss: coordinating
Permanent ink pen
Scissors
Pinking shears
Sewing machine
Tracing paper and marking tool

I Love Quilts

Assembly
¼" seam allowance

1. Sew one square border piece to each end of 6¼" border strips, right sides together.

2. Sew two 4½" border strips to center patch. Press. Pin and sew together top and bottom border pieces to center patch, making certain corners match. Press seams and top.

3. Trace, apply fusible web to, and cut out pieces 1–4 according to General Instructions. Fuse pieces 1, 3, and 4 to background and piece 2 to piece 1, following manufacturer's instructions. Buttonhole-stitch around piece 3. Straight-stitch around piece 4. See Placement Diagram.

4. Outline stitches on assembled quilt and spools using a permanent ink pen.

5. Layer backing, batting, and assembled background. Pin. Straight-stitch layers together. Trim edges with pinking shears.

6. Make one large and one small yo-yo (pieces 5 and 6). Sew on center patch. Tie bows using neutral-colored thread and sew to front of each yo-yo. See photograph.

7. Hang as desired.

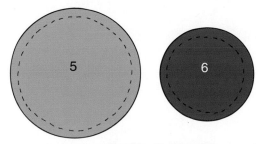

**Yo-Yo Patterns
Enlarge 200%**

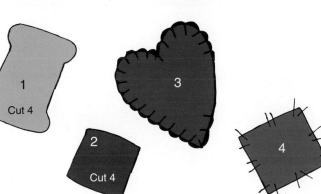

**Motif Patterns
Enlarge 200%**

**Placement Diagram
Enlarge 200%**

Basket of Posies

Assembly
¼" seam allowance

1. Trace, apply fusible web to, and cut out pieces 1–5 according to General Instructions.

2. Fuse pieces 1–5 to background, following manufacturer's instructions. Fuse them in the following order: piece 1, piece 5, pieces 4, pieces 2, and pieces 3. See Placement Diagram.

3. Outline stitches around pieces 1, 2, 4, and 5 using a permanent ink pen. See photograph.

4. Layer backing, batting, and assembled background. Pin. Straight-stitch layers together. Trim edges with pinking shears.

5. Hang as desired.

Materials

Fabric: assorted cottons for motifs
    backing: 9" x 7"
    background: 9" x 7"
Cotton batting: thin bonded, 9" x 7"
Fusible web
Iron and ironing board
Needles
Straight pins
Thread: coordinating
Permanent ink pen
Scissors
Pinking shears
Tracing paper and marking tool

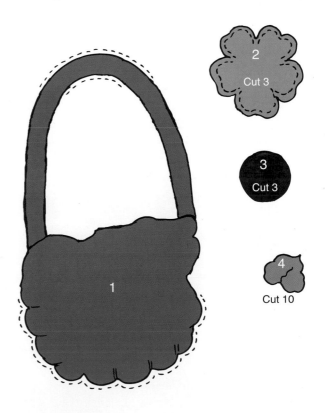

**Motif Patterns
Enlarge 200%**

Placement Diagram
Enlarge 255%

Materials

Fabric: assorted cottons for motifs
    backing: 8" x 10"
    background: 7" x 9"
Cotton batting: thin bonded, 7" x 9"
Fusible web
Iron and ironing board
Needles
Straight pins
Thread: neutral-colored
Pencil
Permanent ink pen
Buttons: medium (3)
Scissors
Tracing paper and marking tool

In the Garden

Assembly

1. Trace, apply fusible web to, and cut out pieces 1–3 according to General Instructions.

2. Fuse pieces 1–3 to background, following manufacturer's instructions. See Placement Diagram.

3. Make three yo-yos (piece 4). Stitch yo-yos in place on background. Stitch buttons to center of yo-yos.

4. Outline stitches around pieces 1–3 and stems using a permanent ink pen.

5. Trace lettering with a pencil. Outline lettering using a permanent ink pen. See Lettering Diagram.

6. Tie bow to handle of piece 1 using neutral-colored thread.

7. Layer backing, batting, and assembled background. Pin. Fold backing to front of quilt. Blind-stitch.

8. Hang as desired.

Lettering Diagram
Enlarge 200%

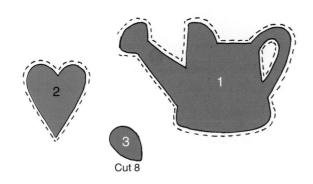

Cut 8

Motif Patterns
Enlarge 200%

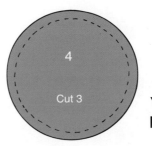

Cut 3

Yo-Yo Pattern
Enlarge 200%

**Placement Diagram
Enlarge 270%**

Materials

Fabric: assorted cottons for motifs
    backing: muslin, 8" x 7"
    background: muslin, 8" x 7"
Cotton batting: thin bonded, 8" x 7"
Fusible web
Iron and ironing board
Needles
Straight pins
Thread: coordinating
Permanent ink pen
Scissors
Pinking shears
Tracing paper and marking tool

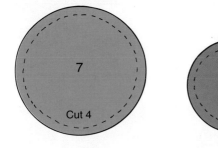

**Yo-Yo Patterns
Enlarge 200%**

Watering Can

Assembly

1. Trace, apply fusible web to, and cut out pieces 1–6 according to General Instructions.

2. Fuse pieces 1–6 to background, following manufacturer's instructions. See Placement Diagram.

3. Layer backing, batting, and assembled background. Pin. Straight-stitch layers together. Trim edges with pinking shears.

4. Make four large and four small yo-yos (pieces 7 and 8). Stitch large yo-yos on background. Stitch small yo-yos to center of large yo-yos.

5. Outline stitches, bee's wings, and antennas using a permanent ink pen.

6. Hang as desired.

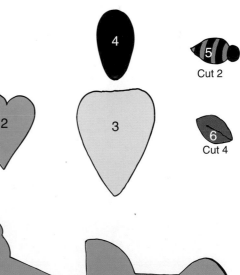

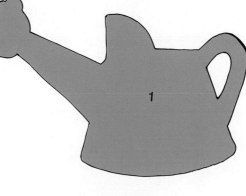

**Motif Patterns
Enlarge 200%**

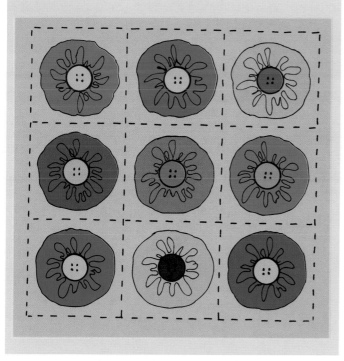

Placement Diagram
Enlarge 200%

Materials

Fabric: assorted flannel prints and plaids
    background: muslin, 8" x 8"
Cotton batting: thin bonded, 8" x 8"
Buttons: small (9)
Needles
Straight pins
Embroidery floss: coordinating
Linen jute or small natural cording
Disappearing ink pen
Glue: fabric
Ruler
Scissors
Tracing paper and marking tool
Frame: wooden, with 7" opening
Foam mounting board
Masking tape

Nine-Square Yo-Yo

Assembly

1. Using a ruler and a disappearing ink pen, measure and mark a 6" square in middle of background. Divide into nine 2" squares.

2. Pin background to batting. Sew a running stitch to form a pattern of nine 2" squares. Remove pins. See Placement Diagram.

3. Make yo-yos. *Note: Flannel fabric is thicker than regular cotton fabric so the centers will not draw up small and tight. However, the buttons will cover the openings.* Glue a yo-yo in the center of each 2" square.

4. Sew buttons to yo-yo centers using linen jute or small natural cording.

5. Place assembled quilt top right side down. Place mounting board on top of batting. Tape to secure. Mount and secure in frame.

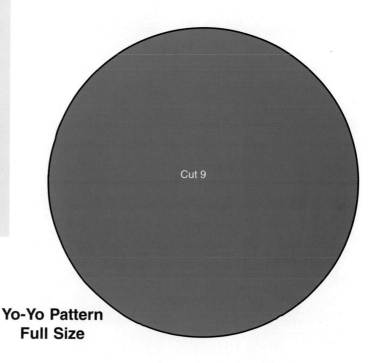

Cut 9

Yo-Yo Pattern
Full Size

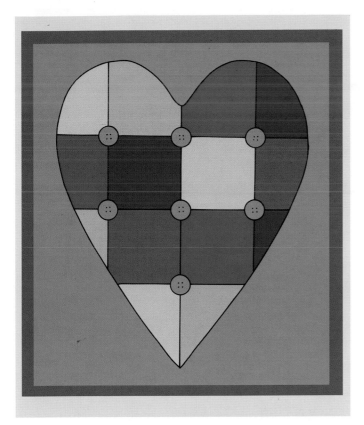

**Placement Diagram
Enlarge 270%**

Materials

Fabric:
  assorted flannel squares: 2½" x 2½" (14)
  background: 9" x 10¾"
  outside borders: 2½" x 11" (2); 2½" x 15" (2)
Cotton batting: thin bonded, 9" x 10¾"
Fusible web
Iron and ironing board
Needles
Straight pins
Embroidery floss: coordinating
Linen jute or small natural cording
Buttons: small (7)
Scissors
Tracing paper and marking tool
Sewing machine
Glue: fabric

Patchwork Heart

Assembly
¼" seam allowance

1. Arrange and sew flannel squares together. Cut out heart shape from assembled squares. See Placement Diagram for pattern to cut out heart shape.

2. Apply fusible web to background. Center and fuse background to batting, following manufacturer's instructions.

3. Pin assembled heart to center of background. Blanket-stitch around edge of heart. See photograph.

4. Sew longer border strips to sides of background, using ½" seam allowance. If necessary, trim ends of strips. Sew shorter border strips to top and bottom of background. Fold the top and bottom to back side of quilt. Tuck raw edges under batting and glue to secure.

5. Sew buttons to corners of each square using linen jute or small natural cording.

6. Hang as desired.

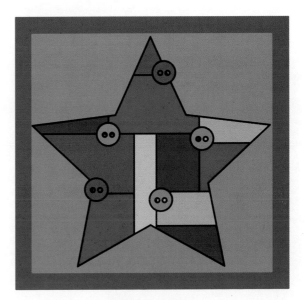

**Alternative
Patchwork Design**

Placement Diagram
Enlarge 260%

Materials

Fabric: assorted cottons for motifs
    backing: 11" x 7½"
    background: 11" x 7½"
    patch behind cow: fabric and felt, 5½" x 5"
    patch behind milk bottle:
        fabric and felt, 2¾" x 5½"
    bow: 10" x 1"
Cotton batting: thin bonded, 11" x 7½"
Fusible web
Iron and ironing board
Needles
Straight pins
Embroidery floss: coordinating
Twine: 4"
Glue: fabric
Scissors
Pinking shears
Tracing paper and marking tool

Buttercup

Assembly

1. Cut out background, backing, batting, and patches using pinking shears.

2. Trace and apply fusible web to pieces 1–14 according to General Instructions. Cut out pieces 1–16.

3. Straight-stitch patches to background. Layer backing, batting, and background. Pin. Straight-stitch layers together. Trim with pinking shears.

4. Fuse pieces 1–14 to patches, following manufacturer's instructions. See Placement Diagram.

5. Straight-stitch pieces 15–16 to assembled quilt.

6. Make four yo-yos (piece 17) and glue to quilt.

7. Cross-stitch cow's eyes.

8. Tie knot in end of twine and glue in place for cow's tail.

9. Tie a bow from fabric strip and glue to front of milk bottle.

10. Hang as desired.

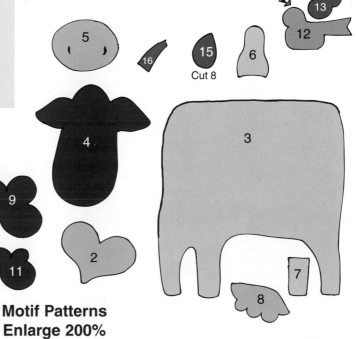

Yo-Yo Pattern
Enlarge 200%

Motif Patterns
Enlarge 200%

Placement Diagram
Enlarge 235%

Materials

Fabric: assorted cottons for motifs
    backing: off-white felt, 8½" x 8"
    background: 8½" x 8"
Fusible web
Iron and ironing board
Needles
Straight pins
Thread: coordinating
Embroidery floss: coordinating
Buttons: small (4)
Glue: craft
Scissors
Tracing paper and marking tool
Decorative wooden bee

Honeycomb

Assembly

1. Trace and apply fusible web to piece 1 according to General Instructions. Cut out pieces 1–3.

2. Fuse honeycomb pieces to background, following manufacturer's instructions. See Placement Diagram.

3. Straight-stitch around honeycomb. See photograph.

4. Straight-stitch leaves to background.

5. Make four yo-yos (piece 3) and sew to corners of background.

6. Sew button to center of each yo-yo.

7. Layer backing and assembled quilt. Pin. Straight-stitch layers together.

8. Glue wooden bee to quilt.

9. Hang as desired.

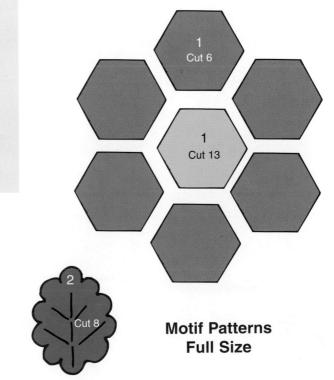

Motif Patterns
Full Size

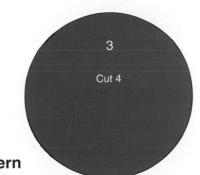

Yo-Yo Pattern
Enlarge 200%

Placement Diagram
Enlarge 135%

Materials

Fabric: assorted cottons for motifs
    backing: 5½" x 7"
    background: 4½" x 6"
Cotton batting: thin bonded, 4½" x 6"
Needles
Straight pins
Embroidery floss: coordinating
Linen jute
Cording
Button: medium (1); large (4)
Twig: 2½" (1); 6" (1)
Scissors
Pinking shears
Tracing paper and marking tool

Ripe Apple

Assembly

1. Cut out pieces 1–2 and backing using pinking shears.
2. Straight-stitch edge of piece 1 to background using linen jute. Sew button on piece 1. Straight-stitch leaves to background down the center. See Placement Diagram.
3. Sew 2½" twig with an "X"-stitch for apple stem on top of the apple and between the two leaves.
4. Layer backing, batting, and assembled quilt. Pin. Fold backing to front of quilt and herringbone-stitch layers together.
5. Sew a button to each corner of assembled quilt.
6. Tie remaining twig to top of quilt using cording for hanging.

Motif Patterns
Full Size

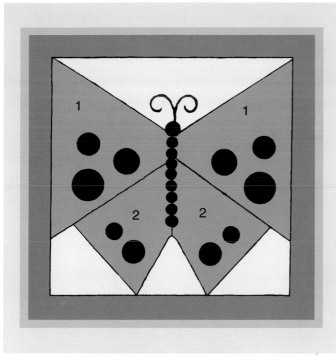

Placement Diagram
Enlarge 200%

Materials

Fabric: assorted cottons for motifs
    backing: 11½" square
    outside borders: 5½" x 2¼" (2); 2¼" x 8½" (2)
    center patch: 5½" square
Cotton batting: thin bonded, 9½" square
Needles
Straight pins
Thread: coordinating
Embroidery floss: coordinating
Beads: 6mm (8); 8mm (1)
Buttons: small (4); medium (2);
    large (2); decorative (2)
Iron and ironing board
Sewing machine
Tracing paper and marking tool

Button Butterfly

Assembly
¼" seam allowance

1. Cut out pieces 1–2.
2. Fold edges of pieces 1–2 under ¼". Press. Blind-stitch to center patch. See Placement Diagram.
3. Pin and sew side borders to center patch. Press.
4. Pin and sew top and bottom borders to center patch. Press.
5. Blanket-stitch around butterfly wings. See photograph.
6. Sew buttons and beads on butterfly. Straight-stitch antennas. Make a French knot at the end of each antenna.
7. Herringbone-stitch along top and bottom of borders. See photograph.
8. Layer backing, batting, and assembled quilt. Pin. Fold backing to front of quilt and straight-stitch layers together.
9. Hang as desired.

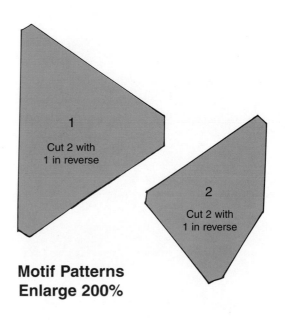

Motif Patterns
Enlarge 200%

**Placement Diagram
Enlarge 200%**

Primitive House

Assembly

1. Cut out pieces 1–8.

2. Pin piece 1 to background. Straight-stitch to background. Randomly stitch grassy areas. See Placement Diagram.

3. Pin pieces 2–6 to background. Blanket-stitch pieces 2–3 and 6 to background, and piece 4 to piece 2. Straight-stitch piece 5 to piece 2. Sew small button for door knob. Sew heart button on roof.

4. Glue piece 7 to background. Pin and straight-stitch around piece 8. Make French knots on tree for apples.

5. Straight-stitch smoke coming out of chimney.

6. Sew moon and star buttons to assembled quilt.

7. Place assembled quilt right side down. Place batting on top. Place back of frame on top of batting. Mount and secure in frame.

Materials

Fabric: assorted wool and felt for motifs
    background: flannel, 5" x 7"
Cotton batting: thin bonded, 5" x 7"
Needles
Straight pins
Thread: coordinating
Embroidery floss: coordinating
Buttons: stars (3); moon (1); heart (1); small (1)
Glue: fabric
Frame: wooden, 5" x 7"
Scissors
Tracing paper and marking tool

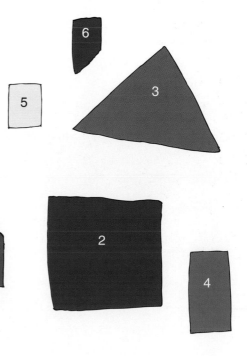

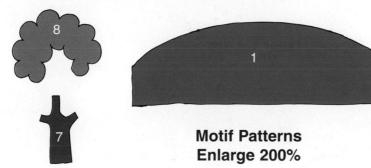

**Motif Patterns
Enlarge 200%**

**Placement Diagram
Enlarge 200%**

Materials

Fabric: assorted cottons for motifs
    background: 7" x 7"
    outside borders: 8¾" x 1¼" (2); 7" x 1¼" (2)
Cotton batting: thin bonded, 8" x 8"
Fusible web
Iron and ironing board
Needles
Straight pins
Thread: coordinating
Embroidery floss: coordinating
Scissors
Sewing machine
Tracing paper and marking tool
Pillow form

**Motif Patterns
Enlarge 200%**

Morning Rooster

Assembly
¼" seam allowance

1. Trace, apply fusible web to, and cut out pieces 1–6 according to General Instructions.

2. Fuse pieces 1–6 to background, following manufacturer's instructions. See Placement Diagram.

3. Sew side borders to background, right sides together. Press. Sew top and bottom borders to background. Top and bottom borders will overlap the side borders. Press. See photograph.

4. Pin batting to assembled background. Straight-stitch sun rays and rooster legs. Lazy daisy-stitch rooster feet, flower petals, and leaves. Straight-stitch flower stems. Make French knots for flower centers. Straight-stitch around rooster body. Remove pins.

5. Fold and press border edges under ¼". Sew assembled quilt to the top of a favorite pillow by blind-stitching around outside borders.

Cock-A-Doodle

Placement Diagram
Enlarge 220%

Materials

Fabric: assorted cottons for motifs
    patches: 4½ x 4½" (4)
    strips: 1¾" x 8"; 1¼" x 8"
Cotton batting: thin bonded, 8" x 10"
Fusible web
Iron and ironing board
Needles
Thread: coordinating
Straight pins
Embroidery floss: coordinating
Pencil
Scissors
Sewing machine
Tracing paper and marking tool
Frame: wooden, 8" x 10"
Foam mounting board
Masking tape

Assembly
¼" seam allowance

1. Trace, apply fusible web to, and cut out pieces 1–4 according to General Instructions.
   Note: Bottom right rooster is positioned in opposite direction.

2. Sew patches, right sides together. Press open.

3. Sew two strips together along one long edge. Press open.

4. Sew strips along bottom edges of patches, right sides together. Press open.

5. Fuse pieces 1–4 to patches, following manufacturer's instructions. See Placement Diagram.

6. Layer batting and assembled quilt. Pin. Straight-stitch layers together. Make French knots on top left rooster. Straight-stitch roosters' feet.

7. Trace lettering with a pencil. Backstitch lettering. See Lettering Diagram. Sew rooster tracks along bottom strip using straight stitches.

8. Place assembled quilt right side down. Place mounting board on top of batting. Tape to secure. Mount and secure in frame.

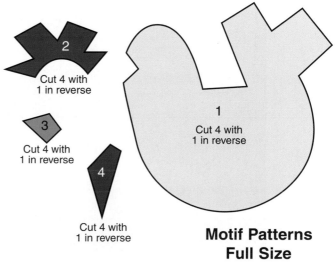

Cut 4 with 1 in reverse (2)

Cut 4 with 1 in reverse (3)

Cut 4 with 1 in reverse (4)

Cut 4 with 1 in reverse (1)

Motif Patterns
Full Size

COCK-A-DOODLE-DOO

Lettering Diagram
Enlarge 200%

289

Cherry Pie Patch Pattern

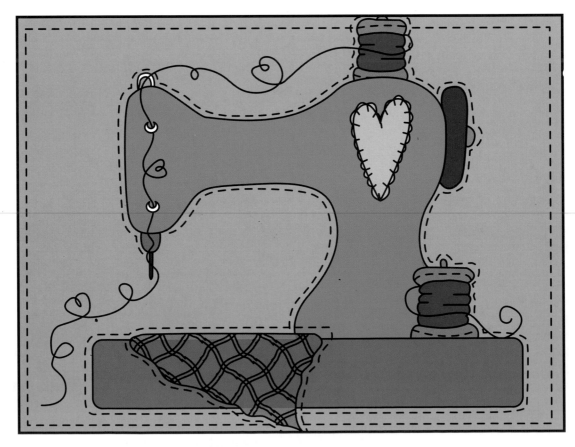

I'd Rather Be Sewing Pattern

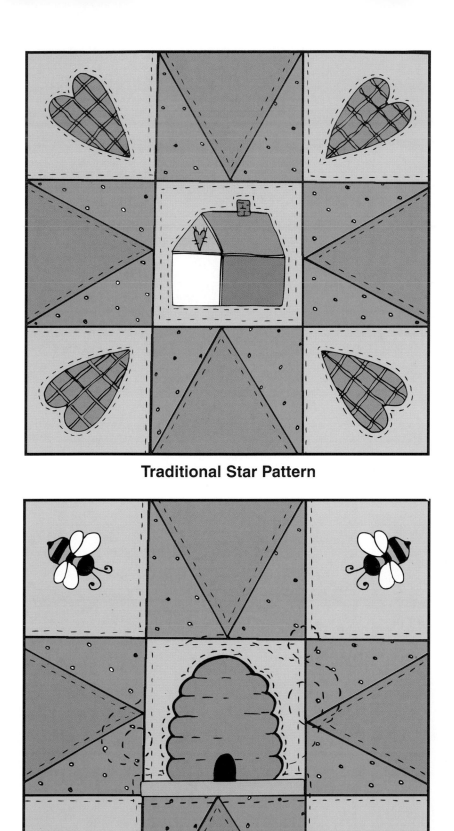

Traditional Star Pattern

Beehive Pattern

Country Patch Patterns

Pumpkin Patch Pattern

Country Santa Pattern

Winter Patches Pattern

Summer Garden Pattern

Garden Gatherings Pattern

293

Gardening Angel Pattern

I Believe In Angels Pattern

Teddy Bear Repair Pattern

294

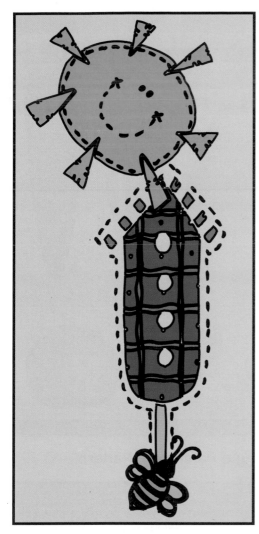

Bee House Pattern

Patchwork Rooster Pattern

Watermelon Pattern

Sunny Sunflowers Pattern

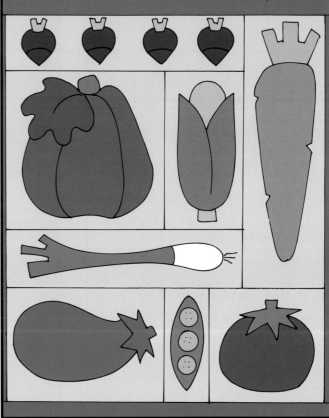

Veggie Patchwork Pattern

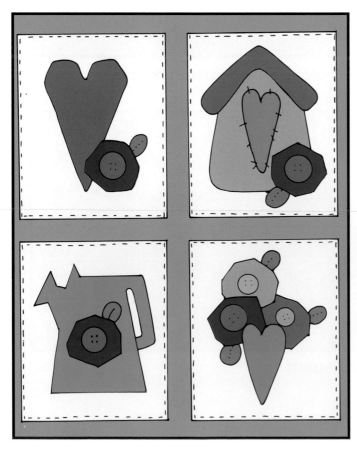

Country Garden Squares Pattern

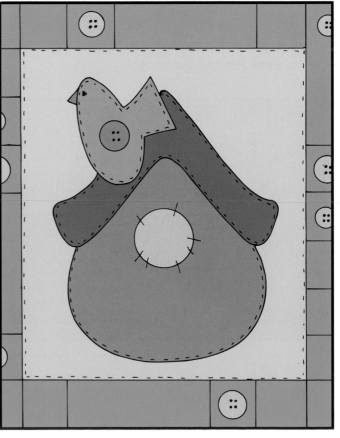

Country Birdhouse Pattern

We Love Cats Pattern

Bird on Birdhouse Pattern

Grandpa's Barn Pattern

Flowers In Pot Pattern

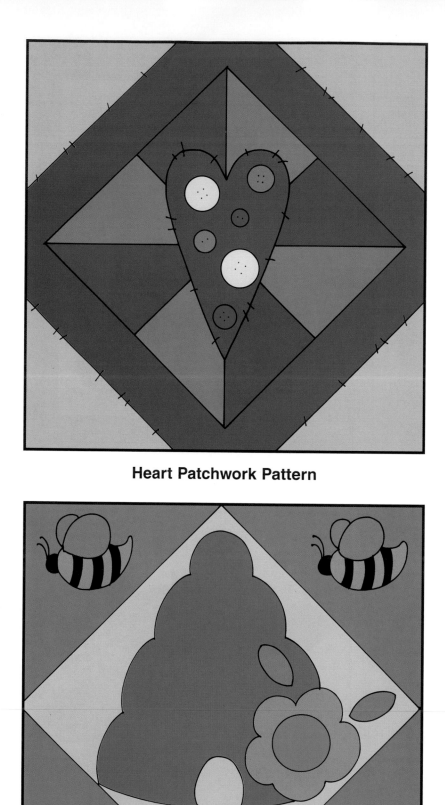

Heart Patchwork Pattern

Beehive Pattern

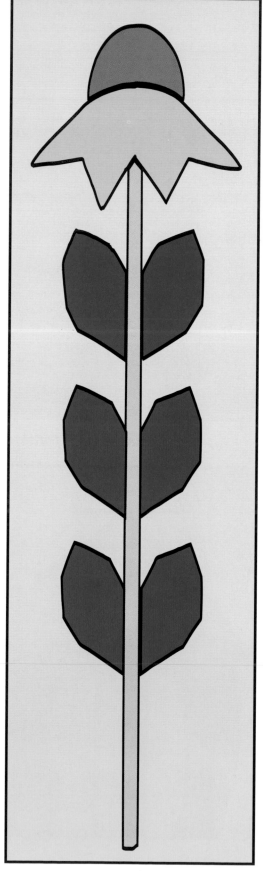

Single Sunflower Pattern

Pine Tree Retreat Pattern

Canes, Trees & Stockings Pattern

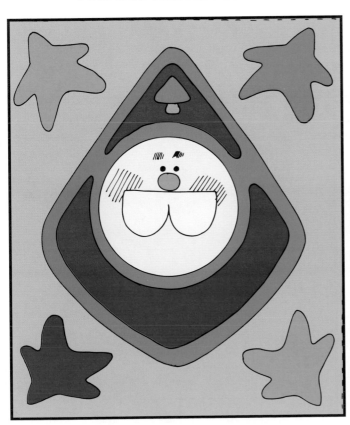

Stenciled Santa Pattern

Angels Pattern

Beehive & Strawberries Pattern

Honey Pot Pattern

Patches the Cat Pattern

Forest Friends Pattern

300

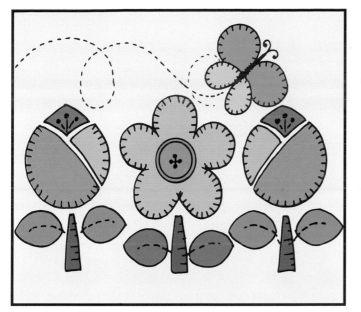

Signs of Spring Pattern

Victorian Charm Pattern

Rain Rain Go Away Pattern

Forget-Me-Not Pattern

Wish'n I Were Fish'n Pattern

Welcome Home Pattern

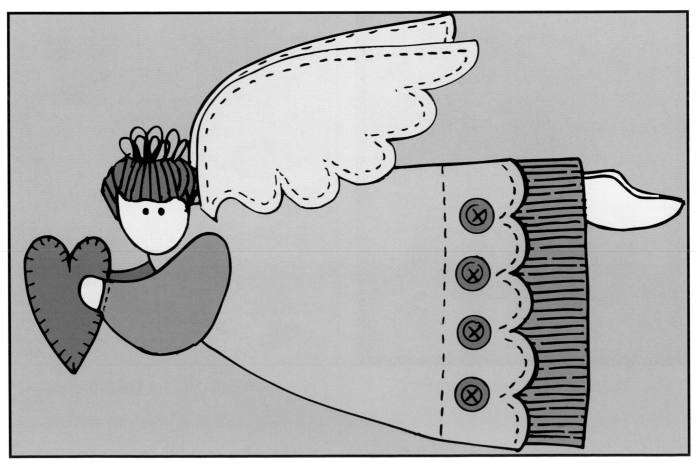

Angel In Flight Pattern

Girls Love Flowers Pattern

Sweetheart Sampler Pattern

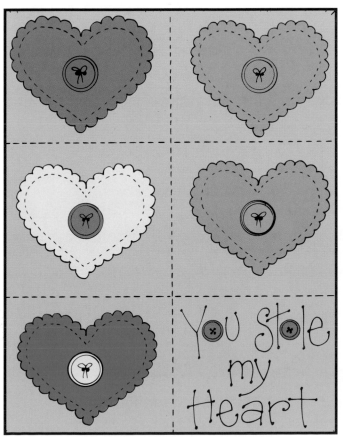

You Stole My Heart Pattern

Mender of Broken Hearts Pattern

303

Christmas Mittens Pattern

Crazy Patch Pattern

Patchwork Snowman Pattern

Tis' the Season Pattern

**Woodland
Night
Pattern**

Catch of the Day Pattern

Home In Heart Pattern

Home is where the ♥ is.

Home Is Where the Heart Is Pattern

Home Tweet Home Pattern

Raggedy Pals Pattern

307

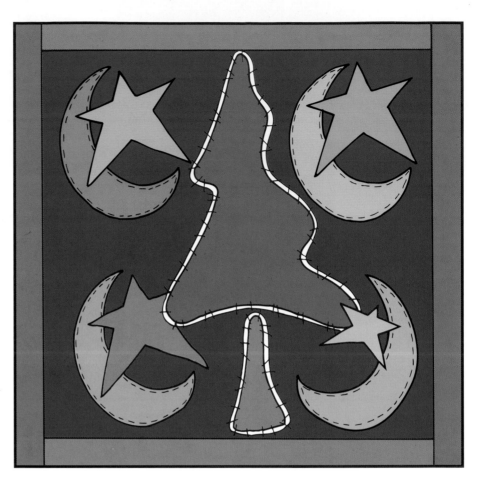

**Moon
Night
Pattern**

Scarecrow with Pumpkins Pattern

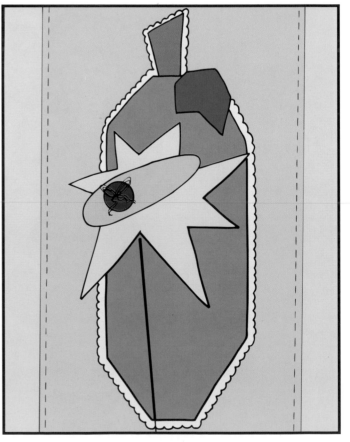

Pumpkin with Sunflower Pattern

308

Baby's Asleep Pattern

Warm Hands . . . Warm Heart Pattern

Barnyard Friends Pattern

Country Bird Pattern

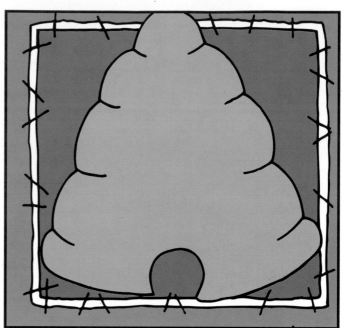

Country Beehive Pattern

Country Bee Pattern

Country Birdhouse Pattern

Two-Hour Nature Craft Projects

Getting Started ...

Air Drying Long-Stemmed Flowers & Leaves

Materials

❧ Bundles of fresh flowers & leaves

❧ String or rubberbands

❧ Spare room, garage, or shed

Instructions

1. Gather six to ten stems and tie string around ends (or use rubberband) to secure bundle.

2. Hang bundles upside-down in a spare room, garage, or shed. Make certain the bundles are hung in a dry environment, preferably out of the sun to avoid bleaching.

3. Allow to dry thoroughly.

Air Drying Short-Stemmed Flowers & Leaves

Materials

❧ Loose fresh flowers & leaves

❧ Window screen

❧ Bricks (4)

❧ Spare room, garage, or shed

Instructions

1. Place window screen up on four bricks in a spare room, garage, or shed. Make certain the window screen is placed in a dry environment, preferably out of the sun to avoid bleaching.

2. Place loose flowers and leaves on top of window screen without overlapping.

3. Allow to dry thoroughly.

Drying Flowers & Leaves Slowly with Silica Gel

Materials

- Loose fresh flowers & leaves
- Silica gel
- Container, metal, glass, or plastic
- Paintbrush, soft

Instructions

1. Place one inch of silica gel (moisture-absorbent crystals) into container.

2. Place loose flowers and leaves on top of silica gel without overlapping.

3. Cover loose flowers and leaves with a thin layer of silica gel just until flowers and leaves are covered.

4. Repeat process until container is full.

5. Allow to dry thoroughly; check every other day.

6. Using a soft paintbrush, whisk away any lingering silica gel crystals.

Drying Flowers & Leaves Quickly with Silica Gel

Materials

- Loose fresh flowers & leaves
- Silica gel
- Container, microwave-safe
- Microwave oven
- Paintbrush, soft

Instructions

1. Place one inch of silica gel into container.

2. Place loose flowers and leaves on top of silica gel without overlapping.

3. Cover loose flowers and leaves with a thin layer of silica gel just until flowers and leaves are covered.

4. Place container in microwave oven and heat on medium for one to two minutes.

5. Remove and allow to stand for 30 minutes.

6. Using a soft paintbrush, whisk away any lingering silica gel crystals.

Pressing Flowers & Leaves

Materials

- ❧ Loose fresh flowers & leaves
- ❧ Plywood: $1/4$"-thick squares (2)
- ❧ Cardboard, corrugated
- ❧ Watercolor paper or absorbent paper
- ❧ Acrylic paints
- ❧ Tweezers
- ❧ Toothpick
- ❧ Craft glue
- ❧ Découpage glue, optional
- ❧ Paintbrush
- ❧ Flat screws, $1 1/2$" (4)
- ❧ Wing nuts (4)
- ❧ Drill with $1/8$" drill bit
- ❧ Scissors

Instructions for Making Flower Presses

1. Each flower press consists of two plywood squares, four flat screws, and four wing nuts. Note: The size of the flower press (the plywood squares) is determined by the size of the flowers or leaves to be pressed.

2. Drill one hole in each corner of each plywood square with drill and $1/8$" drill bit.

3. Using a paintbrush, paint plywood squares with acrylic paints as desired.

4. If desired, embellish one side of each plywood square with pressed flowers and leaves by gluing them on and then applying découpage glue over the top according to manufacturer's directions.

Instructions for Pressing Flowers & Leaves

1. Cut cardboard and watercolor paper into circles with scissors, using the size of the plywood squares to determine the diameter of the circles. Note: Cut several of each.

2. Begin by placing one plywood square on working surface. Next, place one cardboard circle on top of plywood square. Next, place one watercolor paper circle on top of cardboard. Next, place fresh flower or leaf to be pressed.

3. Place another watercolor paper circle on top of fresh flower or leaf, followed by another cardboard circle.

4. Repeat process until flowers and leaves are each between watercolor paper and cardboard circles. Note: Keep the flower press to a stacked height of about one inch or less.

5. Place the remaining plywood square on top of last cardboard circle.

6. Holding flower press together firmly, place flat screw into drilled hole in each corner.

7. Place wing nuts on flat screws and tighten until flower press appears tight enough that flowers and leaves are being pressed adequately.

8. Allow to press for seven to ten days.

9. Carefully remove pressed flowers and leaves from between watercolor circles.

Making Wreaths

Materials

- ❧ Grapevines
- ❧ Twigs, green
- ❧ Branches, green
- ❧ Copper wire:
     19-gauge
- ❧ Floral wire

Instructions for Grapevine Wreaths

1. Soak grapevines in water until pliable.

2. Place grapevines together with ends staggered slightly and bend into desired shape.

3. Hold grapevines in place and wrap the longest grapevine around the shaped grapevines, making certain all grapevines are secured. Tuck in stray ends.

Instructions for Green Twig & Branch Wreaths

1. Bend green twigs or branches into desired shape and secure them with copper or floral wire.

2. Allow wreath to sit in the sun for several days for green twigs or branches to dry thoroughly.

Embellishing Wreaths

Materials

- ❧ Wreath
- ❧ Embellishments
- ❧ Ribbon
- ❧ Floral wire
- ❧ Hot glue gun & glue sticks
- ❧ Scissors

Instructions

1. Choose desired embellishments — dried and fresh flowers and greenery, nuts, and pinecones are a few among many to choose from.

2. Divide embellishments into groups for easy access.

3. Begin by arranging the largest items on the wreath and, using a hot glue gun and glue sticks, hot-glue in place.

4. Repeat process for remaining embellishments, from largest to smallest.

5. Tie ribbon in a bow according to instructions for Making Multi-Loop Bows on page 320.

6. Using hot glue gun and glue sticks, hot-glue bow to wreath or, using floral wire, secure bow in place. Cascade ribbon tails down.

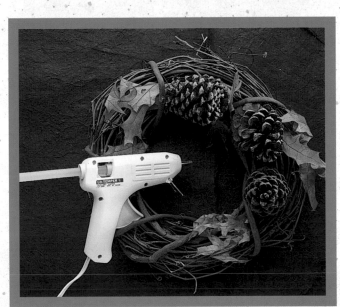

What is Beeswax?

Beeswax is a very pliable, natural substance that is secreted by bees and creates the honeycomb that actually holds the honey.

The honey is extracted by heating the honeycomb until the honey runs free from the honeycomb shell. Then the honeycomb, or beeswax, is cleaned and ready to be used.

The color of beeswax ranges in shades, but always has a dull-yellow or amber coloring.

What is Candle Wax?

Candle wax is wax that has a hardening additive. It melts at a higher temperature than paraffin wax.

The color of candle wax is translucent, but can be changed with candle dyes.

What is Paraffin Wax?

Paraffin wax is a soft wax. It melts at a lower temperature than candle wax.

The color of paraffin wax is translucent, but can be changed with candle dyes.

Generally, paraffin wax is too soft for making decorative candles, but is ideal for re-dipping candles or sealing bottles.

Using Candle Dyes

Candle wax and paraffin wax colors can be changed simply by adding a candle dye. Candle dyes come in several colors and will render a rich and vibrant shade.

Old candles and crayons can be used as candle dyes, however the shade of color will be a tint rather than a deep color.

Using Candle Fragrance Oils

Candle fragrance oils can be purchased and have been specially formulated to be used in candle making. Always refer to manufacturer's directions. *Caution: Never use alcohol- or water-based fragrances for scenting candles, they will cause the hot wax to pop and explode.*

Melting Wax

Materials

- Saucepan, double-boiler, or crockpot
- Tin can
- Pliers
- Heat source
- Beeswax, candle wax, or paraffin wax

Instructions

1. Place enough water in saucepan, double-boiler, or crockpot to adequately heat sides of tin can.

2. Place on stove or plug-in heating appliance and heat on low. *Note: Higher temperatures will burn the wax and/or cause the hot wax to pop and explode.*

3. Place wax in tin can and place tin can in saucepan, double-boiler, or crockpot. *Note: Do not get water in the wax.*

4. Wax will slowly begin to melt. *Caution: If wax begins to smoke it is being melted too quickly at too high a temperature — remove from heat immediately as hot wax will ignite. Note: Melted wax is very difficult to remove from pans, utensils, and clothing. Use old items that can be discarded.*

5. When wax is completely melted and ready to use, carefully remove tin can containing melted wax from hot water with pliers. *Caution: The melted wax and the tin can will be very hot and can cause serious burns.*

Re-dipping Candles

Materials

- ❧ Saucepan, double-boiler, or crockpot
- ❧ Tin can
- ❧ Pliers
- ❧ Heat source
- ❧ Paraffin wax
- ❧ Salad tongs
- ❧ Waxed paper

Instructions

1. Melt paraffin wax according to instructions for Melting Wax

2. Using pliers (or needle-nose pliers), pick up candles by candlewicks. Quickly place candle into tin can containing melted wax until candle has been completely submerged. <u>Note: Dip candles into hot wax only once unless indicated otherwise.</u>

3. Using salad tongs, remove candle from hot wax and place on waxed paper to cool thoroughly.

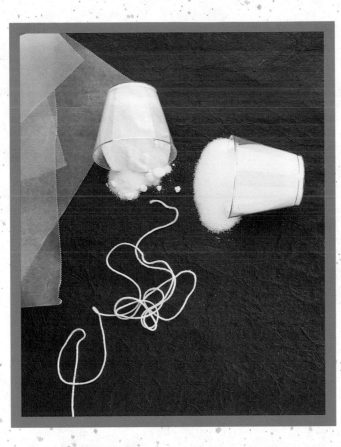

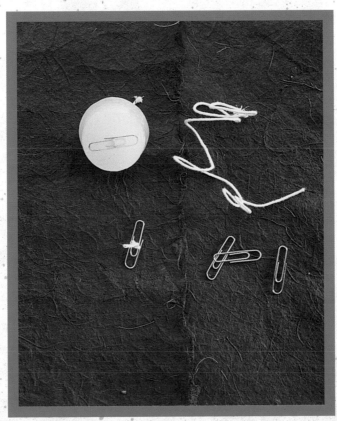

Making & Using Candlewicks

Materials

- ❧ Borax: 2 tablespoons
- ❧ Salt: 1 tablespoon
- ❧ Water: 1 cup
- ❧ Container
- ❧ Cord, cotton
- ❧ Candle mold
- ❧ Paper clips
- ❧ Scissors

Instructions

1. Place Borax, salt, and water in container and soak cord overnight.

2. Remove cord from solution and allow cord to dry thoroughly.

3. Cut candlewick to desired length with scissors.

4. Insert candlewick through a paper clip and fold lengthwise. Twist ends together.

5. Place paper clip in bottom of candle mold.

6. Pour hot wax into candle mold and hold onto end of candlewick until the wax sets enough that candlewick cannot sink back into the wax.

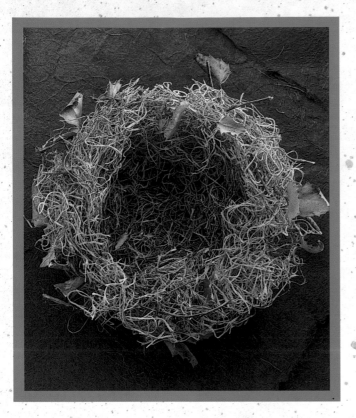

Making Bird Nests

Materials

- Spanish moss
- Leaves, dried
- Twigs
- Acrylic spray, matte
- Adhesive spray

Instructions

1. The amount of Spanish moss needed depends on the desired size of bird nest.

2. Form bird nest by hollowing out center of Spanish moss, pushing excess out toward the sides.

3. Spray bird nest with adhesive spray and slightly press Spanish moss so it adheres to itself.

4. Randomly add dried leaves and twigs.

5. Allow adhesive spray to dry thoroughly.

6. To seal bird nest, spray with matte acrylic spray.

7. Allow acrylic spray to dry thoroughly.

Making Wasp Nests

Materials

- Styrofoam egg: small
- Toilet paper, white
- Acrylic paints: Dark gray Light gray
- Paintbrush
- Spray bottle
- Craft knife
- Pencil

Instructions

1. Cut $^1/_4$" off pointed end of styrofoam egg with craft knife.

2. Make a $^1/_2$" deep hole in flat end of styrofoam egg with a pencil.

3. Tear toilet paper sheets into three or four strips. Wet strips with spray bottle and wrap around and inside hole in styrofoam egg, allowing a few strips to pull away from sides of styrofoam egg.

4. Allow toilet paper to dry thoroughly.

5. Using a paintbrush, make rings around styrofoam egg with dark gray acrylic paint.

6. Repeat process with light gray acrylic paint, blending paints as desired.

7. Allow paint to dry thoroughly after each step.

Painting Wooden Eggs

Materials

❧ Wooden eggs
❧ Acrylic paints:
　Black
　Cream
　Gold
　Sandstone
❧ Paintbrush
❧ Toothbrush
❧ Foam plate
❧ Acrylic spray, gloss

Instructions

1. Place a small dab of each acrylic paint color on a foam plate.

2. Using a paint-brush, load bristles with cream and sandstone acrylic paints.

3. Using up and down strokes, paint wooden eggs.

4. Allow paint to dry thoroughly.

5. Using a paint-brush, load bristles with gold.

6. Streak paint on eggs making certain gold does not stand out. Note: Colors should blend, yet show through individually.

7. Allow paint to dry thoroughly.

8. Lightly dip tooth-brush in black. Hold toothbrush six inches from eggs and spatter by running a finger up the tooth-brush bristles.

9. Allow paint to dry thoroughly.

10. To seal wooden eggs, spray with gloss acrylic spray.

11. Allow acrylic spray to dry thoroughly.

Making Multi-Loop Bows

Materials

- ❦ Ribbon
- ❦ Floral wire
- ❦ Scissors

Instructions

1. Cut ribbon to desired length with scissors.

2. Leaving a length of ribbon for a tail, make a figure eight. Loop size should be determined by the size of the desired bow.

3. Holding ribbon in the center, make another figure eight on top of the first one.

4. Repeat process until the desired number of loops are formed. Leave a length of ribbon for a tail equivalent to the length of the first tail.

5. Pinch center of ribbon bow and gather center loops together.

6. Tightly wrap floral wire around center of bow to secure.

7. Pull each loop and shape as desired. If necessary, trim floral wire with scissors.

Cutting & Oxidizing Metal

Materials

- ❦ Vinegar: 1 cup
- ❦ Salt: ¹/₂ cup
- ❦ Water: ¹/₂ cup
- ❦ Metal
- ❦ Saucepan
- ❦ Tin snips

Instructions

1. Using tin snips, cut metal into desired shapes. <u>Note: To avoid jagged edges, keep tin snips deep in the cut and do not withdraw the blades until entire cut is complete.</u>

2. Place vinegar, salt, and water in saucepan. Place metal shapes in oxidizing solution and soak outside overnight. Make certain metal shapes are submerged in oxidizing solution. <u>Note: Do not soak inside — adequate ventilation is imperative.</u>

3. Remove metal shapes from oxidizing solution and allow metal shapes to dry thoroughly. <u>Caution: The metal shapes will have sharp edges that can cause serious cuts.</u>

Making Spiced Ornaments

Materials

- ❦ Ground cinnamon: 1 cup
- ❦ Ground cloves: 1 tablespoon
- ❦ Ground nutmeg: 1 tablespoon
- ❦ Applesauce: ³/₄ cup
- ❦ All-purpose glue: 2 tablespoons
- ❦ Water: ³/₄ to 1 cup
- ❦ Jute, waxed
- ❦ Toothpick
- ❦ Cookie cutters
- ❦ Mixing bowl
- ❦ Wooden spoon
- ❦ Cookie sheet

Instructions

1. Place ground cinnamon, ground cloves, ground nutmeg, applesauce, all-purpose glue, and ³/₄ cup water in a mixing bowl. Mix with a wooden spoon to make a dough that has the consistency of cookie dough. If necessary, add more water by teaspoonful.

2. Cover bowl and refrigerate dough for two hours.

3. Working on a clean surface that has been sprinkled with ground cinnamon, knead dough until smooth and press flat.

4. Cut dough into desired shapes with cookie cutters.

5. Using a toothpick, make a hole near the top of each ornament for hanging. Note: When ready, hang with waxed jute.

6. Place dough shapes on a cookie sheet and bake at 200° F (93° C) for two hours, turning shapes every half hour.

Making Natural Soap

Materials

- Water: 1¼ cups
- Lye: 4 tablespoons
- Coconut oil: 3 tablespoons
- Sunflower oil: 3½ tablespoons
- Olive oil: 3 tablespoons
- Herbal oil: 1½ teaspoons
- Food coloring: 2 drops, optional
- Oatmeal, fine: 4 tablespoons, optional
- Honey: 2 tablespoons, optional
- Glass bowl
- Saucepan
- Wooden spoon
- Wire whisk
- Rubber gloves
- Newspaper
- Waxed paper
- Candle molds or small baking tins

Instructions

1. Working over newspaper, place water in a glass bowl. <u>Note: Do not use a metal bowl; lye will eat the metal.</u>

2. Carefully pour lye into water and stir with a wooden spoon until lye dissolves. Set aside. <u>Caution: Lye is an alkali that can cause serious burns. Rubber gloves should be worn at all times when working with lye. If lye should come into contact with the skin, immediately wash affected areas with cold water. Vinegar or lemon juice will help ease the pain from the burn.</u>

3. Place oils in a saucepan and heat on low until oil is lukewarm.

4. Pour lukewarm oil into glass bowl containing lye mixture, stirring constantly.

5. If desired, add food coloring. Beat together with wire whisk until thick.

6. Pour mixture into candle molds or baking tins and set aside for 24 hours.

7. Remove soap from candle molds or baking tins and wrap in waxed paper.

8. Store in a cool place for three weeks to allow soap to harden thoroughly.

9. If desired, add oatmeal and honey to lye mixture to make natural oatmeal soap.

Glossary of Drieds ...

Ammobium
(Ammobium
alatum)

Calendula
(Calendula
officinalis)

Caspia
(Miniature
Statice)

Cedar Rose
(Deodara
rosa)

Cedar Tips
(Deodara)

Cockscomb
(Celosia
argentea)

Corn Flowers
(Centaurea
montana)

Deer Moss
(Cladonia
rangiferina)

Eucalyptus
(Eucalyptus
gunnii)

Fern
(Plumosa)

Foxtail Millet
(Panicum
miliaceum)

Galoxa Leaf
(Galeax)

*Garlic Bulb
(Allium
sativum)*

*German Statice
(Limonium
globus)*

*Globe
Amaranth*

*Heather
(Calluna
vulgaris)*

*Juniper Berries
(Juniperus
sabina)*

*Lantern
Pods*

*Larkspur
(Consolida
ambigua)*

*Lavender
(Lavendula
angustifolia)*

*Lemon Leaf
(Citrus
limonium)*

*Licopodium
or Princess Pine*

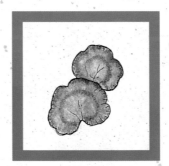

*Mushrooms
(Trametes
vericolor)*

*Myrtle Leaf
(Myrtus
communis)*

*Nigella or
Love in a Mist*

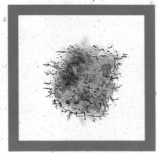

*Oregon Moss
(Sphagnum)*

*Pepper Berries
(Clelthra
alnifloia)*

*Pinecones
(Pinus)*

Pomegranate
(Punica granatum)

Poppy Pods
(Papaver orientale)

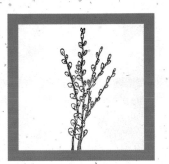

Pussy Willows
(Salix discolor)

River Birch Cones
(Betula)

Rosebuds
(Rosa)

Rose hips
(Rosa gallica)

Safflower
(Carthamus tinctorius)

Spanish Moss
(Tillandria usneoides)

Star Anise
(Pimpinella anisum)

Statice Sinuata
(Limonium sinuata)

Straw Flowers
(Helichrysum bracteatum)

Sunflower Seed Head
(Helianthus annus)

Sunflowers
(Helianthus)

Wheat Stem
(Triticum)

Wild Grass
(Gramineae)

Yarrow
(Achillea millefolium)

Helpful Hints ...

❧ When making dried floral arrangements, use styrofoam or floral foam that has been made for drieds. Foam that has been made for fresh floral arrangements will not work because it deteriorates easily and will not hold drieds permanently.

❧ When using deer moss, Oregon moss, or Spanish moss in dried floral arrangements, soak the moss in a bucket of water. This will make the moss soft and pliable and eliminate airborne particles.

❧ When using deer moss, Oregon moss, or Spanish moss in dried floral arrangements, allow some wisps of moss to show through for an enhanced look of nature.

❧ Garlic bulbs maintain their freshness for about three months. Once the garlic bulbs begin to turn lavender in color, it is time for them to be used. Simply remove the garlic bulbs from the dried arrangement and replace them with fresh ones.

❧ When using fresh fruits, dip them in lemon juice before drying to prevent the fruit from darkening in color.

❧ Before drying fragile flowers, greenery, grasses, grains, and pods, spray with a fixative such as hair spray to seal surfaces.

❧ When working with fresh flowers, cut stems at an angle with sharp scissors and immediately place in a bucket of cool water for several hours before using.

❧ When displaying fresh flowers, an aspirin added to the flower vase can prolong the life of the fresh flowers. It is recommended that the water in the flower vase be changed and another aspirin added every one or two days.

❧ Embellished candles are best used for decorative purposes only.

❧ Never allow a candle to burn lower than three inches of display height and never leave a candle unattended.

❧ After time, dried flowers begin to look dull and unnatural. When this happens, try steaming the dried flowers back to life.

❧ Small bird nests make fun decorative accessories. Place them on top of drapery rods, along window sills, and on top of doorways.

❧ Do not display potpourri on window sills as direct sunlight fades its color.

❧ When displaying potpourri, always keep out of reach of children and pets.

Candlelight ...

Pinecone Firestarters

Materials

- Pinecones
- Candle wax
- Candle dyes, optional
- Candle fragrance oils, optional
- Saucepan
- Tin can
- Pliers
- Salad tongs
- Waxed paper

Instructions

1. Melt wax according to instructions for Melting Wax on page 316. If desired, add candle dyes and fragrance oils.

2. Using salad tongs, dip pinecones upside-down into hot wax. Dip each pinecone twice.

3. Remove pinecones from hot wax and place on waxed paper to cool thoroughly.

4. A pine scent will enhance the aroma once the pinecones begin to burn. _Caution: If the pinecones are extremely dry, they will pop and crackle while they burn and will likely send out sparks._

Santa Sticks

Materials

- Cinnamon sticks
- Acrylic paints:
  Black
  Caucasian flesh
  Red
  White
- Paintbrush
- Raffia
- Straight pin

Instructions

1. Using a paintbrush, paint $1/2$" of one end of each cinnamon stick with Caucasian flesh acrylic paint for Santa's face.

2. Paint Santa's beard and hair with white.

3. Paint end of cinnamon stick with red for Santa's hat.

4. Using the head of a straight pin, dot Santa's eyes with black. Dot Santa's nose and cheeks with red. Dot a pompon on Santa's hat with white.

5. Allow paint to dry thoroughly after each step.

6. Repeat process for each cinnamon stick.

7. Gather Santa Sticks and tie raffia around center to secure bundle.

Pinecone Cupcake Firestarters

Materials

- Pinecones
- Candle wax
- Candle dyes, optional
- Candle fragrance oils, optional
- Embellishments, as desired
- Cupcake tin, non-stick
- Saucepan
- Tin can
- Pliers
- Salad tongs
- Waxed paper

Instructions

1. Melt wax according to instructions for Melting Wax on page 316. If desired, add candle dyes and fragrance oils.

2. Pour hot wax into cupcake tin, $2/3$ full.

3. Place one pinecone, facing up, in the center of each "cupcake" and push down into hot wax.

4. Place cupcake tin in refrigerator to cool for about one hour.

5. Remove cupcake tin from refrigerator and place in a cold water bath. This helps loosen wax around edges.

6. One at a time, pick up each "cupcake" by the bottom with salad tongs. Dip pinecones upside-down into hot wax. Dip each pinecone twice.

7. Remove pinecones from hot wax and place on waxed paper to cool thoroughly.

8. Embellish pinecone cupcakes as desired.

Molded Beehive Candle

Materials

- ❧ Beehive with bees candle mold
- ❧ Beeswax
- ❧ Candlewick
- ❧ Saucepan
- ❧ Tin can
- ❧ Pliers
- ❧ Waxed paper

Instructions

1. Melt wax according to instructions for Melting Wax on page 316.

2. Place candlewick in bottom of candle mold. Home-made candlewicks can be made according to instructions for Making & Using Candlewicks on page 317.

3. Pour hot wax into candle mold and hold onto end of candlewick until the wax sets enough that candlewick cannot sink back into the wax.

4. Allow wax to cool for about 15 minutes before removing candle from candle mold.

5. Remove candle from candle mold and place on waxed paper to cool thoroughly.

Pressed Flower Candle

Materials

- ❧ Candle: any size
- ❧ Pressed flowers
- ❧ Pressed greenery
- ❧ Tweezers
- ❧ Toothpick
- ❧ Craft glue
- ❧ Découpage glue
- ❧ Paintbrush

Instructions

1. Using tweezers, pick up pressed flowers and greenery.

2. Using a toothpick, apply craft glue to back sides of pressed flowers and greenery.

3. Carefully arrange pressed flowers and greenery on front of candle.

4. Allow glue to dry thoroughly.

5. Using a paintbrush, apply découpage glue over pressed flowers and greenery on front of candle according to manufacturer's directions.

Re-dipped Flower Candles

Materials

- Candles: any size
- Pressed flowers
- Pressed greenery
- Raffia, optional
- Tweezers
- Toothpick
- Craft glue
- Paraffin wax
- Saucepan
- Tin can
- Pliers
- Salad tongs
- Waxed paper

Instructions

1. Using tweezers, pick up pressed flowers and greenery.

2. Using a toothpick, apply craft glue to back sides of pressed flowers and greenery.

3. Carefully arrange pressed flowers and greenery on front of candles.

4. Allow glue to dry thoroughly.

5. Melt wax according to instructions for Melting Wax on page 316.

6. Dip embellished candles into hot wax according to instructions for Re-dipping Candles on page 317.

7. Using salad tongs, remove candles from hot wax and place on waxed paper to cool thoroughly.

8. If desired, tie raffia around candles and tie raffia in bows.

Re-dipped Cinnamon Candle

Materials

- Candle: any size
- Cinnamon sticks
- Raffia
- Toothpick
- Craft glue
- Paraffin wax
- Saucepan
- Tin can
- Pliers
- Salad tongs
- Waxed paper
- Scissors

Instructions

1. Break cinnamon sticks into uniform lengths.

2. Using a toothpick, apply craft glue to back sides of cinnamon sticks.

3. Carefully arrange cinnamon sticks around candle.

4. Allow glue to dry thoroughly.

5. Tie raffia around candle to secure cinnamon sticks.

6. Melt wax according to instructions for Melting Wax on page 316.

7. Dip embellished candle into hot wax according to instructions for Re-dipping Candles on page 317.

8. Using salad tongs, remove candle from hot wax and place on waxed paper to cool thoroughly.

9. Tie more raffia around candle.

10. Trim ends of raffia with scissors.

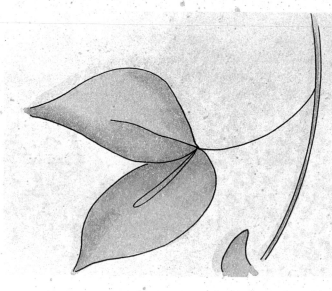

Re-dipped Bay Leaf Candle

Materials

- Candle: any size
- Bay leaves, dried
- Raffia
- Toothpick
- Craft glue
- Paraffin wax
- Saucepan
- Tin can
- Pliers
- Salad tongs
- Waxed paper
- Scissors

Instructions

1. Using a toothpick, apply craft glue to back sides of bay leaves.

2. Carefully arrange bay leaves around candle.

3. Allow glue to dry thoroughly.

4. Tie raffia around candle to secure bay leaves.

5. Melt wax according to instructions for Melting Wax on page 316.

6. Dip embellished candle into hot wax according to instructions for Re-dipping Candles on page 317.

7. Using salad tongs, remove candle from hot wax and place on waxed paper to cool thoroughly.

8. Tie more raffia around candle.

9. Trim ends of raffia with scissors.

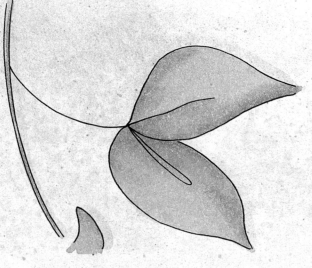

Log Candles

Materials

- ❧ Logs: any size
- ❧ Candle wax
- ❧ Candle dyes, optional
- ❧ Candle fragrance oils, optional
- ❧ Candlewicks
- ❧ Raffia or jute
- ❧ Saucepan
- ❧ Tin can
- ❧ Pliers
- ❧ Drill with 3" forstner bit

Instructions

1. Drill 3"-diameter holes in tops of logs with drill and forstner bit. The holes can be any depth desired, but it is recommended that the bottom 2" of logs remain undrilled. _Note: A forstner bit is a wide drill bit that makes a flat bottom if not allowed to penetrate through the entire log or piece of wood._

2. Melt wax according to instructions for Melting Wax on page 316. If desired, add candle dyes and fragrance oils.

3. Place candlewick in bottom of each drilled hole. Homemade candlewicks can be made according to instructions for Making & Using Candlewicks on page 317.

4. One at a time, pour hot wax into drilled hole of each log. Hold onto end of candlewick until the wax sets enough that candlewick cannot sink back into the wax.

5. Allow wax to cool thoroughly.

6. Tie raffia or jute around logs.

7. Tie raffia or jute in a bow.

Spiced Ornament Candle

Materials

- Candle: any size
- Ground cinnamon: 1 cup
- Ground cloves: 1 tablespoon
- Ground nutmeg: 1 tablespoon
- Applesauce: $3/4$ cup
- All-purpose glue: 2 tablespoons
- Water: $3/4$ to 1 cup
- Jute, waxed
- Toothpick
- Cookie cutter, heart-shaped
- Mixing bowl
- Wooden spoon
- Cookie sheet

Instructions

1. Make heart-shaped spiced ornaments according to instructions for Making Spiced Ornaments on page 321.

2. String heart-shaped spiced ornaments onto jute so they hang nicely.

3. Tie jute around candle.

Cinnamon & Jute Candle

Materials

- Candle: any size
- Cinnamon sticks
- Jute: 2-ply & 3-ply
- Craft glue

Instructions

1. Tie 2-ply jute around candle and tie knots at each end.

2. Break cinnamon sticks into various lengths.

3. Apply craft glue to cinnamon sticks and glue to 2-ply jute all the way around candle.

4. Allow glue to dry thoroughly.

5. Tie 3-ply jute around candle to secure cinnamon sticks.

6. Tie 3-ply jute in a bow and tie knots at each end.

Cupcake Candles

Materials

- ❦ Cedar chips
- ❦ Potpourri
- ❦ Rosebuds & rose petals, dried
- ❦ Orange slices, dried
- ❦ Candle wax
- ❦ Candle dyes, optional
- ❦ Candle fragrance oils, optional
- ❦ Candlewicks
- ❦ Cupcake tin, non-stick
- ❦ Saucepan
- ❦ Tin can
- ❦ Pliers
- ❦ Waxed paper

Instructions

1. Melt wax according to instructions for Melting Wax on page 316. If desired, add candle dyes and fragrance oils.

2. Fill cupcake tin ¹/₃ full with cedar chips, potpourri, rosebuds and rose petals, or orange slices.

3. Place candlewick in bottom of each "cupcake." Homemade candlewicks can be made according to instructions for Making & Using Candlewicks on page 317.

4. Pour hot wax into cupcake tin until full. Hold onto end of each candlewick until the wax sets enough that candlewick cannot sink back into the wax.

5. Place cupcake tin in refrigerator to cool for about one hour.

6. Remove cupcake tin from refrigerator and place in a cold water bath. This helps loosen wax around edges.

7. Carefully remove candles from cupcake tin.

8. Cupcake candles are generally used as firestarters. See Pinecone Cupcake Firestarters on page 329.

336

Woodland Candle Box

Materials

- ❧ Candle: 8" high
- ❧ Papier-mâché box with lid, hexagon: 6"-diameter
- ❧ Styrofoam block: 4"-square x 3"-thick
- ❧ Oregon moss
- ❧ Pomegranate, dried
- ❧ Poppy pods, dried
- ❧ Nuts, assorted
- ❧ Pinecones
- ❧ Cinnamon sticks: 12"-long (8)
- ❧ Grapevine wreath: 3"-diameter
- ❧ Jute: 3-ply
- ❧ Spray stain, green
- ❧ Craft glue

Instructions

1. Spray papier-mâché box and lid with spray stain.

2. Allow spray stain to dry thoroughly.

3. Place lid on bottom of box.

4. Tie jute around sides of box and lid to secure lid to box.

5. Apply craft glue to bottom of candle and glue into one corner of box.

6. Apply craft glue to bottom of styrofoam block and glue into box next to candle.

7. Allow glue to dry thoroughly.

8. Apply craft glue to top and sides of styrofoam block and glue Oregon moss around it.

9. Apply craft glue to the pomegranate, poppy pods, nuts, pinecones, and cinnamon sticks.

10. Carefully arrange the pomegranate, poppy pods, nuts, pinecones, and cinnamon sticks on styrofoam block and inside box around candle.

11. Apply craft glue to grapevine wreath and glue into box next to candle.

12. Allow glue to dry thoroughly.

13. Tie three jute bows and randomly tie knots in tails.

14. Using craft glue, glue bows into center of arrangement.

15. Allow glue to dry thoroughly.

Gift Candles

Materials

- Tapered candles: 12" (2)
- Orange slices, dried
- Straw flowers
- Raffia
- Tissue paper
- Cardboard: 3" x 14"
- Craft glue

Instructions

1. Tear edges of tissue paper.

2. One at a time, roll centers of candles in tissue paper.

3. Place wrapped candles on cardboard.

4. Apply craft glue to orange slices and straw flowers.

5. Carefully arrange orange slices and straw flowers on front of wrapped candles.

6. Allow glue to dry thoroughly.

7. Tie raffia around cardboard, candles, and orange slices.

8. Tie raffia in a bow.

338

Dried Flowers ...

Dried Sunflower Basket

Photograph on page 35.

Materials

- ❦ Decorative basket
- ❦ Sunflowers, dried
- ❦ Yarrow, dried
- ❦ Larkspur, dried
- ❦ Nigella, dried
- ❦ Poppy pods, dried
- ❦ Eucalyptus, silver dollar
- ❦ Lemon leaves, dried
- ❦ Spanish moss
- ❦ Raffia
- ❦ Floral foam for drieds, to fit inside basket
- ❦ Floral pins
- ❦ Copper wire: 19-gauge
- ❦ Watering can, tin: miniature
- ❦ Hot glue gun & glue sticks

Instructions

1. Place floral foam inside basket, making certain it fits tightly all the way around the edges.

2. Using floral pins, cover floral foam with Spanish moss until it is completely covered.

3. Beginning with the largest flowers, carefully arrange sunflowers, yarrow, larkspur, nigella, poppy pods, eucalyptus, and lemon leaves in basket in a triangular shape. Push dried flowers and greenery into floral foam. Make certain the arrangement is even on both sides.

4. Tie raffia in a bow.

5. Using hot glue gun and glue sticks, hot-glue bow to side of basket.

6. Form a copper wire loop and thread it through handle of watering can.

7. Twist copper wire at top to secure, leaving a two-inch long tail.

8. Push copper wire tail into floral foam, hanging watering can on top of raffia bow.

Christmas Corsage

Materials

- ❦ Pine garland: 8" length
- ❦ Licopodium
- ❦ Globe amaranth, dried
- ❦ Cockscomb, dried
- ❦ River birch cones
- ❦ Hot glue gun & glue sticks
- ❦ Corsage pin

Instructions

1. Using pine garland, form a tight circle. Twist tightly to make a base for the corsage.

2. Using hot glue gun and glue sticks, hot-glue licopodium to pine garland base.

3. Carefully arrange and hot-glue cockscomb, globe amaranth, and river birch cones on top of licopodium.

4. Pin to garment with a corsage pin.

Kissing Ball

Materials

- ❦ Globe amaranth, dried
- ❦ Nigella, dried
- ❦ Safflowers, dried
- ❦ Cedar roses
- ❦ Oregon moss
- ❦ Styrofoam ball: 3"-diameter
- ❦ Wired ribbon, 1"-wide, purple
- ❦ Floral wire
- ❦ Corsage pin
- ❦ Craft glue
- ❦ Hot glue gun & glue sticks
- ❦ Scissors

Instructions

1. Apply craft glue to styrofoam ball and glue Oregon moss around it until it is completely covered.

2. Allow glue to dry thoroughly.

3. Tie wired ribbon in a bow according to instructions for Making Multi-Loop Bows on page 320.

4. Using hot glue gun and glue sticks, hot-glue bow to top of styrofoam ball. Cascade ribbon tails over styrofoam ball and hot-glue in place.

5. Carefully arrange and hot-glue globe amaranth, nigella, safflowers, and cedar roses, evenly, around styrofoam ball on top of Oregon moss.

6. Cut wired ribbon into one 12" length with scissors. Fold wired ribbon in half. Tie loose ends of wired ribbon in a knot. Attach knotted end to center top of styrofoam ball with a corsage pin to make a loop for hanging.

Fantasy Ball

Materials

- ❦ Rosebuds, dried
- ❦ Straw flowers
- ❦ Eucalyptus (4)
- ❦ Statice sinuata
- ❦ Pepper berries, dried
- ❦ Pinecones
- ❦ Styrofoam ball: 12$\frac{1}{2}$"-diameter
- ❦ Paper ribbon, 3"-wide, tan
- ❦ Wired ribbon, $\frac{5}{8}$"-wide, pink iridescent
- ❦ Floral wire
- ❦ Corsage pin
- ❦ Découpage glue
- ❦ Paintbrush
- ❦ Hot glue gun & glue sticks
- ❦ Scissors

Instructions

1. Unravel paper ribbon. Cut into three 12$\frac{1}{2}$" lengths with scissors.

2. Cut wired ribbon into two 42" lengths and one 12" length with scissors.

3. Cut eucalyptus into one 10" length and three 6" lengths with scissors.

4. Beginning and ending at the center, wrap one 12$\frac{1}{2}$" length of paper ribbon around styrofoam ball. Repeat process for two remaining 12$\frac{1}{2}$" lengths of paper ribbon, overlapping previous ribbon and completely covering styrofoam ball.

5. Using a paintbrush, apply découpage glue over paper ribbon according to manufacturer's directions.

6. Unravel more paper ribbon and tie in a bow according to instructions for Making Multi-Loop Bows on page 320.

7. Using hot glue gun and glue sticks, hot-glue bow to top of styrofoam ball. Cascade ribbon tails over styrofoam ball and hot-glue in place.

8. Hot-glue 10" length of eucalyptus to top center of styrofoam ball so it hangs freely and curves down one side. Hot-glue all three 6" lengths of eucalyptus, evenly, to top center of styrofoam ball.

9. Carefully arrange and hot-glue straw flowers, statice sinuata, and pepper berries to styrofoam ball as desired.

10. Tie wired ribbon in two bows according to instructions for Making Multi-Loop Bows on page 320. Form ten 1$\frac{1}{2}$" loops from each 42" length of wired ribbon, leaving six-inch tails, and secure with floral wire.

11. Using hot glue gun and glue sticks, hot-glue one bow to each side of paper ribbon bow. Cascade ribbon tails down and hot-glue in place.

12. Hot-glue one rosebud and one pinecone into center of paper ribbon bow.

13. Carefully arrange and hot-glue remaining rosebuds and pinecones to styrofoam ball as desired.

14. Fold 12" length of wired ribbon in half. Attach center to top of styrofoam ball with a corsage pin. Tie loose ends of wired ribbon in a knot, leaving two-inch tails, to make a loop for hanging.

Dried Pansy Lampshade

Materials

- ❦ Pansies, dried
- ❦ Spray paint, lavender
- ❦ Tweezers
- ❦ Toothpick
- ❦ Craft glue
- ❦ Lamp with lampshade

Instructions

1. Dry pansies according to instructions for Drying Flowers and Leaves with Silica Gel on page 313.

2. Lightly spray lampshade with lavender spray paint.

3. Allow spray paint to dry thoroughly.

4. Using tweezers, pick up pansies.

5. Using a toothpick, apply craft glue to back sides of pansies.

6. Carefully arrange pansies around lampshade, overlapping petals as desired.

7. Allow glue to dry thoroughly.

Dried Wreath of Many Colors

Materials

- Grapevine wreath
- Eucalyptus
- Yarrow, dried
- Ammobium, dried
- Larkspur, dried
- Lantern pods, dried
- Straw flowers
- Caspia
- German statice
- Statice sinuata
- Pepper berries, dried
- Licopodium
- Fern, dried
- Raffia
- Hot glue gun & glue sticks

Instructions

1. Using hot glue gun and glue sticks, hot-glue eucalyptus, evenly, around outer edge of wreath.

2. Carefully arrange and hot-glue yarrow, evenly, around wreath.

3. Tie several raffia bows.

4. Using hot glue gun and glue sticks, hot-glue bows around wreath.

5. Hot-glue ammobium, larkspur, lantern pods, straw flowers, caspia, German statice, statice sinuata, pepper berries, licopodium, and fern around wreath until it is completely covered.

6. Hot-glue several strands of raffia to lower right hand corner of wreath.

Acorn & Pinecone Wreath

Materials

- Grapevine wreath
- Eucalyptus
- Yarrow, dried
- Acorns
- Pinecones
- Lantern pods, dried
- Oak leaves, dried
- Licopodium
- Raffia
- Acrylic spray, gloss
- Hot glue gun & glue sticks

Instructions

1. Using hot glue gun and glue sticks, hot-glue eucalyptus, diagonally, around outer edge of wreath.

2. Carefully arrange and hot-glue yarrow, evenly, around wreath.

3. Hot-glue acorns, pinecones, lantern pods, oak leaves, and licopodium around wreath until it is completely covered.

4. Spray wreath with acrylic spray.

5. Allow acrylic spray to dry thoroughly.

6. Tie raffia in a bow.

7. Using hot glue gun and glue sticks, hot-glue bow to lower left hand corner of wreath.

House of Dried Flowers

Materials

- Shadow box, house-shaped
- Poppy pods, dried
- Rosebuds, dried
- Roses, dried
- Globe amaranth, dried
- Statice sinuata
- Pepper berries, dried
- Oregon moss
- Deer moss
- Tree bark
- Hot glue gun & glue sticks

Instructions

1. Using hot glue gun and glue sticks, hot-glue tree bark to shadow box for roofs.

2. Randomly hot-glue deer moss on sections of roofs.

3. Hot-glue Oregon moss into each section of shadow box.

4. Carefully arrange and hot-glue poppy pods, rosebuds, roses, globe amaranth, statice sinuata, and pepper berries into shadow box on top of Oregon moss.

Rosebud Potpourri

Materials

- Ammobium, dried: 1 cup
- Cedar tips, dried: 1 cup
- Corn flowers, dried: 2 cups
- Globe amaranth, dried: 1 cup
- Lavender, dried: 4 cups
- Lemon grass, dried: 1 cup crushed
- Orris root, dried: 2 tablespoons
- Pepper berries, dried: 1 cup
- River birch cones: 1 cup
- Rosebuds, dried: 1 cup
- Rose hips, dried: 1 cup
- Rose petals, dried: 2 cups crushed
- Star anise, dried: 1 cup
- Fragrance oils: lavender, 1 ounce; rose essence, 1 ounce
- Container

Instructions

1. Mix all ingredients together in container with hands.

2. As fragrance dissipates, add more fragrance oils to dried mixture.

3. Keep out of direct sunlight as potpourri will fade.

Rosebud Potpourri Birdhouse

Materials

- ❧ Birdhouse on wooden dowel with base
- ❧ Rosebud potpourri
- ❧ Lavender, dried
- ❧ Acrylic paint, pink
- ❧ Paintbrush
- ❧ Wired ribbon, 1"-wide, silver-lavender ombré
- ❧ Floral wire
- ❧ Craft glue
- ❧ Hot glue gun & glue sticks
- ❧ Scissors

Instructions

1. Using a paintbrush, paint birdhouse, wooden dowel, and base with pink acrylic paint.

2. Allow paint to dry thoroughly.

3. Apply craft glue to roof of birdhouse and glue rosebud potpourri on it until it is completely covered. See Rosebud Potpourri on page 347.

4. Apply craft glue to base of birdhouse and glue rosebud potpourri on it until it is completely covered.

5. Allow glue to dry thoroughly.

6. Apply craft glue to front of birdhouse and glue lavender on it until it is completely covered.

7. Allow glue to dry thoroughly.

8. Tie wired ribbon in a bow according to instructions for Making Multi-Loop Bows on page 320.

9. Using hot glue gun and glue sticks, hot-glue bow to top of wooden dowel just below birdhouse. Cascade ribbon tails down each side.

Rosebud Bird's Nest

Materials

- ❧ Spanish moss
- ❧ Leaves, dried
- ❧ Twigs
- ❧ Oregon moss
- ❧ Rosebuds, dried
- ❧ Caspia
- ❧ Wired ribbon, ³⁄₄"-wide, lavender iridescent
- ❧ Floral wire
- ❧ Acrylic spray, matte
- ❧ Adhesive spray
- ❧ Craft glue
- ❧ Hot glue gun & glue sticks
- ❧ Scissors

Instructions

1. Make bird's nest according to instructions for Making Bird Nests on page 318.

2. Using three twigs, form a teardrop. Wire at top with floral wire to secure.

3. Apply craft glue to top of teardrop and glue Oregon moss on it.

4. Apply craft glue to bottom of bird's nest and glue to bottom of teardrop.

5. Allow glue to dry thoroughly.

6. Using hot glue gun and glue sticks, hot-glue rosebuds and caspia on top of Oregon moss and on each side of bird's nest, adding more rosebuds to one side of bird's nest than the other.

7. Tie wired ribbon in a bow according to instructions for Making Multi-Loop Bows on page 320.

8. Using hot glue gun and glue sticks, hot-glue bow at top of teardrop. Cascade ribbon tails down each side and hot-glue in place.

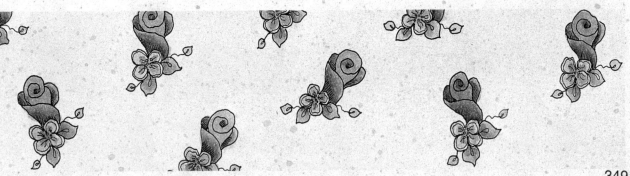

Rosebud Topiary

Materials

- ❧ Oregon moss
- ❧ Rosebuds, dried
- ❧ Cinnamon stick: 8"-long
- ❧ Styrofoam balls: 2$\frac{1}{2}$"-diameter; 3"-diameter
- ❧ Creamer & saucer
- ❧ Wired ribbon, $\frac{5}{8}$"-wide, lavender
- ❧ Floral wire
- ❧ Craft glue
- ❧ Hot glue gun & glue sticks
- ❧ Scissors

Instructions

1. Using hot glue gun and glue sticks, hot-glue 3"-diameter styrofoam ball into creamer.

2. Push cinnamon stick into center of styrofoam ball.

3. Push 2$\frac{1}{2}$"-diameter styrofoam ball on top of cinnamon stick.

4. Apply craft glue to styrofoam balls and glue Oregon moss around them until both are completely covered.

5. Allow glue to dry thoroughly.

6. Using hot glue gun and glue sticks, hot-glue rosebuds to moss-covered styrofoam ball at top of cinnamon stick until it is completely covered.

7. Tie wired ribbon in a bow according to instructions for *Making Multi-Loop Bows* on page 320.

8. Using hot glue gun and glue sticks, hot-glue bow to top of cinnamon stick just below styrofoam ball. Cascade ribbon tails down and hot-glue in place.

9. Hot-glue creamer to saucer.

Rosebud Lampshade

Materials

- ❧ Lamp shade, natural paper
- ❧ Spray stain, oak
- ❧ Spanish moss
- ❧ Leaves, dried
- ❧ Twigs
- ❧ Rosebuds, dried
- ❧ Rose leaves, dried
- ❧ Heather
- ❧ Cording, plum
- ❧ Acrylic spray, matte
- ❧ Adhesive spray
- ❧ Hot glue gun & glue sticks

Instructions

1. Make bird's nest according to instructions for *Making Bird Nests* on page 318.

2. Lightly spray edges of lamp shade with spray stain.

3. Allow spray stain to dry thoroughly.

4. Gather heather and tie cording around center to secure bundle.

5. Tie cording in a bow.

6. Using hot glue gun and glue sticks, hot-glue heather bundle to front of lamp shade at an angle.

7. Hot-glue bird's nest on top of heather bundle.

8. Carefully arrange rosebuds and rose leaves on heather and hot-glue in place.

Rosebud Box Lid

Materials

- ❧ Papier-mâché box with lid, hexagon
- ❧ Corrugated paper
- ❧ Oregon moss
- ❧ Rosebuds, dried
- ❧ Craft glue

Instructions

1. Apply craft glue to edges of box lid and glue corrugated paper around it. Apply craft glue to top of box lid and glue Oregon moss on it until it is completely covered.

2. Apply craft glue to rosebuds.

3. Carefully arrange rosebuds on top of Oregon moss.

4. Allow glue to dry thoroughly.

Rosebud & Ribbon Wooden Eggs

Materials

- ❧ Wooden eggs
- ❧ Acrylic paints
- ❧ Paintbrush
- ❧ Toothbrush
- ❧ Foam plate
- ❧ Acrylic spray, gloss
- ❧ Rosebuds, dried
- ❧ Licopodium
- ❧ Mesh ribbon
- ❧ Toothpick
- ❧ Craft glue
- ❧ Spanish moss, optional
- ❧ Decorative egg carton, optional

Instructions

1. Paint wooden eggs according to instructions for Painting Wooden Eggs on page 319.

2. Tie mesh ribbon around each egg and glue with craft glue to secure.

3. Allow glue to dry thoroughly.

4. Using a toothpick, apply craft glue to back sides of rosebuds and licopodium.

5. Carefully arrange rosebuds and licopodium on front of eggs on top of lace.

6. Allow glue to dry thoroughly.

7. If desired, make one dozen rosebud and lace wooden eggs and display in a decorative egg carton. Spanish moss can be added in the bottom of each "egg cup" to enhance the beauty of the painted and embellished eggs.

Fresh Flowers ...

Roses in a Moss Vase

Photograph on page 353.

Materials

- Roses, fresh
- Baby's breath, fresh
- Spiral picks
- Oregon moss
- Decorative charm
- Mesh ribbon, 2"-wide, gold
- Poster board, green
- Vase, round
- Craft glue
- Hot glue gun & glue sticks
- Pencil
- Measuring tape
- Stapler & staples
- Scissors

Instructions

1. Measure vase height and the circumference around vase with measuring tape.

2. Using a pencil, draw a pattern on poster board using the dimensions plus 1" added to length.

3. Cut out pattern with scissors.

4. Arrange roses, baby's breath, and spiral picks inside vase.

5. Apply craft glue to poster board pattern and cover with Oregon moss until it is completely covered.

6. Allow glue to dry thoroughly.

7. Place poster board around vase, overlapping one inch, and staple to secure.

8. Place vase with fresh flower arrangement inside moss-covered "tube."

9. Tie mesh ribbon around moss-covered tube and tie in a bow.

10. Using hot glue gun and glue sticks, hot-glue ribbon and bow to secure. Cascade ribbon tails down and hot-glue in place.

11. Hot-glue decorative charm to front of moss-covered tube just below center of bow.

Curtain Tie Back

Materials

- Freesia stems, fresh
- Fern stems, fresh
- Baby's breath, fresh
- Sheer ribbon, 3"-wide
- Floral wire
- Corsage pins
- Scissors

Instructions

1. Gather fern stems together and hold tightly around bottom.

2. Gather baby's breath and place on top of fern stems.

3. Place freesia stems on top of baby's breath and cut stems to about 10 inches.

4. Wrap floral wire around bottom of stems to secure bundle.

5. Tie sheer ribbon in a bow according to instructions for Making Multi-Loop Bows on page 320.

6. Wire bow around fresh flower bundle.

7. Pin arrangement to curtain with corsage pins.

8. Note: This tie back will stay fresh for no longer than six to eight hours; it is recommended that this tie back be assembled one hour prior to displaying.

Rose Wreath

Materials

- Roses, fresh
  pink (12)
  purple (12)
  yellow (12)
- Tulips, fresh (6)
- Freesia stems,
  fresh (6)
- Ivy stems,
  fresh (2)
- Fern stems,
  fresh (2)
- Foam floral
  wreath,
  8"-diameter
- Floral preservative:
  1 tablespoon
- Leather gloves
- Pan, shallow
- Pruning shears

Instructions

1. Fill pan with cold water and add floral preservative.

2. Place foam floral wreath into pan of cold water.

3. Wearing leather gloves, clip rose stems to about 2" in length with pruning shears.

4. Remove foam floral wreath from pan of cold water and place on a flat working surface.

5. Beginning on the inside edge, firmly push roses into wet foam floral wreath.

6. Repeat process until all roses have been placed evenly around wreath.

7. Repeat process for remaining fresh flowers and greenery until all have been used and the wreath is completely covered.

8. *Note: This wreath will stay fresh for no longer than one day; it is recommended that this wreath be assembled one hour prior to displaying.*

*Of all the wonderful things
in the wonderful Universe of God,
nothing seems to me more surprising*

than the planting of a seed in the Earth and the blessings thereof.

— *Adapted from Celia Thaxter, An Island Garden*

Flowers in Fresh Fruit Vases

Materials

- ❧ Flowers, fresh
- ❧ Vases, transparent
- ❧ Limes, fresh
- ❧ Lemons, fresh
- ❧ Oranges, fresh
- ❧ Slicer
- ❧ Kettle

Instructions

1. Slice limes, lemons, and oranges with a slicer into a kettle of cold water.

2. Rinse each slice to remove acid and pulp.

3. Fill vases half full of fresh, cold water.

4. Add some lime, lemon, and orange slices to vases.

5. Arrange fresh flowers inside vases as desired.

6. Add remaining lime, lemon, and orange slices to vases, around arrangements.

7. Fill vases with cold water.

Fresh Flowers Displayed in a Clay Pot & Matching Chair

Materials

- Flowers, fresh
- Vase
- Clay pot
- Wooden chair
- Acrylic paints
- Paintbrush

Instructions

1. Paint clay pot and wooden chair to match with acrylic paints.

2. Allow paints to dry thoroughly.

3. Fill vase ⅔ full with cold water.

4. Arrange fresh flowers inside vase as desired.

5. Place vase inside clay pot.

6. Hang wooden chair on wall, upside-down.

7. Place clay pot containing fresh flower arrangement into the bottom of the wooden chair.

Beans & Seeds ...

Citrus & Sunflowers in a Jar Full of Beans

Materials

- Canning jar: two-quart
- Chile beans: to fill jar
- Sunflowers, dried
- Orange slices, dried
- Garlic bulbs (6)
- Leather fern, dried
- Lemon leaves, dried
- Spanish moss
- Curly willow twigs
- Cinnamon sticks: 12"-long (4)
- Wooden dowels: $1/8$"-diameter, 12"-long (12); $1/4$"-diameter, 12"-long (6)
- Styrofoam ball: 3"-diameter
- Raffia
- Birdhouse on wooden dowel, prepainted
- Coffee pot lid
- Wired ribbon, $2^1/4$"-wide, blue checkered
- Floral wire
- Floral tape, white
- Craft glue
- Hot glue gun & glue sticks
- Scissors

Instructions

1. Fill jar with chile beans.

2. Using hot glue gun and glue sticks, hot-glue styrofoam ball into jar.

3. Apply craft glue to styrofoam ball and glue Spanish moss around it until it is completely covered. Allow some Spanish moss to hang down sides of jar.

4. Push twigs into styrofoam ball.

5. Allow glue to dry thoroughly.

6. Carefully arrange sunflowers, leather fern, and lemon leaves on styrofoam ball. Push sunflowers, leather fern, and lemon leaves into styrofoam ball.

7. Using floral tape, wrap all wooden dowels.

8. Insert $1/4$"-diameter wooden dowels into bottoms of garlic bulbs.

9. Using hot glue gun and glue sticks, hot-glue orange slices to $1/8$"-diameter wooden dowels.

10. Push wooden dowels with garlic bulbs and orange slices on them into styrofoam ball.

11. Braid several strands of raffia and tie knots at each end.

12. Tie raffia braid around neck of jar.

13. Fray ends of raffia.

14. Tie wired ribbon in a bow according to instructions for Making Multi-Loop Bows on page 320.

15. Using hot glue gun and glue sticks, hot-glue bow to right hand side of jar just below neck. Cascade ribbon tails down and hot-glue in place.

16. Position raffia braid on right hand side of jar in center of bow.

17. Gather cinnamon sticks and tie raffia around center to secure bundle.

18. Using hot glue gun and glue sticks, hot-glue cinnamon sticks into side of arrangement.

19. Hot-glue coffee pot lid on top of cinnamon sticks.

20. Push birdhouse on wooden dowel into center of arrangement.

21. Fill hole in front of birdhouse with Spanish moss.

Pinecone & Sunflower Seed Star Ornament

Materials

- Pinecones (5)
- Sunflower seeds (5)
- Pecan
- Mustard seeds
- Jute, waxed
- Cardboard
- Craft glue
- Hot glue gun & glue sticks
- Scissors

Instructions

1. Cut a 1"-diameter cardboard circle with scissors.

2. Using hot glue gun and glue sticks, hot-glue pinecones to outside of cardboard circle to form a star.

3. Hot-glue pecan to cardboard circle inside center of pinecone star.

4. Hot-glue sunflower seeds on top of pinecones to form a star.

5. Apply craft glue to pecan and cover with mustard seeds.

6. Allow glue to dry thoroughly.

7. Attach jute for hanging.

Cinnamon Stick & Fennel Seed Star Ornament

Materials

- Papier-mâché star
- Cinnamon sticks
- Pinecones: tiny
- Fennel seeds
- Jute, waxed
- Craft glue

Instructions

1. Apply craft glue to top of papier-mâché star.

2. Carefully arrange cinnamon sticks around outside edges of star, breaking cinnamon sticks into various lengths as necessary.

3. Allow glue to dry thoroughly.

4. Apply craft glue to top of papier-mâché star.

5. Carefully arrange pinecones around inside edge of cinnamon sticks. Cover remaining area with fennel seeds.

6. Allow glue to dry thoroughly.

7. Attach jute for hanging.

Lima Bean Birdhouse

Materials

- Birdhouse with one or more openings
- Leaves, dried
- Berries, dried
- Twigs
- Lima beans
- Wooden hearts
- Craft glue

Instructions

1. Crumble leaves.

2. Apply craft glue around and inside opening(s) on birdhouse.

3. Carefully sprinkle crumbled leaves around and inside opening(s) on birdhouse.

4. Glue berries, twigs, and lima beans in or near opening(s) on birdhouse.

5. Glue wooden hearts on birdhouse as desired.

6. Allow glue to dry thoroughly.

Sunflower Seed & Barbed Wire Hanger

Materials

- ❦ Sunflower seed head, dried
- ❦ Nuts, assorted
- ❦ Pinecones
- ❦ Cinnamon sticks
- ❦ Log slab
- ❦ Barbed wire
- ❦ Hammer
- ❦ Nails
- ❦ Craft glue
- ❦ Hot glue gun & glue sticks

Instructions

1. Bend barbed wire and nail to sides of log slab to make a handle for hanging.

2. Apply craft glue to back side of sunflower seed head and glue to top of log slab, centered.

3. Allow glue to dry thoroughly.

4. Carefully arrange nuts, pinecones, and cinnamon sticks around right side of sunflower seed head.

5. Using hot glue gun and glue sticks, hot-glue nuts, pinecones, and cinnamon sticks in place.

Fruits & Nuts ...

Dried Fruit in a Jar

Photograph on page 69.

Materials

- Jar with cork
- Currants, dried
- Pineapple, dried
- Dates, dried
- Golden raisins
- Cranberries, dried
- Licopodium
- Cedar rose
- Pinecones
- Raffia
- Cording, gold
- Hot glue gun & glue sticks

Instructions

1. Layer dried fruit in jar as desired.

2. Place cork on jar.

3. Tie raffia around jar just below cork.

4. Tie raffia in a bow.

5. Carefully arrange and hot-glue licopodium, cedar rose, and pinecones on top of raffia bow.

6. Tie cording in a bow and hot-glue into center of arrangement on top of raffia bow.

Woodland Potpourri

Not Photographed

Materials

- Acorns & acorn hulls
- Bay leaves, dried
- Nuts, assorted
- Pinecones
- Pomegranates, dried
- Poppy pods, dried
- River birch cones
- Rose hips, dried
- Fragrance oil: potpourri, 1 ounce
- Container

Instructions

1. Mix all ingredients together in container with hands.

2. As fragrance dissipates, add more fragrance oil to dried mixture.

3. If desired, display a seed pomander on top of potpourri or tie a few cinnamon sticks together with raffia and place on top of potpourri.

Citrus & Spice Potpourri

Materials

- Cinnamon sticks, broken: 2 cups
- Grapefruit slices, dried: 1 cup
- Calendula, dried: 1 cup
- Orange rind
- Orange slices, dried: 1 cup
- Orris root, dried: 1 tablespoon
- River birch cones: 1 cup
- Rose hips, dried: 1 cup
- Spiced ornaments, heart-shaped & star-shaped
- Star anise, dried: 1 cup
- Fragrance oil: tangerine, 1 ounce
- Cookie cutters, heart-shaped & star-shaped
- Container

Instructions

1. Make heart- and star-shaped spiced ornaments according to instructions for Making Spiced Ornaments on page 15.

2. Using a star-shaped cookie cutter, cut stars from orange rind.

3. Allow orange rind stars to dry thoroughly.

4. Mix all ingredients together in container with hands.

5. As fragrance dissipates, add more fragrance oil to dried mixture.

Citrus & Spice Potpourri in a Jar

Materials

- Jar with cork
- Pressed flowers
- Pressed greenery
- Cinnamon stick
- Orange slice, dried
- Citrus & spice potpourri
- Raffia
- Ground cinnamon: 1 cup
- Ground cloves: 1 tablespoon
- Ground nutmeg: 1 tablespoon
- Applesauce: $3/4$ cup
- All-purpose glue: 2 tablespoons
- Water: $3/4$ to 1 cup
- Jute, waxed
- Tweezers
- Toothpick
- Craft glue
- Découpage glue
- Paintbrush
- Cookie cutter, heart-shaped
- Mixing bowl
- Wooden spoon
- Cookie sheet

Instructions

1. Fill jar with citrus and spice potpourri. See Citrus and Spice Potpourri on page 366.

2. Make heart-shaped spiced ornaments according to instructions for Making Spiced Ornaments on page 321.

3. String heart-shaped spiced ornaments onto jute so they hang nicely.

4. Place cork on jar. Photograph shows cork removed from jar to show details.

5. Tie raffia around jar just below cork.

6. Place a cinnamon stick in the center and tie raffia in a bow.

7. Hang heart-shaped spiced ornaments from raffia bow.

8. Apply craft glue to back side of orange slice.

9. Carefully arrange orange slice on top of raffia bow.

10. Allow glue to dry thoroughly.

11. Using tweezers, pick up pressed flowers and greenery.

12. Using a toothpick, apply craft glue to back sides of pressed flowers and greenery.

13. Carefully arrange pressed flowers and greenery on top of cork.

14. Allow glue to dry thoroughly.

15. Using a paintbrush, apply découpage glue over pressed flowers and greenery on top of cork according to manufacturer's directions.

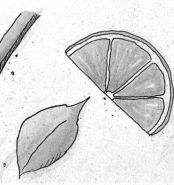

Apples & Juniper Berries in a Crate

Materials

- ❦ Wooden crate, oblong
- ❦ Nigella, dried
- ❦ Apple slices, dried
- ❦ Juniper berries, dried
- ❦ Lantern pods, dried
- ❦ Cinnamon sticks
- ❦ Oregon moss
- ❦ Hot glue gun & glue sticks

Instructions

1. Break cinnamon sticks into uniform lengths.

2. Using hot glue gun and glue sticks, hot-glue Oregon moss into bottom of wooden crate.

3. Carefully arrange and hot-glue nigella around outside edges of wooden crate on top of Oregon moss.

4. Hot-glue apple slices in a border inside nigella, followed by cinnamon sticks and juniper berries. Hot-glue lantern pods into center of juniper berry border.

Apples & Rosebuds in a Basket

Materials

- ❧ Twig basket
- ❧ Apple slices, dried
- ❧ Rosebuds, dried
- ❧ Rose leaves, dried
- ❧ Twigs
- ❧ Baby's breath, dried
- ❧ Oregon moss
- ❧ Floral foam for drieds, to fit inside basket
- ❧ Floral pins
- ❧ Wired ribbon, 1"-wide, red-yellow ombré
- ❧ Floral wire
- ❧ Hot glue gun & glue sticks
- ❧ Scissors

Instructions

1. Place floral foam inside basket, making certain it fits tightly all the way around the edges.

2. Using floral pins, cover floral foam with Oregon moss until it is completely covered.

3. Using hot glue gun and glue sticks, hot-glue rosebuds, rose leaves, and baby's breath into basket.

4. Hot-glue apple slices around edges of basket and into center of arrangement.

5. Push twigs into floral foam.

6. Tie wired ribbon in a bow according to instructions for Making Multi-Loop Bows on page 320.

7. Using hot glue gun and glue sticks, hot-glue bow to top of basket. Cascade ribbon tails down each side and hot-glue in place.

Apples & Cinnamon Sticks

Materials

- Apple slices, dried
- Ammobium, dried
- Statice sinuata
- Cinnamon sticks
- Ground cinnamon: 1 cup
- Ground cloves: 1 tablespoon
- Ground nutmeg: 1 tablespoon
- Applesauce: $^3/_4$ cup
- All-purpose glue: 2 tablespoons
- Water: $^3/_4$ to 1 cup
- Wired ribbon, $^3/_4$"-wide, blue-green ombré
- Floral wire
- Jute, waxed
- Toothpick
- Cookie cutter, heart-shaped
- Mixing bowl
- Wooden spoon
- Cookie sheet
- Hot glue gun & glue sticks
- Scissors

Instructions

1. Make heart-shaped spiced ornaments according to instructions for Making Spiced Ornaments on page 321.

2. Gather cinnamon sticks and tie jute around center to secure bundle.

3. Tie wired ribbon in a bow according to instructions for Making Multi-Loop Bows on page 320.

4. Using hot glue gun and glue sticks, hot-glue bow centered on top of cinnamon sticks.

5. Carefully arrange and hot-glue statice sinuata and ammo-bium on top of cinnamon sticks on each side of bow. Make certain the arrangement is even on both sides.

6. Hot-glue apple slices into center of arrangement just above bow.

7. String heart-shaped spiced ornaments onto jute so they hang nicely.

8. Using hot glue gun and glue sticks, hot-glue spiced ornaments into center of arrangement on top of wired-ribbon bow.

Apples & Garlic in a Salt Shaker

Materials

- Salt shaker with lid
- Apple slices, dried
- Garlic bulb
- Ammobium, dried
- Poppy pods, dried
- Myrtle leaves, dried
- Oregon moss
- Cinnamon sticks
- Ground cinnamon: 1 cup
- Ground cloves: 1 tablespoon
- Ground nutmeg: 1 tablespoon
- Applesauce: ³/₄ cup
- All-purpose glue: 2 tablespoons
- Water: ³/₄ to 1 cup
- Styrofoam ball: to fit salt shaker opening
- Wired ribbon, ³/₄"-wide, dark green
- Floral wire
- Copper wire: 19-gauge
- Birdhouse on wooden dowel
- Tree bark
- Jute, waxed
- Toothpick
- Cookie cutter, heart-shaped
- Mixing bowl
- Wooden spoon
- Cookie sheet
- Craft glue
- Hot glue gun & glue sticks
- Scissors

Instructions

1. Make heart-shaped spiced ornaments according to instructions for Making Spiced Ornaments on page 321.

2. Using hot glue gun and glue sticks, hot-glue styrofoam ball into salt shaker.

3. Push wooden dowel with birdhouse attached into center of styrofoam ball.

4. Apply craft glue to styrofoam ball and glue Oregon moss around it until it is completely covered.

5. Allow glue to dry thoroughly.

6. Using hot glue gun and glue sticks, carefully arrange and hot-glue apple slices, garlic bulb, ammobium, poppy pods, myrtle leaves, and cinnamon sticks on top of moss-covered styrofoam ball.

7. Hot-glue tree bark to both sides of birdhouse roof.

8. Form a copper wire loop through one of the holes in top of salt shaker lid.

9. Twist copper wire at top to secure, leaving a two-inch long tail.

10. Push copper wire tail into styrofoam ball, hanging salt shaker lid on side of salt shaker.

11. Tie wired ribbon in a bow according to instructions for Making Multi-Loop Bows on page 320.

12. Using hot glue gun and glue sticks, hot-glue bow into arrangement just above salt shaker lid.

13. String heart-shaped spiced ornaments onto jute so they hang nicely.

14. Using hot glue gun and glue sticks, hot-glue spiced ornaments into arrangement on top of wired-ribbon bow.

Pecan & Nutmeg Wind Chime

Materials

- Pecans
- Whole nutmeg
- Cinnamon sticks
- Jute: 3-ply
- Clay pots: $1/2$"-diameter (3)
- Needle with large eye
- Drill with $1/4$" drill bit
- Scissors

Instructions

1. Drill a hole through center of each nut and cinnamon stick with drill and $1/4$" drill bit.

2. Cut jute with scissors.

3. Tie a knot about 3" down from top to make a loop for hanging.

4. Thread jute onto needle.

5. String one pecan onto jute and tie a knot under it. String three cinnamon sticks onto jute and tie a knot under them. String one whole nutmeg onto jute and tie a knot under it.

6. String one clay pot upside-down onto jute and tie a knot under it. Repeat process for remaining two clay pots.

7. Tie a knot in jute just below rim of third clay pot. String one whole nutmeg onto jute and tie a knot under it. String one pecan onto jute and tie a knot under it.

8. Fray ends of jute.

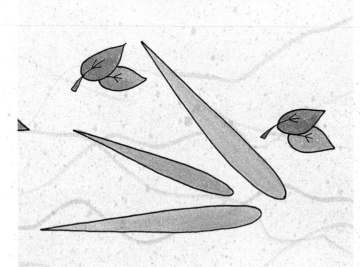

Pinecone & Chestnut Topiary

Materials

- Oregon moss
- Chestnuts
- Nuts, assorted
- Pinecones
- Cinnamon sticks: 8"-long
- Jute: 2-ply
- Clay pot: 4"-diameter
- Styrofoam cone: 3"-diameter
- Styrofoam ball: 4"-diameter
- Craft glue
- Hot glue gun & glue sticks

Instructions

1. Using hot glue gun and glue sticks, hot-glue styrofoam ball into clay pot.

2. Hot-glue four cinnamon sticks together and push into center of styrofoam ball.

3. Push styrofoam cone, pointed end up, on top of cinnamon sticks.

4. Apply craft glue to styrofoam ball and styrofoam cone and glue Oregon moss around them until they are completely covered.

5. Allow glue to dry thoroughly.

6. Break cinnamon sticks into two-inch lengths.

7. Using hot glue gun and glue sticks, carefully arrange and hot-glue chestnuts, nuts, pinecones, and 2"-long cinnamon sticks to moss-covered styrofoam cone at top of cinnamon sticks until it is completely covered.

8. Tie jute around cinnamon sticks.

9. Tie jute in a bow and tie knots at each end.

Cookie Cutter Centerpieces

Materials

- ❦ Cranberries, dried
- ❦ Pinecones
- ❦ Oregon moss
- ❦ Acrylic paints:
    Copper
    Green
- ❦ Sponge
- ❦ Wooden dowels:
    $1/4$"-diameter,
    4"-long (3)
- ❦ Clay pots with
    saucers:
    5"-diameter (3)
- ❦ Cookie cutters,
    metal,
    gingerbread
    man-, tree-,
    and star-shaped
- ❦ Plaster of paris
- ❦ Hammer
- ❦ Nails
- ❦ Hot glue gun &
    glue sticks

Instructions

1. Mix plaster of paris according to manufacturer's directions.

2. Pour plaster of paris into clay pots. Fill to just below rim.

3. Insert wooden dowels into center of each clay pot.

4. Allow plaster of paris to harden.

5. Using a sponge, sponge-paint wooden dowels and clay pots and saucers with acrylic paints.

6. Allow paints to dry thoroughly.

7. Using hot glue gun and glue sticks, hot-glue clay pots to saucers.

8. Hot-glue Oregon moss inside clay pots until plaster of paris is completely covered and the moss is in a mound at the top.

9. Carefully arrange and hot-glue cranberries and pinecones on top of Oregon moss, as desired.

10. If desired, metal cookie cutters can be "aged" by soaking them in water overnight.

11. Center cookie cutters on top of wooden dowels, and nail in place.

12. Using hot glue gun and glue sticks, hot-glue star-shaped cookie cutter to top of tree-shaped cookie cutter.

Pomegranate & Pepper Berries Wreath

Materials

- Pomegranates, dried
- Rosebuds, dried
- Sunflowers, dried
- Garlic bulbs
- Pepper berries, dried
- Cockscomb, dried
- Lemon leaves, dried
- Deer moss
- Twigs
- Branches, green
- Copper wire: 19-gauge
- Wired ribbon, 1 1/2"-wide, purple iridescent
- Floral wire
- Hot glue gun & glue sticks
- Scissors

Instructions

1. Bend green branches into desired shape and secure them with copper wire.

2. Using hot glue gun and glue sticks, carefully arrange and hot-glue lemon leaves around outside edges of wreath.

3. Hot-glue deer moss to wreath inside lemon leaves.

4. Carefully arrange and hot-glue pomegranates, rosebuds, sunflowers, garlic bulbs, pepper berries, and cockscomb to wreath on top of deer moss.

5. Randomly hot-glue twigs into arrangement.

6. Tie wired ribbon in a bow according to instructions for Making Multi-Loop Bows on page 320.

7. Using hot glue gun and glue sticks, hot-glue bow to wreath. Cascade ribbon tails down.

Grapefruit & Apple Garland

Materials

- ❧ Grapefruit slices, dried
- ❧ Apple slices, dried
- ❧ Cinnamon sticks
- ❧ Pinecones
- ❧ Acrylic paint: Yellow-gold
- ❧ Paintbrush
- ❧ Papier-mâché stars
- ❧ Jute, waxed
- ❧ Jute: 2-ply
- ❧ Spray stain, oak
- ❧ Needle with large eye
- ❧ Drill with ¹⁄₈" drill bit

Instructions

1. Using a paint-brush, paint papier-mâché stars with yellow-gold acrylic paint.

2. Allow paint to dry thoroughly.

3. Spray papier-mâché stars with spray stain.

4. Allow spray stain to dry thoroughly.

5. Drill a hole through center of each cinnamon stick and star with drill and ¹⁄₈" drill bit.

6. Tie waxed jute tightly around each pinecone. Tie a knot at ends to make a loop for hanging.

7. Thread 2-ply jute onto needle and tie a knot six inches from one end.

8. String items onto 2-ply jute in the following order: two cinnamon sticks, two pinecones (through waxed jute loops), one grapefruit slice, three apple slices, one more grapefruit slice, two more pinecones, two more cinnamon sticks, and one papier-mâché star. Push down so the first cinnamon stick rests on knot.

9. Repeat process until garland is the desired length and tie a knot six inches from end. If more 2-ply jute is needed to complete garland, tie another piece of 2-ply jute to existing piece and tie a knot to secure. Make certain the needle is on the new piece of 2-ply jute.

10. Double the 2-ply jute at each end and tie a knot to make loops for hanging.

11. Randomly tie two knots at each end of 2-ply jute.

Grapefruit & Bay Leaf Garland

Photograph on page 376.

Materials

- ❧ Grapefruit slices, dried
- ❧ Bay leaves, dried
- ❧ Cinnamon sticks
- ❧ Pinecones
- ❧ Deer moss
- ❧ Clay pots: 3"-diameter
- ❧ Jute, waxed
- ❧ Raffia, optional
- ❧ Needle with large eye
- ❧ Hot glue gun & glue sticks
- ❧ Drill with $^1/_8$" drill bit

Instructions

1. Drill a hole through center of each cinnamon stick and sides of clay pots with drill and $^1/_8$" drill bit.

2. Tie waxed jute tightly around each pinecone. Tie a knot at ends to make a loop for hanging.

3. Thread jute onto needle and tie a large knot six inches from one end.

4. String items onto jute in the following order: one cinnamon stick, several bay leaves, one pinecone (through waxed jute loops), several more bay leaves, one more pinecone, several more bay leaves, three grapefruit slices, several more bay leaves, one clay pot, several more bay leaves, three more grapefruit slices, several more bay leaves, and one more pinecone. Push down so the cinnamon stick rests on knot.

5. Reverse the order without adding a second pinecone to the center.

6. Repeat process until garland is the desired length and tie a knot six inches from end. If more jute is needed to complete garland, tie another piece of jute to existing piece and tie a knot to secure. Make certain the needle is on the new piece of jute.

7. Double the jute at each end and tie a knot to make loops for hanging.

8. Using hot glue gun and glue sticks, hot-glue deer moss inside each clay pot.

9. If desired, randomly tie raffia bows around waxed jute.

Chestnut Garland

Materials

- ❧ Chestnuts
- ❧ Pinecones
- ❧ Jute, waxed
- ❧ Jute: 3-ply
- ❧ Needle with large eye
- ❧ Drill with $^1/_8$" drill bit

Instructions

1. Drill a hole through center of each chestnut with drill and $^1/_8$" drill bit.

2. Tie waxed jute tightly around each pinecone. Tie a knot at ends to make a loop for hanging.

3. Thread waxed jute onto needle and tie a large knot six inches from one end.

4. String items onto waxed jute in the following order: five chestnuts and three pinecones (through waxed jute loops). Push down so the first chestnut rests on knot.

5. Repeat process until garland is the desired length and tie a knot six inches from end. If more waxed jute is needed to complete garland, tie another piece of waxed jute to existing piece and tie a knot to secure. Make certain the needle is on the new piece of waxed jute.

6. Double the waxed jute at each end and tie a knot to make loops for hanging.

7. Tie 3-ply jute in two bows and tie around waxed jute at each end of garland.

Dried Fruit & Pinecone Topiary

Materials

- ❦ Oregon moss
- ❦ Apple slices, dried
- ❦ Orange slices, dried
- ❦ Pomegranates, dried
- ❦ Yarrow, dried
- ❦ Myrtle leaves, dried
- ❦ Pinecones
- ❦ Cinnamon sticks: 8"-long
- ❦ Watering can, tin
- ❦ Styrofoam balls: $2^1/_2$"-diameter; 3"-diameter
- ❦ Wired ribbon, $^3/_4$"-wide, copper iridescent
- ❦ Floral wire
- ❦ Craft glue
- ❦ Hot glue gun & glue sticks
- ❦ Scissors

Instructions

1. Using hot glue gun and glue sticks, hot-glue 3"-diameter styrofoam ball into watering can.

2. Hot-glue three cinnamon sticks together and push into center of styrofoam ball.

3. Push $2^1/_2$"-diameter styrofoam ball on top of cinnamon sticks.

4. Apply craft glue to styrofoam balls and glue Oregon moss around them until both are completely covered.

5. Allow glue to dry thoroughly.

6. Using hot glue gun and glue sticks, carefully arrange and hot-glue apple slices, orange slices, pomegranates, yarrow, myrtle leaves, and pinecones to moss-covered styrofoam ball at top of cinnamon sticks until it is completely covered.

7. Tie wired ribbon in a bow according to instructions for Making Multi-Loop Bows on page 320.

8. Using hot glue gun and glue sticks, hot-glue bow to top of moss-covered styrofoam ball in watering can. Cascade ribbon tails down and hot-glue in place.

9. Carefully arrange and hot-glue pinecones, cinnamon sticks, one apple slice, and one orange slice to top of moss-covered styrofoam ball just behind bow.

Herbs ...

Baby Dill & Chile Pepper Vinegar

Photograph on page 85.

Materials

- ❧ Bottle with wire closure
- ❧ Carrots with carrot tops: thin (3)
- ❧ Baby dill sprig
- ❧ Chile peppers (2)
- ❧ Garlic cloves (2)
- ❧ Vinegar, white: see steps 1 & 2
- ❧ Vinegar, apple cider: see steps 1 & 2
- ❧ Non-iodized salt: 1 teaspoon
- ❧ Sugar, optional: 1 teaspoon
- ❧ Measuring cup: 1 cup
- ❧ Saucepan
- ❧ Funnel
- ❧ Scissors

Instructions

1. To determine how much vinegar the bottle will hold, measure by filling bottle up with water using a measuring cup.

2. The amount of vinegar to be used is based on a 3:1 ratio. Three parts of white vinegar to one part of apple cider vinegar.

3. Wash and sterilize bottle.

4. Place white vinegar, apple cider vinegar, salt, and sugar in a saucepan and bring to a boil.

5. Wash carrots, baby dill sprig, and chile peppers.

6. Trim carrot tops with scissors leaving two to three inches.

7. Remove skins around garlic cloves.

8. Drop chile peppers and garlic cloves into sterilized bottle.

9. Place carrots and baby dill sprig in bottle. The carrots must fit nicely in bottle.

10. Using a funnel, carefully pour hot vinegar into bottle. The chile peppers, garlic cloves, carrots, and baby dill sprig will float to top of bottle, but will settle on bottom in about two weeks. <u>Note: Make certain carrots are submerged in vinegar.</u>

11. Wipe mouth of bottle and seal with wire closure.

12. It is recommended that this vinegar be used within two months.

Wheat & Straw Flowers in a Jar

Photograph on page 85.

Materials

- ❧ Bottle with cork
- ❧ Wheat stem, dried
- ❧ Globe amaranth, dried
- ❧ Mineral or baby oil
- ❧ Funnel
- ❧ Beeswax or paraffin wax
- ❧ Saucepan
- ❧ Tin can
- ❧ Pliers
- ❧ Salad tongs
- ❧ Waxed paper

Instructions

1. Place wheat stem and globe amaranth in bottle.

2. Using a funnel, carefully pour mineral or baby oil into bottle.

3. Wipe mouth of bottle and seal with cork.

4. Melt wax according to instructions for Melting Wax on page 316.

5. Using salad tongs, turn bottle upside-down and dip cork and top of bottle into hot wax several times until desired look is achieved.

Rosemary, Sage & Thyme Vinegar

Photograph on page 85.

Materials

- ❧ Bottle with cork
- ❧ Rosemary stem
- ❧ Sage sprig
- ❧ Thyme sprig
- ❧ Vinegar, white
- ❧ Saucepan
- ❧ Funnel

Instructions

1. Wash and sterilize bottle.

2. Place vinegar in a saucepan and bring to a boil.

3. Wash rosemary stem, sage sprig, and thyme sprig. Pat dry.

4. Place rosemary stem, sage sprig, and thyme sprig in bottle.

5. Using a funnel, carefully pour hot vinegar into bottle. The herbs will float to top of bottle, but will settle on bottom in about two weeks.

6. Wipe mouth of bottle and seal with cork.

7. It is recommended that this vinegar be used within two months.

Garlic & Basil Vinegar

Materials

- ❧ Bottle with cork
- ❧ Garlic cloves (2)
- ❧ Basil, dried: small bunch
- ❧ Rice vinegar, seasoned
- ❧ Saucepan
- ❧ Funnel

Instructions

1. Wash and sterilize bottle.

2. Place rice vinegar in a saucepan and bring to a boil.

3. Remove skins around garlic cloves.

4. Drop garlic cloves into sterilized bottle.

5. Place basil in bottle.

6. Using a funnel, carefully pour hot vinegar into bottle. The garlic cloves and basil will float to top of bottle, but will settle on bottom in about two weeks.

7. Wipe mouth of bottle and seal with cork.

8. It is recommended that this vinegar be used within two months.

Garlic & Basil Vinegar Salad

Not Photographed

Ingredients

- ❧ Romaine lettuce, 4 cups torn
- ❧ Red onion, $1/2$ cup sliced
- ❧ Jumbo olives, 1 can sliced
- ❧ Basil, dried: 2 tablespoons
- ❧ Parsley leaves, 1 teaspoon
- ❧ Feta cheese, $1/2$ cup crumbled
- ❧ Olive oil
- ❧ Garlic & basil vinegar
- ❧ Salt & pepper

Instructions

1. Wash romaine lettuce. Pat dry.

2. Place romaine lettuce, red onion, olives, basil leaves, parsley leaves, and feta cheese in a salad bowl.

3. Toss lightly and add olive oil and garlic and basil vinegar. See Garlic and Basil Vinegar on page 381.

4. Salt and pepper to taste.

Foxtail Millet & Chile Pepper Spray

Materials

- ❧ Foxtail millet, dried
- ❧ Chile peppers, dried
- ❧ Garlic bulb
- ❧ Straw flowers
- ❧ Safflowers, dried
- ❧ Galoxa leaves, dried
- ❧ Raffia
- ❧ Hot glue gun & glue sticks

Instructions

1. Gather foxtail millet and tie raffia around center to secure bundle.

2. Tie raffia in a bow.

3. Using hot glue gun and glue sticks, hot-glue galoxa leaves to foxtail millet bundle just above raffia bow.

4. Carefully arrange and hot-glue chile peppers, garlic bulb, straw flowers, and safflowers on top of galoxa leaves and on top of raffia bow.

Chile Pepper Star

Materials

- Chile peppers, dried
- Garlic bulbs
- Bay leaves, dried
- Branches, straight (5)
- Jute, waxed
- Floral wire

Instructions

1. Arrange branches into a star shape and secure at points with floral wire.

2. Carefully thread chile peppers onto floral wire to create a garland long enough to fit across front of star.

3. Wire chile pepper garland to front of star so it hangs nicely.

4. Carefully thread garlic bulbs and bay leaves onto floral wire to create a garland long enough to fit across front of star.

5. Wire garlic bulb and bay leaf garland to front of star just above chile pepper garland so it hangs nicely.

6. Cover floral wire at star points with jute.

Garlic Bulbs in a Crate

Materials

- ❧ Wooden crate, oblong
- ❧ Pomegranate, dried
- ❧ Ammobium, dried
- ❧ Lantern pods, dried
- ❧ Pinecones
- ❧ Garlic bulbs
- ❧ Nigella, dried
- ❧ Safflowers, dried
- ❧ Cinnamon sticks
- ❧ Oregon moss
- ❧ Raffia
- ❧ Hot glue gun & glue sticks

Instructions

1. Break cinnamon sticks into uniform lengths.

2. Divide wooden crate into eight equal sections with raffia.

3. Using hot glue gun and glue sticks, hot-glue Oregon moss into bottom of wooden crate in all eight sections.

4. Hot-glue the pomegranate into the first section on top of Oregon moss.

5. Hot-glue ammobium into the second section on top of Oregon moss until it is completely full.

6. Hot-glue lantern pods into the third section on top of Oregon moss until it is completely full.

7. Hot-glue pinecones into the fourth section on top of Oregon moss until it is completely full.

8. Hot-glue garlic bulbs into the fifth section on top of Oregon moss.

9. Hot-glue nigella into the sixth section on top of Oregon moss until it is completely full.

10. Hot-glue safflowers into the seventh section on top of Oregon moss until it is completely full.

11. Hot-glue cinnamon sticks into the eighth section on top of Oregon moss until it is completely full.

Garlic Bulb Topiary

Materials

- Garlic bulbs
- Chile peppers, dried
- Bay leaves, dried
- Deer moss
- Raffia
- Wooden dowels: $^1/_8$"-diameter
- Clay pot: 4"-diameter
- Styrofoam cone: 3"-diameter
- Styrofoam ball: 4"-diameter
- Floral tape, white
- Craft glue
- Hot glue gun & glue sticks

Instructions

1. Using hot glue gun and glue sticks, hot-glue styrofoam ball into clay pot.

2. Roll styrofoam cone on top of a hard surface to flatten the point.

3. Using hot glue gun and glue sticks, hot-glue styrofoam cone to styrofoam ball, with the cone point up.

4. Apply craft glue to styrofoam ball and styrofoam cone and glue deer moss

around them until they are completely covered.

5. Allow glue to dry thoroughly.

6. Using floral tape, wrap all wooden dowels.

7. Insert wooden dowels into tops of garlic bulbs.

8. Push wooden dowels with garlic bulbs on them into styrofoam ball. <u>Note: Begin at the top and work down in a circular pattern.</u>

9. Using hot glue gun and glue sticks, carefully arrange and hot-glue chile peppers and bay

leaves to moss-covered styrofoam cone in between garlic bulbs.

10. Tie raffia in a bow and hot-glue to side of clay pot just below arrangement.

Garlic Bulb & German Statice Garland

Materials

- ❧ Garlic bulbs
- ❧ German statice
- ❧ Raffia
- ❧ Hot glue gun & glue sticks
- ❧ Needle with large eye
- ❧ Scissors

Instructions

1. Cut raffia with scissors to twice the desired length. Double strand the raffia and tie a knot at end.

2. Thread double strand of raffia onto needle.

3. String garlic bulbs onto raffia. Push down so the first garlic bulb rests on knot.

4. Leaving a loop at the top for hanging, braid several new strands of raffia. Intertwine around garlic bulbs and tie a knot at the end.

5. Fray ends of raffia.

6. Using hot glue gun and glue sticks, hot-glue German statice to raffia braid in between garlic bulbs.

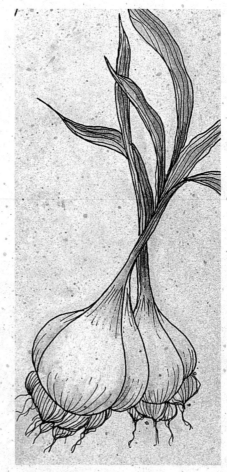

Soaps ...

Stacked Bars of Soap Embellished with Wheat Stem & Cinnamon Stick

Photograph on page 387.

Materials

- Bars of natural soap, round (3)
- Wheat stem, dried
- Pinecones
- Cinnamon stick
- Jute: 3-ply
- Hot glue gun & glue sticks

Instructions

1. Make bars of natural soap according to instructions for Making Natural Soap on page 322.

2. Stack three bars of soap on top of each other.

3. Tie jute around bars of soap twice in each direction.

4. Tie jute in a bow on top of stacked soap.

5. Using hot glue gun and glue sticks, hot-glue wheat, pinecones, and cinnamon stick on top of jute bow.

Wrapped Bar of Soap Embellished with a Raffia Braid & Cinnamon Stick

Photograph on page 387.

Materials

- Bar of natural soap
- Cinnamon stick
- Raffia
- Natural paper
- Cellophane tape
- Hot glue gun & glue sticks

Instructions

1. Make bar of natural soap according to instructions for Making Natural Soap on page 322.

2. Wrap natural paper around bar of soap. Secure with cellophane tape.

3. Braid several strands of raffia and tie knots at each end.

4. Tie raffia braid around bar of soap.

5. Fray ends of raffia.

6. Insert cinnamon stick into raffia braid knot.

Stacked Bars of Soap Embellished with Licopodium & Cinnamon Sticks

Photograph on page 387.

Materials

- Bars of natural soap (3)
- Licopodium
- Cinnamon sticks
- Jute: 3-ply
- Corrugated paper: 1"-wide
- Cellophane tape
- Hot glue gun & glue sticks

Instructions

1. Make bars of natural soap according to instructions for Making Natural Soap on page 322.

2. Stack three bars of soap on top of each other.

3. Wrap corrugated paper around bars of soap. Secure with cellophane tape.

4. Using hot glue gun and glue sticks, hot-glue licopodium and cinnamon sticks on top of corrugated paper.

5. Tie jute around bars of soap once in each direction.

6. Tie jute in a bow at top of stacked soap.

Bars of Soap Embellished with Bay Leaves or Orange Slices

Photograph on page 387.

Materials

- Bars of natural soap
- Bay leaves, dried
- Orange slices, dried
- Raffia
- Natural paper
- Corrugated paper: 1"-wide, optional
- Cellophane tape
- Hot glue gun & glue sticks

Instructions

1. Make bars of natural soap according to instructions for Making Natural Soap on page 322.

2. Wrap natural paper around bars of soap. Secure with cellophane tape.

Continued on page 389.

Bars of Soap Embellished with Pressed Flowers & Greenery

Materials

- ❧ Bars of natural soap, round
- ❧ Pressed flowers
- ❧ Pressed greenery
- ❧ Tweezers
- ❧ Toothpick
- ❧ Craft glue
- ❧ Découpage glue
- ❧ Paintbrush

Instructions

1. Make bars of natural soap according to instructions for Making Natural Soap on page 322.

2. Using tweezers, pick up pressed flowers and greenery.

3. Using a toothpick, apply craft glue to back sides of pressed flowers and greenery.

4. Carefully arrange pressed flowers and greenery on top of bars of soap.

5. Allow glue to dry thoroughly.

6. Using a paintbrush, apply découpage glue over pressed flowers and greenery on top of bars of soap according to manufacturer's directions.

Continued from page 388.

3. If desired, wrap corrugated paper around bars of soap. Secure with cellophane tape.

4. Using hot glue gun and glue sticks, hot-glue bay leaves or orange slices on top of natural or corrugated papers.

5. Tie raffia around bars of soap once in each direction.

6. Tie raffia in a bow on top of soap.

390

Loofah Embellished with Licopodium & Cinnamon Sticks

Materials

- Loofah
- Licopodium
- Cinnamon sticks
- Star anise, dried
- Raffia
- Natural paper
- Corrugated paper: 1"-wide
- Cellophane tape
- Hot glue gun & glue sticks

Instructions

1. Peel loofah and allow to dry completely.

2. Wrap natural paper around loofah. Secure with cellophane tape.

3. Wrap corrugated paper around loofah. Secure with cellophane tape.

4. Using hot glue gun and glue sticks, hot-glue licopodium, cinnamon sticks, and star anise on top of corrugated paper.

5. Tie raffia around loofah.

6. Tie raffia in a bow on top of loofah.

Loofah Embellished with River Birch Twigs & Cones

Materials

- Loofah
- River birch twigs
- River birch cones
- Raffia
- Natural paper
- Corrugated paper: 1"-wide
- Cellophane tape
- Hot glue gun & glue sticks

Instructions

1. Peel loofah and allow to dry completely.

2. Wrap natural paper around loofah. Secure with cellophane tape.

3. Wrap corrugated paper around loofah. Secure with cellophane tape.

4. Using hot glue gun and glue sticks, hot-glue river birch twigs and cones on top of corrugated paper.

5. Tie raffia around loofah.

6. Tie raffia in a bow on top of loofah.

Stacked Bars of Soap Embellished with Wild Grass & Foxtail Millet

Materials

- Bars of natural soap, round (2)
- Wild grass, dried
- Foxtail millet, dried
- Jute: 3-ply
- Hot glue gun & glue sticks

Instructions

1. Make bars of natural soap according to instructions for Making Natural Soap on page 322.

2. Stack two bars of soap on top of each other.

3. Tie jute around bars of soap once in each direction.

4. Tie jute in a bow on top of stacked soap.

5. Using hot glue gun and glue sticks, hot-glue wild grass and foxtail millet on top of jute bow.

Metal Heart Hanger

Materials

- Sheet metal
- Branch
- Grapevine wreath: 4"-diameter
- Steel wire, 19-gauge
- Saucepan
- Vinegar: 1 cup
- Salt: $\frac{1}{2}$ cup
- Water: $\frac{1}{2}$ cup
- Tin snips
- Drill with $\frac{1}{8}$" drill bit

Instructions

1. Cut and oxidize three sheet metal hearts according to instructions for Cutting and Oxidizing Metal on page 320.

2. Drill a hole in the top center of each heart with drill and $\frac{1}{8}$" drill bit.

3. Wrap steel wire around each end of branch to make a handle for hanging.

4. Thread steel wire through drilled hole in each heart. Twist in back of heart to secure, leaving four-inch long tail.

5. Wrap tails around branch two to three times.

6. Unwind grapevine wreath and wrap around branch.

Two-Hour Painted Wood Projects

General Instructions

When creating pieces for this book, every attempt was made to make them legitimate 2-hour projects. This time period excludes shopping for materials and any time spent in preparing woods for painting. I hope you enjoy painting these projects, as much as I enjoyed creating them!

Before You Begin:

Many of the projects in this book call for wood shapes that we have provided dimensions and patterns for use in cutting these shapes. However, anytime you are able to find pre-cut pieces, we recommend you do just that! We want you to get on with the "painting" of these projects—that's why this book was written!

Transferring Patterns:

If you cannot find pre-cut wood shapes you need for a particular project, you will need to cut them from wood using the dimensions and patterns provided for your

use. When doing so, you will trace the patterns from this book onto tracing paper using a pencil. You will use graphite paper to transfer these patterns onto the wood shapes. Be certain that you take all precautions in cutting the wood shapes from the wood—safety always comes first!

After you have cut the wood shapes that you need, lightly sand all edges and rough surfaces with fine- or medium-grit sandpaper. Using a clean, damp cloth, wipe the dust from the sanded shapes.

Spackling / Texturing Techniques:

Using a spackling knife or a metal ruler, apply spackling compound to the surface and texture as desired. Be sure to use a spackling compound that can be painted. Let the spackling compound dry completely before painting. A texturing medium can also be used by following manufacturer's instructions.

Dry Brushing:

You will use a ¹/₂" flat brush to dry brush—make sure the flat brush is indeed dry. Dip the dry, flat brush into the acrylic paint and brush across a piece of paper until most of the paint is removed from the bristles of the brush. Paint the surface. Repeat this process as necessary for coverage desired.

Stenciling:

You can either use a pre-cut stencil or cut one yourself by tracing the pattern onto poster board or a manila envelope and cutting it out carefully with a craft knife or scissors. Using your fingertips, hold the stencil firmly in place on your project.

To get the best results, use a stencil brush as they are designed so that paint can be applied vertically without seeping under the edges. Apply acrylic paint with a gentle, dabbing motion, working well into the edges for a clean line. Don't overload the brush with acrylic paint, but instead "dab" several coats for a more intense color.

Painting with a Toothbrush:

Dip an old toothbrush into the stain or acrylic paint you intend to use. Using your finger, "flip" the mixture onto the project from a distance of about six inches. Let the stain or acrylic paint dry.

Rag Painting Techniques:

Using a clean, dry textured rag or cheesecloth, dip the corner of the rag into acrylic paint and blot the excess paint onto a paper towel. Dab the rag over the surface to be painted, using heavy or light coverage as desired.

Antiquing:

Using an old pie pan, pour a small amount of mineral spirits or paint thinner in one side and a small amount of acrylic paint in the other side. Thin your paint a little at a time.

Using an old brush or a disposable sponge brush, apply this stain over the surface. Let the stain dry for about 30 seconds and, using a rag or old cloth, wipe off the remaining stain.

When covering a large area, do a small portion at a time, overlapping so as to not leave an unwanted pattern. If the stain is too dark, some may be removed with a rag dipped in mineral spirits or paint thinner and if a darker stain is desired, simply repeat the process.

All rags and brushes should be disposed of properly, as the stain mixture makes these items very combustible.

Sponge Painting:

Using a small damp sponge, dip into acrylic paint and "blot" onto paper towels to remove excess paint before "blotting" the surface of the project, using heavy or light coverage as desired.

A Plate
Full of Cherries

This is one of my favorite projects in this book. The simplicity of the design is what appeals to me. Also, the simple coloring will work well in any room of my home. I think the plate would look good on the mantel in my living room, on the antique dresser in my entry, or on the buffet in my dining room. It is nice to have choices in life!

THINGS YOU'LL NEED:

15½" Wooden plate
   with a 3" rim
Ruler
Pencil
Eraser
Tracing paper
Graphite paper
½" Flat brush
1" Sponge brush
Acrylic paint:
   Barnyard red
   Butter pecan
   Linen beige
   Thicket green
Oil paint:
   Burnt umber
Mineral spirits
Rag or old cloth
Fine-point permanent
   black marker
Clear matte spray finish

FOLLOW THESE STEPS:

1 Using a ruler, divide the center of the wooden plate into 1" squares by drawing lines with a pencil.

2 Using the pencil, trace the cherry pattern from page 398 onto tracing paper. Using graphite paper, transfer the pattern onto the plate rim. Refer to the photograph for suggested placement. For variety, you may opt to reverse the pattern for some of the cherries. Draw a leaf next to

the cherries, and vice versa, so that not too many cherries or leaves are together.

3 Using a ½" flat brush, working in the circular direction of the plate rim, paint the plate rim with butter pecan acrylic paint. Apply only one thin coat of paint to allow the wood to be exposed through the paint. Let the paint dry.

4 Paint the squares in the center of the plate, alternating squares with butter pecan acrylic paint and linen beige acrylic paint. Leave a small amount of space around each square, near the pencil markings, unpainted. Refer to Diagram A. Let the paint dry between coats.

5 Paint inside the plate rim, between the center of the plate and the outside rim, with linen beige acrylic paint. Let the paint dry. The back of the plate will not be painted with acrylic paint.

6 Paint the cherries with barnyard red acrylic paint. Paint the leaves and stems with thicket green acrylic paint. Let the paint dry.

7 Mix 1 part of burnt umber oil paint to 4 parts of mineral spirits. Using a 1" sponge brush, paint this stain over the entire plate front and sides. Let the stain dry for about 30 seconds and, using a rag or old cloth, wipe off the remaining stain. Using the stain, repeat the process on the back of the plate.

8 Using an eraser, erase all the exposed pencil lines on the front of the plate. Using a fine-point permanent black marker, draw small circles on the plate rim around the cherries and at the corners of every other square on the center of the plate. Refer to the photograph for suggested placement. Outline and add small dots to the cherries, the stems, and the leaves. Draw a line down the center of each leaf. Dots and lines may vary from cherry to cherry and leaf to leaf. Refer to the photograph for suggested placement.

9 Using clear matte spray finish, spray the front of the plate. Let the spray finish dry. Using the spray finish, repeat the process on the back of the plate. Let the spray finish dry. Apply additional coats of spray finish to the front of the plate if the plate will be used to serve food.

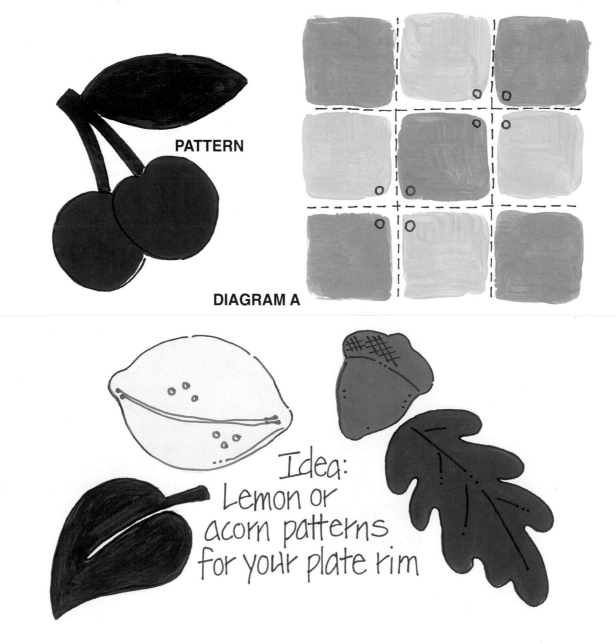

PATTERN

DIAGRAM A

Idea: Lemon or acorn patterns for your plate rim

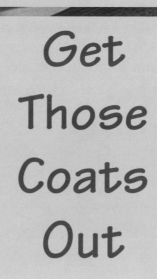

Get
Those
Coats
Out

Get Those Coats Out

This coat rack was purchased by my sister, Nan, with instructions to me to make her something that could hang above her bathroom window with raffia draped from the pegs for a window treatment. As I write this, she hasn't seen it. I am hoping she and her husband, Allen, will approve. If not, I have a few vacant windows.

THINGS YOU'LL NEED:

Coat rack, 30" x 3$\frac{1}{2}$" x $\frac{3}{4}$",
  with five 3" wooden pegs
4 Trees,
  5" x 10" x $\frac{1}{8}$" balsa wood
$\frac{3}{4}$" Masking tape
$\frac{1}{2}$" Flat brush
1" Sponge brush
Spackling knife or metal ruler
Spackling compound
Fine-grit sandpaper
Clean cloth
Acrylic paint:
  Acorn brown
  Butter pecan
  Dark green
  Mint green
Oil paint:
  Burnt umber
Mineral spirits
Rag or old cloth
Glue gun and glue sticks
Clear matte spray finish

FOLLOW THESE STEPS:

1 Cut the trees from the $\frac{1}{8}$" balsa wood. Use the tree pattern from page 401. Refer to the General Instructions for transferring patterns. Using $\frac{3}{4}$" masking tape, tape around all the front edges of the coat rack. Be sure the masking tape is pushed down securely on the wood so that paint cannot seep under the edges of the tape.

2 Using either a spackling knife or a metal ruler, spackle inside the masking tape lines and around the

wooden pegs with spackling compound. Texture the trees with spackling compound. Refer to the General Instructions for spackling and texturing techniques. Let the spackling compound dry completely.

3 Using fine-grit sandpaper, lightly sand all spackled and textured surfaces. Using a clean, damp cloth, wipe the dust from the coat rack and the trees.

4 Using a $\frac{1}{2}$" flat brush, paint some areas of the trees and all of the tree edges with dark green acrylic paint. Paint the remaining areas of the trees with mint green acrylic paint. Refer to the pattern. Repeat the process on the coat rack with acorn brown and butter pecan acrylic paints. Let the paint dry between coats.

5 Dry-brush the trees and coat rack with butter pecan acrylic paint. Refer to the General Instructions for dry brushing techniques.

6 Paint the wooden pegs with acorn brown acrylic paint. Let the paint dry.

7 Mix 1 part of burnt umber oil paint to 3 parts of mineral spirits. Using a 1" sponge brush, paint this stain over the painted coat rack. Let the stain dry for about 30 seconds and, using a rag or old cloth, wipe off the remaining stain. Using the stain, repeat the process on the wooden pegs and the trees.

8 Using a glue gun, attach the trees to the coat rack between the wooden pegs. Two of the trees are attached over the holes where the nails or screws go to hang the coat rack. If you are hanging the coat rack in this manner, you may want to hang it, and then attach the trees.

9 Remove the masking tape. Using clear matte spray finish, spray the coat rack and the trees. Apply a second coat of spray finish to the coat rack and trees. Let the spray finish dry between coats.

PATTERN

Idea: Instead of trees how about

a planter or a teddy bear for the baby's room!

Picture Perfect

I love stars. Our Wyoming ranch is 22 miles from the closest town. Without the interruption of earthly light, the stars are abundant and beautiful. Their brilliance makes me ponder all of life's mysteries ... and wonder why I'm up so late when I have to get up early to feed the orphaned calves. Who knows what this has to do with this frame!

THINGS YOU'LL NEED:

6 Wooden balls,
 1/2" diameter
Wooden frame,
 4 1/2" x 5 1/2"
 with 1 3/4" x 2 3/4" opening
1" Sponge brush
1/2" Flat brush
Fine-grit sandpaper
Clean cloth
Acrylic paint:
 Black
 Navy
Medium-point permanent
 gold marker
Glue gun and glue sticks
Clear matte spray finish

DIAGRAM A

FOLLOW THESE STEPS:

1 Remove the backing and the glass from the frame.

2 Using fine-grit sandpaper, lightly sand the frame. Using a clean, damp cloth, wipe the dust from the frame.

3 Using a 1/2" flat brush, paint the inside edges by the frame opening with black acrylic paint. Using a 1" sponge brush, paint the front and outside edges of the frame with navy acrylic paint. Let the paint dry.

4 Using a medium-point permanent gold marker, color the six wooden balls. Let the marker dry.

5 Using the medium-point permanent gold marker, make spirals and stars on the frame. Use small dots to create the image. Refer to Diagram A.

6 Using a glue gun, attach the wooden balls to the top of the frame. Refer to the photograph for placement.

7 Using clear matte spray finish, spray the frame and the wooden balls. Apply a second coat of spray finish to the frame and wooden balls. Let the spray finish dry between coats.

8 Return the glass to the frame. Insert your favorite photograph and return the backing to the frame.

Planted Pots

My brother, Mike, and his wife, Linda, have the green thumbs in my family. These little pots will look good in their tidy new kitchen greenhouse window. And, chances are, the plants will live!

THINGS YOU'LL NEED:

3 Clay pots,
   3½" diameter
Pencil
Tracing paper
Graphite paper
1" Sponge brush
Small pointed brush
Acrylic paint:
   Butter pecan
   Sedona clay
   Dark green
Clear matte spray finish

FOLLOW THESE STEPS:

1 Using a 1" sponge brush, paint the body of two clay pots and the top rim of the third clay pot with dark green acrylic paint. Apply as many coats as necessary to cover. Let the paint dry between each coat.

2 Using a small pointed brush, paint three horizontal stripes around the rim of one of the clay pots that has an unpainted top rim. Allow the brush stroke to become thinner and thicker as you paint.

3 Using a pencil, trace the heart pattern below onto tracing paper. Using graphite paper, transfer the pattern onto the rims of the two remaining clay pots. Eleven hearts should be transferred onto each clay pot.

4 Using the small pointed brush, paint the hearts on the clay pot that has been painted dark green with butter pecan acrylic paint. Paint the hearts on the clay pot that has the top rim painted dark green with Sedona clay acrylic paint.

PATTERN

5 Using the small pointed brush, paint small dots with dark green acrylic paint between the butter pecan colored hearts—approximately five dots. Paint small dots with butter pecan acrylic paint between the Sedona clay colored hearts. Paint dots around the top and the bottom of the rim that has the horizontal lines with butter pecan acrylic paint. Refer to the photograph for suggested placement.

6 Using clear matte spray finish, spray the clay pots. Apply a second coat of spray finish to the clay pots. Let the spray finish dry between coats. Plant your favorite flowers.

Idea: Change the coloring & patterns on the rims of the pots. Paint planters to match. Don't be afraid to experiment with color!

Mama Kitty on My Mind

I have a 13-year-old black cat named Mama Kitty. She is stuck-up and demanding, but I love her. She adopted all of our dogs and keeps their faces spit-shined. She can create some fantastic doggie-dos with cat saliva. When the alarm rings, it will remind me of Mama Kitty, long after she is gone.

THINGS YOU'LL NEED:

Wooden clock,
 4¹⁄₄" square x 2" deep
4 Finials, 1" x 4"
3 Cats,
 2" x 4" x ³⁄₄" pine
³⁄₄" Masking tape
¹⁄₂" Flat brush
Fine-grit sandpaper
Clean cloth
Acrylic paint:
 Black
 Mustard, optional
Glue gun and glue sticks
Clear matte spray finish

FOLLOW THESE STEPS:

1 Cut the cats from the ³⁄₄" pine. Use the cat pattern below. Refer to the General Instructions for transferring patterns.

2 Using fine-grit sandpaper, lightly sand the clock and the cats. Using a clean, damp cloth, wipe the dust from the clock and the cats.

3 Using ³⁄₄" masking tape, cover the clock mechanism.

4 Using a ¹⁄₂" flat brush, paint the finials and the cats with black acrylic paint.

5 Using the ¹⁄₂" flat brush, paint the clock the color of your choice — I chose mustard acrylic paint. Apply as many coats as necessary to cover. Let the paint dry between coats.

6 Using a glue gun, attach one finial to each corner on the bottom of the clock. Attach the cats to the top of the clock. Refer to the photograph for suggested placement. Two cats should be facing one direction and the other cat should be facing the opposite direction.

7 Using clear matte spray finish, spray the clock. Let the spray finish dry. Remove the masking tape from the clock mechanism, insert the batteries, and set the time!

PATTERN

A Holder with a Heart

It was fun to use a wooden object made for a sole purpose and turn it into something else. This was the first time I had ever used a rubber stamp and I was amazed at how well stamping worked with acrylic paint.

THINGS YOU'LL NEED:

Wooden tissue box holder,
  5" wide x 5³/₄" tall
4 Wooden finials,
  1¹/₂" diameter x 2" tall
Heart, rubber stamp or
  stencil, 1¹/₄" square
Ruler
Pencil
¹/₂" Flat brush
1" Sponge brush
Small pointed brush
Stencil brush, if stenciling
Fine-grit sandpaper
Clean cloth
Acrylic paint:
  Butter pecan
  Thicket green
Oil paint:
  Burnt umber
Mineral spirits
Rag or old cloth
Old toothbrush
Glue gun and glue sticks
Clear matte spray finish

FOLLOW THESE STEPS:

1 Turn the tissue box holder upside down so the hole is on the bottom. Starting at the bottom, measure 1⁵/₈" squares—three across, three high—with a ruler and mark with a pencil. The middle squares may be slightly larger. Leave a ⁵/₈" border at the top. Using the pencil, draw three inverted triangles above each square on the ⁵/₈"

border—nine inverted triangles on each side. Refer to Diagram A. Draw the inverted triangles on the remaining sides.

2 Using a 1" sponge brush, paint the inside and the edges of the tissue box holder with thicket green acrylic paint. Paint the wooden finials, which will be used as the planter's legs, with thicket green acrylic paint. Using a ¹/₂" flat brush, paint all of the "tan" squares with butter pecan acrylic paint. Refer to Diagram A. Paint the remaining squares with thicket green acrylic paint. Let the paint dry between coats. Don't worry about uneven lines; if a small amount of wood shows through between the paint, it will absorb the stain you will apply later and will enhance the project.

3 Using a small pointed brush, paint all of the bottom triangles with butter pecan acrylic paint. Paint all of the upper triangles with thicket green acrylic paint. Add dots of thicket green acrylic paint to the butter pecan colored triangles. Add dots of butter pecan acrylic paint to the thicket green colored triangles. Let the paint dry between coats. Refer to the photograph for suggested placement.

4 If you are using a rubber stamp, apply acrylic paint to the rubber stamp using the 1/2" flat brush. You will need to apply acrylic paint to the rubber stamp before stamping each square. Stamp all of the butter pecan colored squares on all four sides of the tissue box holder with a thicket green colored heart. Stamp all of the thicket green colored squares on all four sides of the tissue box holder with a butter pecan colored heart. If

you are using a stencil, repeat the same color pattern as described. Press the stencil against each square before you apply acrylic paint with a stencil brush. Refer to the General Instructions for stenciling.

5 Using fine-grit sandpaper, lightly sand all the edges of the wooden finials. Using a clean, damp cloth, wipe the dust from the legs.

6 Mix 1 part of burnt umber oil paint to 4 parts of mineral spirits. Using the 1" sponge brush, paint this stain over the tissue box holder and the wooden finials. Let the stain dry for about 20 to 30 seconds and, using a rag or old cloth, wipe off the remaining stain. Leave the stain in the grooves. Apply more burnt umber color to the butter pecan colored areas than to the thicket green colored areas.

7 Using a glue gun, attach one wooden finial to each corner on the top of the tissue box holder (which is now the bottom). Hold in place until se-

cure. Refer to the photograph for suggested placement.

8 Dip an old toothbrush into the burnt umber oil paint / mineral spirits stain. Using your finger, "flip" the mixture onto the tissue box holder from a distance of about six inches. Using this technique, paint the tissue box holder on all sides. Refer to the General Instructions for painting with a toothbrush. Let the stain dry.

9 Using clear matte spray finish, spray the tissue box holder. Apply a second coat of spray finish to the tissue box holder. Make sure the inside of the tissue box holder is well coated with spray finish to repel water. Let the spray finish dry between coats. The hole in the bottom of the tissue box holder will allow water to run through the plant and not accumulate in the "planter." Plant your favorite flower in a clay pot and place the clay pot inside the planter. It is recommended that this "planter" be used indoors.

DIAGRAM A

410

Peek-
a-Boo

Peek-a-Boo

I bought a ceramic mirror in Park City, Utah, over twenty years ago that had one little bird perched looking into the bottom of the mirror. When I saw these little birds on a wire, I knew they would work for me in using the concept to create my own design. The mirror is just the right size to see if you have birdseed in your teeth!

THINGS YOU'LL NEED:

Wooden frame,
  9$^1/_2$" square
  with 4$^1/_2$"-square opening
Mirror, 5" x 5" square
2 Wooden birds with wire
  attached to the bottom,
  2$^1/_2$" long x 1" high
  x $^3/_4$" deep
Miniature Americana
  window shutters,
  4$^1/_2$" long x 1$^1/_4$" wide
4 Variegated
  green / rust beads, $^1/_2$"
$^1/_2$" Flat brush
1" Sponge brush
Small pointed brush
Spackling knife or metal ruler
Spackling compound
Fine-grit sandpaper
Clean cloth

Acrylic paint:
  Barnyard red
  Black
  Mint green
  Mustard
  White
Oil paint:
  Burnt umber
Mineral spirits
Rag or old cloth
Glue gun and glue sticks
Clear matte spray finish
Masking tape or
  small brad nails
  and hammer

FOLLOW THESE STEPS:

1 Using either a spackling knife or a metal ruler, spackle the wooden frame with spackling compound. Refer to the General Instructions for spackling and texturing techniques. Let the spackling compound dry completely.

2 Using fine-grit sandpaper, lightly sand all spackled surfaces. Using a clean, damp cloth, wipe the dust from the frame.

3 Using a 1" sponge brush, paint over parts of the spackled side of the frame and the edges with mint green acrylic paint. Refer to Diagram A. Repeat this process using white acrylic paint. Allow some of the raw wood to remain exposed.

4 Using the 1/2" flat brush, paint one bird with barnyard red acrylic paint. Paint the second bird with mustard acrylic paint. Using a small pointed brush, paint the birds' eyes with black acrylic paint. Paint the barnyard red colored bird's beak with mustard acrylic paint. Paint the mustard colored bird's beak with black acrylic paint.

5 Mix 1 part of burnt umber oil paint to 4 parts of mineral spirits. Using the 1" sponge brush, paint this stain over the frame and sides. Let the stain dry for about 30 seconds and, using a rag or old cloth, wipe off the remaining stain. If the frame is too dark, wipe it with mineral spirits to lighten. Repeat this process on the birds.

6 Using a glue gun, glue the wire on the bottom of the barnyard red colored bird down one side of the frame—under where the shutter is to be placed. Leave enough wire so that the bird can bend to look inside the mirror that will be placed in the frame. Glue the wire on the bottom of the second bird from the opposite corner up. Attach one shutter over the top of each wire, aligning the edge with the inside edge of the frame. Hold in place until secure. Attach the beads. Refer to the photograph for suggested placement.

7 Using clear matte spray finish, spray the frame and the birds. Apply a second coat of spray finish to the frame and birds. Let the spray finish dry between coats.

8 Insert the mirror in the frame and secure with masking tape or small brad nails hammered into the sides of the frame.

Idea: Use a doll house window over the mirror or a photograph instead of shutters...the birds will still be able to see inside...

DIAGRAM A

What to Do with Ugly Fruit

Everywhere you shop, it seems you run into ugly wooden fruits and vegetables! I took some of these, painted them, and made this whimsical box. This project is quite different from the rest. I just kept changing things and experimenting until I got something I liked. It was the first time I had ever used spray glitter on anything.

THINGS YOU'LL NEED:

Round bentwood box with lid,
  6" diameter x 3" high
6 Wooden balls, 1"
4 Wooden pears,
  1½" diameter
  (large end) x 2" tall
2 Wooden apples with stems,
  2" x 2" round
3 Silk leaves
Measuring tape
Pencil
½" Flat brush
Acrylic paint:
  Barnyard red
  Lavender
  Light gray
  Moon yellow
  White
  Wrought iron black
Gold spray glitter
Glue gun and glue sticks

FOLLOW THESE STEPS:

1 Using a ½" flat brush, paint the inside and the outside of the round bentwood box and lid with white acrylic paint. Paint the rim of the lid with moon yellow acrylic paint. Apply only one coat of acrylic paint to the bentwood box and lid. Paint the fruits: 1" wooden balls with lavender acrylic paint, wooden pears with moon yellow acrylic paint, wooden apples with barnyard red acrylic paint, and the apple stems with wrought iron black acrylic paint. Apply additional coats of acrylic paint until full coverage is achieved. Let the paint dry between coats.

2 Using a measuring tape, measure around the bottom of the box. Using a pencil, mark at each ½". Add ½" marks all the way to the top of the box. Any discrepancy in the width of the last ½" mark will be covered by the lid. Without using a ruler, draw vertical lines from the top marks to the bottom marks. Starting at the top of the box, measure down ½" three times. Using the pencil, mark these distances about four times around the box. Without using a ruler, draw a line from one ½" mark to the next, until you've drawn a circle around the box. Repeat at each ½" mark. Refer to the photograph. Without using a ruler, draw squares on the lid ½" apart, starting from the center.

3 Using the ½" flat brush, paint alternating squares on the lid and the outside of the box with wrought iron black acrylic paint. Make only two brush strokes per square. Pull the brush down from one side; then turn and pull toward the brush stroke. The sides should be even with the outside edge of the brush. Apply only one coat of acrylic paint to these squares. Let the paint dry.

4 Without measuring, draw squares around the edge of the lid. Don't worry about them being perfectly square. Paint the squares with barnyard red acrylic paint. Apply only one coat of acrylic paint to these squares. Paint diagonal lines over the edge of the barnyard red squares with moon yellow acrylic paint to create a diamond. Make sure the paint is thin so the barnyard red acrylic paint will show through the moon yellow acrylic paint and look almost gray. Refer to Diagram A. Let the paint dry between coats.

5 Dry-brush the pears, apples, and lavender balls (grapes) with light gray acrylic paint. Refer to the General Instructions for dry brushing.

6 Using the pencil, draw a 4" square on the bottom of the box. Using a glue gun, attach one pear (with the small part of the pear to the box) to each corner of the 4" square. The pears will be the legs on the box.

7 Using the glue gun, attach the apples, the grapes, and the leaves to the top of the lid. Refer to the photograph for placement.

8 Using gold spray glitter, spray the inside and the outside of the box and lid. Let the spray glitter dry.

DIAGRAM A

416

Simple But Shapely

I had all of these little wooden finials and spools which were really crafted for other purposes. They were in a bucket by my desk for a long, long time. Finally I picked them up and started inserting one piece into another and gluing them together. Because they are lightweight, I thought they would make ideal Christmas tree ornaments.

THINGS YOU'LL NEED:

Variety of wooden finials,
　with at least one flat edge
Variety of wooden wheels
Variety of wooden plugs
1/2" Flat brush
Acrylic paint:
　Metallic gold
　White
Fine-point permanent
　gold marker
Glue gun and glue sticks
Metallic gold spray
Newspaper
Embellishments,
　your choice

FOLLOW THESE STEPS:

1 Using a glue gun, attach the finials, the wheels, and/or the plugs to create an ornament. Make sure it isn't too heavy to hang on a tree branch.

2 Using a 1/2" flat brush, paint alternating areas of each ornament with white acrylic paint. Apply a second coat of white acrylic paint to the ornaments. Let the paint dry between coats. Paint the remaining areas of each ornament with metallic gold acrylic paint. Let the paint dry.

3 Using a fine-point permanent gold marker, draw the design of your choice onto the white areas of each ornament. Refer to Diagram A. Let the marker dry.

4 Lay the painted ornaments on newspaper. Using metallic gold spray, spray one side of each ornament. Let the metallic spray dry. Turn the ornaments over to spray the other side. Let the metallic spray dry between coats. Embellish as desired.

DIAGRAM A

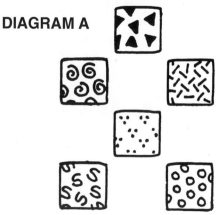

Celestial
Fantasy

Celestial Fantasy

I made this plate for my friend Beverly White. She was sitting at the table watching me paint and said she wanted the plate when I was through using it for the book. Gladly, I agreed. It was flattering to know someone liked my work. We were on a golf vacation, but as the book deadline drew nearer, I had to create wooden projects wherever we went!

THINGS YOU'LL NEED:

12½" wooden plate
   with a decorative rim and
   8" center section
Ruler
Pencil
½" Flat brush
Acrylic paint:
   Metallic gold
   Navy blue
Medium-point permanent
   gold marker
Clear matte spray finish

FOLLOW THESE STEPS:

1 Using a ½" flat brush, paint the entire top side of the wooden plate with navy blue acrylic paint. Paint the inside section of the back side of the wooden plate with navy blue acrylic paint. Paint the outside rim on the back of the wooden plate with metallic gold acrylic paint. Apply additional coats of acrylic paint until full coverage on the plate is achieved. Let the paint dry between coats.

2 Using a pencil, draw a 3¼" circle in the middle of the plate. Starting at the outside of the circle, draw a line in a circular motion until you reach the center of the plate. This will create the center of the sun. Refer to the photograph. From the outside of the circle, using a ruler, measure nine 1" lines around the edges of the 3¼" circle. Leave about ¼" between the circle and the lines you will draw. From the end of each 1" mark, draw a diagonal line to the outside edge of the navy blue area so the lines meet to form a triangle. These are the sun's rays. Refer to the photograph. Using a medium-point permanent gold marker, draw an irregular line to outline the triangles you just created. Fill

420

the triangles, leaving some of the navy blue exposed through the permanent gold marker. Refer to the photograph. Draw an irregular line over the circular line in the center of the sun. Expand the line so that only about $1/4$" of navy blue shows between the circular lines. Leave some of the navy blue exposed through the permanent gold marker.

3 Using the pencil, draw four moons on the rim of the plate. Draw stars of differ-

ent sizes between the moons. Don't worry about the moons and stars being irregular in shape and size. Using the permanent gold marker, fill in the moons, leaving some of the navy blue exposed through the permanent gold marker. Completely fill in the stars. Make dots around the moons and the stars on the rim of the plate. Refer to the photograph for suggested placement.

4 Using the permanent gold marker, paint the inside

decorative trim between the outside rim of the plate and the center of the plate. Paint the outside edge of the plate. Let the marker dry.

5 Using clear matte spray finish, spray the back side of the plate. Let the spray finish dry. Spray the front side of the plate. Apply additional coats of spray finish to the front of the plate if the plate will be used to serve food.

Idea: try a different design

moon, sailboat or design

on the center of the plate

Where's the Goose That Laid These Golden Eggs?

I think this is one of my favorites. The colors are rich and, because they are different from typically pastel Easter eggs, I leave my dozen displayed in my dining room year-round. I get a kick out of visitors who are so inclined to lift an egg and even tap it on the edge of my table. Some day I'll add a few real eggs and really get an unexpected reaction!

THINGS YOU'LL NEED:

12 Wooden eggs, approximately 2¹/₂" long x 2" wide at the center
12-cup egg carton
¹/₂" Flat brush
Fine-grit sandpaper
Clean cloth
Acrylic paint:
　Metallic gold
　Navy blue
　Wicker white
Old toothbrush
Fine-point permanent gold marker
Textured cloth
Clear matte spray finish
Newspaper
Paper towels
Raffia

FOLLOW THESE STEPS:

1 Using fine-grit sandpaper, lightly sand all the wooden eggs. Using a clean, damp cloth, wipe the dust from the eggs.

2 Using a ¹/₂" flat brush, paint four wooden eggs with navy blue acrylic paint, four wooden eggs with wicker white acrylic paint, and four wooden eggs with metallic gold acrylic paint. Apply three coats of acrylic paint to each egg. Let the paint dry completely between coats.

3 One of the metallic gold colored eggs should be left solid gold. The three remaining metallic gold colored eggs should be painted with wicker white acrylic paint, by dipping an old toothbrush into the wicker white acrylic paint. Using your finger, "flip" the acrylic paint onto all sides of the eggs from a distance of about six inches. Refer to the General Instructions for painting with a toothbrush. Let the paint dry.

4 Using a fine-point permanent gold marker, paint one of the wicker white colored eggs and one of the navy blue colored eggs with each of the designs in Diagram A.

5 On the remaining wicker white colored eggs and the remaining navy blue colored eggs, dip a textured cloth into a small amount of metallic gold acrylic paint, and, after patting the cloth almost dry onto paper towels, "pat" the paint onto the eggs. Refer to the General Instructions for rag painting techniques.

6 Place the painted wooden eggs on newspaper. Using clear matte spray finish, spray the eggs. Let the spray finish dry. Turn the eggs over and spray again. Apply a second coat of spray finish to the eggs. Let the spray finish dry between coats.

7 Place a small amount of raffia into the bottom of each "egg cup" in the egg carton and place the painted eggs into the egg carton.

DIAGRAM A

Idea: More patterns and color combos

Metric Equivalency Chart

mm-millimetres cm-centimetres
inches to millimetres and centimetres

inches	mm	cm	inches	cm	inches	cm
⅛	3	0.3	9	22.9	30	76.2
¼	6	0.6	10	25.4	31	78.7
½	13	1.3	12	30.5	33	83.8
⅝	16	1.6	13	33.0	34	86.4
¾	19	1.9	14	35.6	35	88.9
⅞	22	2.2	15	38.1	36	91.4
1	25	2.5	16	40.6	37	94.0
1¼	32	3.2	17	43.2	38	96.5
1½	38	3.8	18	45.7	39	99.1
1¾	44	4.4	19	48.3	40	101.6
2	51	5.1	20	50.8	41	104.1
2½	64	6.4	21	53.3	42	106.7
3	76	7.6	22	55.9	43	109.2
3½	89	8.9	23	58.4	44	111.8
4	102	10.2	24	61.0	45	114.3
4½	114	11.4	25	63.5	46	116.8
5	127	12.7	26	66.0	47	119.4
6	152	15.2	27	68.6	48	121.9
7	178	17.8	28	71.1	49	124.5
8	203	20.3	29	73.7	50	127.0

yards to metres

yards	metres	yards	metres	yards	metres	yards	metres	yards	metres
⅛	0.11	2⅛	1.94	4⅛	3.77	6⅛	5.60	8⅛	7.43
¼	0.23	2¼	2.06	4¼	3.89	6¼	5.72	8¼	7.54
⅜	0.34	2⅜	2.17	4⅜	4.00	6⅜	5.83	8⅜	7.66
½	0.46	2½	2.29	4½	4.11	6½	5.94	8½	7.77
⅝	0.57	2⅝	2.40	4⅝	4.23	6⅝	6.06	8⅝	7.89
¾	0.69	2¾	2.51	4¾	4.34	6¾	6.17	8¾	8.00
⅞	0.80	2⅞	2.63	4⅞	4.46	6⅞	6.29	8⅞	8.12
1	0.91	3	2.74	5	4.57	7	6.40	9	8.23
1⅛	1.03	3⅛	2.86	5⅛	4.69	7⅛	6.52	9⅛	8.34
1¼	1.14	3¼	2.97	5¼	4.80	7¼	6.63	9¼	8.46
1⅜	1.26	3⅜	3.09	5⅜	4.91	7⅜	6.74	9⅜	8.57
1½	1.37	3½	3.20	5½	5.03	7½	6.86	9½	8.69
1⅝	1.49	3⅝	3.31	5⅝	5.14	7⅝	6.97	9⅝	8.80
1¾	1.60	3¾	3.43	5¾	5.26	7¾	7.09	9¾	8.92
1⅞	1.71	3⅞	3.54	5⅞	5.37	7⅞	7.20	9⅞	9.03
2	1.83	4	3.66	6	5.49	8	7.32	10	9.14

INDEX